Se...

Boss Grady's ... Prayers of Sherkin, White Woman Street, The Only True History of Lizzie Finn, The Steward of Christendom

'Sebastian Barry's plays are about history, but not in any very obvious or familiar sense ... The history that informs these plays is a history of counter-currents, of lost strands, of untold stories. Against the simple narrative of Irish history as a long tale of colonisation and resistance, Barry releases more complex stories of people who are, in one way or another, a disgrace to that history ... In Sebastian Barry's luminous plays, grace and disgrace are not opposites but constant companions.' Fintan O'Toole

Boss Grady's Boys: 'Barry's writing has a subtlety which puts *Boss Grady's Boys* into a different league from the vast majority of plays that have been written about rural Ireland since Synge.' *Sunday Press*

Prayers of Sherkin: 'Offers as rich a weave of words, images and ideas as has been seen in years ... the play is like a gentle requiem for a dead community, as it conjures visions of a world that might have been and a people fixed too rigidly in their own love and lore.' *Irish Times*
'In beautiful and languid language, it captures those moments of change in a way that no historian could, the moment at which ideology and cherished doctrine are discarded for the sake of survival. It could stand as a parable for the end of the twentieth century as well as for the nineteenth in which it is set ... This is a haunting and evocative play and it lingers with you long after the curtain goes down.' *Sunday Independent*

White Woman Street: 'Weaving together a Western, a haunting myth-like story, and a very Irish drama of exile (all the characters have a keen sense of being culturally displaced), the play is engrossing ... Barry's strength as a dramatist is best observed in the way he makes tragic and comic feeling grate against each other.' *Independent*

The Only True History of Lizzie Finn: 'The play, based on Barry's own great-great-grandmother, shows he has the capacity to generate strong emotion and to discover in his ancestors a metaphor for Irish history ... Barry uses Lizzie's dilemma to explore the economic decay of the 1890s landowning class and the whaleboned snobberies of rural Ireland ... Barry's poetic gift is constantly in evidence.' *Guardian*

The Steward of Christendom: 'No piece of theatre yet seen on the Irish stage has presented the viewpoint of the Irish Catholic loyalist of eighty years ago with such acute sensitivity, such marvellous intellectual, historical and dramatic integrity ... This is a quite wonderful play which brilliantly re-opens a hitherto closed chapter of Irish history. It is lyrical and profound, extremely funny and extraordinarily observant; and above all it is hauntingly sad. This is one of the great Irish tragedies, and all the more tragic because true.' *Irish Times*
'A beautiful play that would bring tears to the driest eye and it confirms Barry as an exceptional writer with a poetic gift.' *Financial Times*

Sebastian Barry was born in Dublin in 1955 and lives in County Wicklow. He was elected to Aosdana in 1989 and was Ansbacher Writer-in-Residence at the Abbey Theatre, Dublin, in 1990. His plays include *The Pentagonal Dream* (Damer Theatre, Dublin, 1986); *Boss Grady's Boys* (Abbey Theatre, Peacock stage, Dublin 1988), which won the first BBC/Steward Parker Award; *Prayers of Sherkin* (Abbey Theatre, Peacock stage, Dublin, 1990); *White Woman Street* (Bush Theatre, London, 1992); *The Steward of Christendom* (Royal Court Theatre Upstairs, London, 1995), which won numerous awards including the Writers' Guild Award for Best Fringe Play of 1995, the London Critics' Circle Award for Best New Play, Lloyds' Private Banking Playwright of the Year Award and was nominated for an Olivier Award; and *The Only True History of Lizzie Finn* (Abbey Theatre, Dublin, 1995). He has also published several works of poetry and fiction.

Methuen Contemporary Dramatists
include

Peter Barnes (three volumes)
Sebastian Barry
Edward Bond (six volumes)
Howard Brenton
   (two volumes)
Richard Cameron
Jim Cartwright
Caryl Churchill (two volumes)
Sarah Daniels (two volumes)
Nick Darke
David Edgar (three volumes)
Ben Elton
Dario Fo (two volumes)
Michael Frayn (two volumes)
Paul Godfrey
John Guare
Peter Handke
Jonathan Harvey
Declan Hughes
Terry Johnson (two volumes)
Bernard-Marie Koltès
David Lan
Bryony Lavery
Doug Lucie
David Mamet (three volumes)

Martin McDonagh
Duncan McLean
Anthony Minghella
   (two volumes)
Tom Murphy (four volumes)
Phyllis Nagy
Anthony Nielsen
Philip Osment
Louise Page
Joe Penhall
Stephen Poliakoff
   (three volumes)
Christina Reid
Philip Ridley
Willy Russell
Ntozake Shange
Sam Shepard (two volumes)
Wole Soyinka (two volumes)
David Storey (three volumes)
Sue Townsend
Michel Vinaver (two volumes)
Michael Wilcox
David Wood (two volumes)
Victoria Wood

SEBASTIAN BARRY

Plays: 1

Boss Grady's Boys
Prayers of Sherkin
White Woman Street
The Only True History of Lizzie Finn
The Steward of Christendom

*Introduced by Fintan O'Toole
with a preface by the author*

Methuen Drama

METHUEN CONTEMPORARY DRAMATISTS

10 9 8 7 6 5 4 3

First published in Great Britain in 1997 ✔
by Methuen Publishing Limited
215 Vauxhall Bridge Road, London SW1V 1EJ

Boss Grady's Boys first published in 1989 by the Raven Arts Press, Dublin,
Ireland; published in 1991 by Methuen Drama in one volume with *Prayers of
Sherkin* as a Methuen New Theatrescript
Boss Grady's Boys copyright © 1989 by Sebastian Barry
Prayers of Sherkin copyright © 1991 by Sebastian Barry
*White Woman Street, The Only True History of Lizzie Finn, The Steward of
Christendom* first published together in one volume in 1995 by Methuen
Drama; copyright © 1995 by Sebastian Barry

This collection and Preface copyright © 1997 by Sebastian Barry ✔
Introduction copyright © 1997 by Fintan O'Toole

The authors have asserted their moral rights

A CIP catalogue record for this book
is available from the British Library
ISBN 0 413 71120 X

Typeset by Wilmaset Ltd, Birkenhead, Wirral
Printed in Great Britain by Cox & Wyman Ltd, Reading, Berkshire

Methuen Publishing Limited Reg. No. 3543167

Caution

Contents

Sebastian Barry:
Chronology

1982 *Macker's Garden*, a short novel

1983 *The Water-Colourist*, a book of poetry
      Time Out of Mind and *Strappado Square*, two short novels

1985 *The Rhetorical Town*, a book of poetry
      Elsewhere, a children's novel

1986 *The Pentagonal Dream* produced at the Damer Theatre,
      Dublin

1987 *The Engine of Owl-Light*, a novel

1988 *Boss Grady's Boys* produced on the Peacock stage at the
      Abbey Theatre, Dublin; won the first BBC/Steward
      Parker Award

1989 *Fanny Hawke Goes to the Mainland Forever*, a book of
      poetry

1990 *Prayers of Sherkin*, produced on the Peacock stage at the
      Abbey Theatre, Dublin

1992 *White Woman Street* produced at the Bush Theatre,
      London

1995 *The Steward of Christendom* produced at the Royal
      Court Theatre Upstairs, London; won numerous
      awards, including the Writers' Guild Award for Best
      Fringe Play of 1995, the London Critics' Circle Award
      for Best New Play, the *Guardian*'s Best Play of 1995,
      Lloyds' Private Banking Playwright of the Year
      Award; nominated for an Olivier Award
      The Only True History of Lizzie Finn produced by the
      Abbey Theatre, Dublin

Introduction
A True History of Lies

Some time in the late 1980s, Irish theatre shifted in unexpected and at first confusing ways. For thirty years, it had been, for the most part, a theatre of social change, full of startling conflicts between tradition and modernity, old worlds and new. The stage had been swept by epic convulsions, and the audience could watch as actors on it came to represent not just individuals but forces. History was being played out in the hearts and minds, giving Irish theatre a heroic, at times almost Shakespearean edge. Opposites met in great, tragic collisions. And then, quite suddenly, something else entirely was happening on the stage. In the plays of Sebastian Barry, not only was there a new voice, but it was speaking a different theatrical language, evocative rather than explicit, poetic rather than realistic, intent, not on making the familiar conflicts of everyday life strange, but on making the strange familiar.

In these luminous plays, the drama comes, not from public conflicts, but from the human dignity that survives the loss of public meanings. Opposites do not collide but melt into each other. Grace and disgrace, for instance, are constant companions. Sebastian Barry fills the stage with prodigal people, long lost to the wider world. They are history's leftovers, men and women defeated and discarded by their times. The central characters of these plays are dotards, cultists, desperadoes, madmen: a member of a bizarre sect, an enforcer for a discredited regime, an exotic dancer married to declassed landlord, a cowboy who suspects that he is, deep inside, a redskin. They are misfits, anomalies, outlanders.

Yet each is also marked by an amazing grace. They are, in the mundane meaning of grace, possessed in their different ways of extraordinary emotional elegance, expressed in words that are baroque and meticulous at the same time. With infinite effort, they form themselves from moment to moment in the words they speak, letting us hear behind those words the rigorous syntax of their interior lives. And they are also, in the religious sense, full of grace, touched by some kind of inexplicable tenderness that rescues them from oblivion and grants them an equivocal but unmistakable blessing.

Sebastian Barry's plays are about history, but not in any very obvious or familiar sense. Much of Irish theatre since Sean O'Casey has had a direct relationship to public events. Either directly or indirectly virtually all of the major plays written in Ireland this century have reflected on the large-scale public conflicts that have shaped individual destinies on the island. First the conflict between Britishness and Irishness (or Protestantism and Catholicism) and then the conflict between tradition and modernity in independent Ireland echoed through the theatre. The plays themselves tended, inevitably, to be full of the resounding clash of epic forces. We came to expect an especially turbulent kind of drama in Ireland, and we were not disappointed.

Sebastian Barry's extraordinary theatrical history of anomalous people, sustained over the five plays in this volume, marks a striking departure from these precedents. By the late 1980s, when he found his voice in the theatre, the old conflicts were losing their grip. On the one hand, the contest between Britishness and Irishness had run itself into the barren and blood-soaked ground of sectarian strife in Northern Ireland. On the other, the epic clash of tradition and modernity in the Republic of Ireland was becoming an unequal match. Insofar as it still exits, traditional Ireland is alienated, angular and embattled, as strange, with its moving statues and paranoid visions, as any avant-garde has ever been. Its image in the theatre is no longer the proud, confident, dangerous Bull McCabe of John B. Keane's *The Field*, but Barry's odd, sad, comic, encircled Boss Grady's Boys, holed up and waiting for death.

Such a vision of traditional Ireland cannot be the source of great, sweeping dramatic confrontations, and there was every reason to believe that Irish theatre would gradually dwindle. That it has instead found a new way of being alive on stage, a new source of theatrical power that does not depend on outward epic conflict, is Sebastian Barry's mighty achievement. In these plays, external conflict is almost entirely absent. They are, like the great plays of the Irish revival in the early part of this century, essentially poetic, relying on the power of theatre to evoke a world through language rather than assert it through action.

And they are that oddest and most unexpected of things at the end of the twentieth century − works of great formal beauty. They persuade and hold their audience, not through naturalistic illusions, baroque displays of emotion or titanic struggles of historic forces, but through containing all their turbulences within the most delicate and poised of structures, an invisible scaffolding of words and syntax. These plays happen in the space between the ordered serenity of the language on the one hand and the instability of the world in which they are spoken on the other.

In this, Barry is much closer to, say, William Butler Yeats than he is to the Irish playwrights of the 1960s and 1970s. These plays could almost have the same opening line as Yeats's 'At the Hawk's Well': 'I call to the eye of the mind...', for they have a ritual quality of evocation, of spirits called up before our eyes rather than invented from moment to moment on the stage. It is significant that most of the plays are prefigured in Sebastian Barry's slim volume of poems *Fanny Hawke Goes to the Mainland Forever*, published in 1989 by Raven Arts Press. Barry's original impulse is poetic, and that impulse carries through in the sheer depth of language in the plays, and in their linguistic containment of violent feeling, so reminiscent of Wordsworth's description of poetry as 'emotion recollected in tranquillity'. The language of the plays is tough, lucid and superbly theatrical, but it always retains that remarkable linguistic tranquillity that makes them poetic.

This is not to say that Sebastian Barry's plays are refined creations from which the roughage of time and place, of Irish history and Irish land, have been winnowed out. On the contrary, these are emphatically public plays, up to their necks in the matter of Ireland. Behind *Boss Grady's Boys* and *The Only True History of Lizzie Finn* lies the decline of the Protestant landlord class in Ireland in the late nineteenth century and the War of Independence in the early twentieth. *Prayers of Sherkin*, more obliquely but no less movingly, marks the end of an English culture in Ireland. *The Steward of Christendom* is lit by the flames of Ireland's great conflict between capital and labour, the 1913 Lockout, and the withdrawal of Britain from the south of Ireland in 1922. And *White Woman Street* pivots on the irony of Irish natives, dispossessed on this side of the Atlantic, slaughtering and dispossessing Native Americans on the other side. All of these plays are set against a background of recent wars. These are history plays, deeply imbued with the taint of spilt blood. Their beauty arises not from any precious turning away from history, but in spite of an unflinching acknowledgement of history's horrors.

But the sense of both time and place in these plays is very much that of the late twentieth century. It is no accident that *Prayers of Sherkin*, with its elegiac sense of the collapse of a world founded on a utopian vision, could almost be a play about the fall of communism and the end of the Cold War. For Sebastian Barry writes from a perspective in which both the grand narrative of history and the framework of fixed ways of understanding the world are falling apart. The history that informs them is a history of obscurities and counter-currents, of lost strands, and untold stories.

As Lizzie Finn asks, 'What's our history, Robert, but something like that poor Frank James had, a true history of lies, and written by nobody, as you told me yourself? There'll be nobody in the wide world to remember us, child, and all that will remain of us is an echo, a strain of dancing music, and the memory of a man that loved his brothers and his people, who was given a heart as restless as a frightened dog by wars and accidents. So what odds where we are?' The plays themselves are such echoes of a dead music, audible to us when the sounds of wars and accidents have faded.

It is not that the old story of Ireland and England is absent from these plays, just that the gravitational pull of a third place – America – bends its trajectory out of shape. Just as Ireland itself is glimpsed from offshore in *Prayers of Sherkin*, the big moments of its twentieth-century history seem, throughout these plays, to loom momentarily on the horizon before the tide turns and the narrative drifts in other directions. The Easter Rising is a bit of meaningless, disconnected news about 'Fire and ruin in Dublin' told to Trooper O'Hara by an American Indian. Michael Collins, the creator of Independent Ireland, enters *Boss Grady's Boys* with dreams of 'a country that would nurture us', but that country is, for the brothers, lost somewhere between New York and Freedonia. Collins appears again to Thomas in *The Steward of Christendom*, a man who watches the birth – and the death – of a nation, but ends up pining for his daughter in Ohio.

Against the simple narrative of Irish history as a long tale of colonisation and resistance, Barry releases more complex stories in which it is by no means clear who is the native and who the foreigner. Again and again in these plays, those most charged of categories are confounded. Thomas Dunne and his dead son in *The Steward of Christendom* belong to the long tradition of Irishmen in British uniforms. Robert Gibson in *Lizzie Finn* and Trooper O'Hara in *White Woman Street* are Irishmen who are also veterans of wars of colonisation, not on the side of the natives, but that of the colonisers. In the poem from which the latter play derives, 'Trooper O'Hara at the Indian Wars', the narrator says that

> Yesterday, today, tomorrow
> we kill wild native bowmen
> savager surely than the English found us
> I hope, or this is fratricide.

And in the play itself, O'Hara puts it more simply: 'The English had done for us, I was thinking, and now we're doing for the Indians.' The Irish are, in this surreal history, both cowboys and Indians. That crucial ambivalence, revealed in America, is the reason the Wild West keeps breaking into Barry's Ireland: the echoes of the James Boys in *Prayers of Sherkin* and *Lizzie Finn*, the guest appearance of

Gary Cooper in the mundane guise of Mr Smith in *The Steward of Christendom*; Blakely's vision of buffalo roaming the Sligo hills in *White Woman Street*; the role of Buffalo Bill in *Lizzie Finn*; the end of *Boss Grady's Boys*, where Mick imagines his hill farm on the Cork-Kerry border surrounded by Indians. A mythic Wild West acts throughout these plays as a prism, breaking the light of Irish history into the most startling and sometimes the most beautiful of colours.

And if historical time is not simple and stable in the plays, neither is place. The plays are, of course, utterly Irish, but they also acknowledge the terrifying truth that Ireland can no longer be imagined as a fixed place. In *Prayers of Sherkin* Fanny Hawke, speaking of Sherkin Island, but touching on an image that serves for the bigger island of Ireland, asks her brother 'Do you not feel that this island is moored only lightly to the sea-bed, and might be off for the Americas at any moment?' The Ireland of the plays collected here is also moored but lightly to the sea-bed.

In *Boss Grady's Boys* Josey inhabits a jumbled country of memories and desires for which there are no maps. Lizzie Finn and Robert Gibson trail Ireland, England and Africa behind them, and they belong to a journey rather than a fixed homeland. Lizzie is both a stranger and a native in County Kerry, placed and displaced at the same time. Trooper O'Hara is at home on the range, his Ireland an incongruous Sligo recollected from the Wild West. And the country in Thomas Dunne's disordered head is a lost land somewhere between London and Dublin, an English Ireland that has disappeared beneath the waves of revolution.

The thread that runs through all of these plays, indeed, is the ambiguity of belonging. The fundamental opposition of Irish history – native on one side, foreigner on the other – is subverted in these figures who defy history by being at the same time both inhabitants and strangers. Lucinda Gibson tells Robert in *Lizzie Finn* that 'people are very simple and they like to know who they are talking to'. But the plays themselves tell us that people are far from simple and that it is impossible to know who you are talking to. Boss Grady's boys are rooted in the land, but where do they really live? Is

Fanny Hawke, born on Sherkin Island but speaking no native tongue, an Irishwoman? Does Lizzie Finn belong in her native Corkaguiney, to which she returns as an exotic stranger? Is Thomas Dunne, proud Irishman and loyal servant of the Crown, a rightful inhabitant of the new State? Is Trooper O'Hara a white warrior or a dark native, a bringer of order or an outlaw?

The answer, or rather the impossibility of answering, is both the curse and the blessing of these people. They are made vulnerable by their own placelessness. Because they cannot be properly defined by the categories in which history moves, they are always in danger of being lost. It is not for nothing that Thomas Dunne, who has lost a kingdom and is now dependent on his three daughters, reminds us of King Lear on the heath as an 'unaccommodated man . . . no more but such a poor bare forked animal'. Stripped of the things that adorn and cover up our bare humanity – nation, place, property – Barry's central characters stand exposed to the cold winds of history.

But that very nakedness is also their salvation. Robert Gibson tells Lizzie Finn that 'It's only history chooses a person's circumstance . . . We are all very much equal under the clothes that history lends us.' The plays place great weight on this imagery of clothing – Mick's work as a tailor for the madhouse, Thomas Dunne being measured for his asylum suit, Lizzie Finn's star-spangled stage knickers – but only to draw our attention to the reality of the poor bare forked animal underneath, to the naked equality of embodied humanity. By facing up to that naked vulnerability, Barry is also able to say 'only history', to see history as the borrowed clothing beneath which his people can retain their invulnerable grace.

Because they have no clear, simple historical meaning, the people of the plays are able to escape history's relentless drive to obliterate their memory. Barry's people are the footnotes, the oddities, the quirks of history. The tide of time sweeps them beyond familiar ground, and their part is but to surrender to its implacable swell. In *The Steward of Christendom*, for instance, the central public image is that of the surrender of

Dublin Castle to Michael Collins in 1922. The surrender
marks the end, not just of Thomas Dunne's public role, but
of his meaning for history. The world in which he had a
meaning was lost in that moment of surrender. He is fit only
for oblivion. Yet, in the end, his disordered mind allows him
to remember himself, to call himself to the eye of the mind.

   The miracle of each of these plays is that as each piece of
human flotsam floats by we see its head still above water,
kept buoyant by an invisible ring of words and tenderness.
These historically meaningless people come to mean everything to us. In remembering them for us, Sebastian Barry
has played to theatre's simplest and most astonishing strength
– its power to defy the darkness by lighting up our minds with
the unquenchable glow of lost lives.

FINTAN O'TOOLE
September 1996

Preface

I am in fear as a playwright of facts and dates and I will never make an historian, even though the reading of good history, of the kind written by Tacitus or for that matter by the Irish historian Roy Foster, can have the same effect on the hairs at the back of the neck as poetry. But you can't go looking for the pertinences and the changing lights of a play, they must gather about of their own accord, hang round the corners of what you think and say, maybe for a long time, and never be asked to explain themselves, or be orderly, intelligent and truthful.

The materials of a play are often so unlikely you'd be almost ashamed to admit to their origins. A pair of shirt studs from the thirties seemed to anchor *The Steward of Christendom* for me on my table. I was able to write *Boss Grady's Boys* because a good man in Kenmare brought up some swedes and spuds to me one night because he thought I might need the comfort of them, he thought I was unhappy and they would cure the unhappiness.

It is all a mystery to me really but diligent research in the annals of national libraries has not been my practice. I am content, I am forced, to try and guess the shape of things in the ordinary dark. I am interested not so much in the storm as the queer fresh breeze that hits suddenly through the grasses in the ambiguous time before it. And though I call these plays family plays of a sort, and though many of the people of the plays carry the names of people that once lived and from whom I am accidentally descended, nevertheless they exist here in an afterlife, in another life, in a gallery of pictures painted freely, darkly.

They are ghost plays, if ghosts are the images lingering of the vanished and the dead, in the two-and-sixpenny box-camera of the cranium. This process is not allied to any grand design of thinking and purpose, but to those times spent as a child lying in bed imagining for myself streets and fields and people I dearly wanted to see, most likely in the country, and felt far from, cherished places I missed and was able to wander about in that fashion, stuck in the peace and absence of a Victorian suburb of Dublin. It's only a small leap from there to walking about places I have never been, nor could ever have.

After the first production of *Boss Grady's Boys* the manager of the Abbey Theatre joked that I should retire and be the only happy Irish playwright on record. Eamon Kelly and Jim Norton were ideal as *Boss Grady's Boys*. I have never really got over the shock of watching them become Josey and Mick. They shocked me and I stayed in the theatre because of that shock, because there didn't seem to be any gap after a while between actor and character. They cleared the field of the play and were content to stand authentically in it.

I had little hope of writing *Prayers of Sherkin* because I knew nothing about Fanny Hawke beyond her evocative name and the fact or remembered fact, probably not the same thing, that she left her people to marry my great-grandfather, a lithographer in Cork City. For a long time I thought of her standing on the little pier of Sherkin, just about to make her decision, a youngish woman in the dark of a Cork evening, unimportant, on her own, and far away in time. It wasn't long before the thought struck me that if she hadn't crossed that narrow stretch of water, I wouldn't exist myself, a small matter in itself maybe but of some importance to me. Therefore the play is a sort of calling over that water to her, to come, to come.

I set *White Woman Street* in Ohio, not only because there is a street of that name in a little place called Roscoe Village, but because the man who gave me the germ of the play lived in Ohio, an expatriate Irishman called Barney Moloney, who was, in the Irish phrase, a wonderful man. He was a wonderful man.

And I thought, I would have sworn, that I knew Ohio ever

so slightly, in that I had a memory of crossing into Ohio from Iowa by a bridge across the Missouri river. Now as any person knows who has their bearings in this world, Ohio is a couple of states east of Iowa, as one of the actors gently pointed out to me. So this play is no western, nor even a mid-western, but a veritable eastern.

The Only True History of Lizzie Finn is not a costume drama, though there are costumes in it. I feel sure it could be played with everyone in colourless cloth and one costume each and the devil take the hindmost and that would certainly get around the difficulty of the quick changes. In many a draft I tried to make better theatrical sense of these changes and make the play behave itself for a director. In the end you submit to the clamour, the quiet, insistent, indifferent clamour of the play you see in your head. It is a short play of some ninety minutes and for me is the most haunted of a haunted group of plays.

And I would like to record my joy in working with Donal McCann who is a world in himself, one eye a writer's, the other a painter's, and the one at the back of his head . . . God only knows. Time turns and the actor of actor appears, a sort of rescuer to the writer, a sort of father/brother . . . Well, difficult to describe. The playwright gets his salt and may or may not be worth it because he serves the gods of theatre, those beings outside time and victors over time that inhabit with forceful ease the uneasy heaven of the stage. Their souls jostle against their heels.

Whether a writer seeks Innokenty Smoktunovsky of the Moscow Arts or Gérard Depardieu or Max Von Sydow in secret dreams of casting, it can rarely be arranged for the immaculate prince to attend. But one such occasion was when Donal McCann came through Chelsea in his black leather jacket to break his back (almost) and exhibit his heart and soul with magnificent generosity in those dark, magical, dangerous, bright rehearsals for *The Steward of Christendom*.

I have spent the last ten years on these five plays in a sequence of commissions and adventures stemming from the very happy time of *Boss Grady's Boys*. The worst exclusion for me now would be exclusion from the theatre, where a strange fire sears off the ego and the soaring fountain of actors at work amazes and restores the writer.

SEBASTIAN BARRY
July 1996

Boss Grady's Boys

To Philip Casey

Characters

Mick, *sixties, small, slight. Hair still dark.*
Josey, *seventies, larger than his brother* **Mick**, *sandy-white hair.*
Mrs Molloy, *sixties, ample.*
Mrs Swift, *sixties, grey, trim.*
Mr Reagan, *sixties, meagre.*
Father, *Boss Grady, medium height, stocky, bellied, in his sixties.
Father of* **Mick** *and* **Josey**.
Mother, *late twenties, tallish, scraggy, long thin reddish face.*
Girl, *eighteen, small, undernourished, unappealing, thin hair, almost
bald.*

The play is set on a forty-acre hill-farm in the Cork/Kerry
border.

Boss Grady's Boys was first performed at the Abbey Theatre (Peacock stage), Dublin, on 22 August 1988 with the following cast:

Mick	Jim Norton
Josey	Eamon Kelly
Mrs Molloy	Maureen Toal
Mrs Swift	Máire O'Neill
Mr Reagan	Gerard McSorley
Father	Oliver Maguire
Mother	Bríd Ní Neachtain
Girl	Gina Moxley

Directed by Caroline FitzGerald
Designed by Carol Betera
Lighting by Tony Wakefield
Music by Thomas McLaughlin

Note on the first production

In the first production, the stage was arranged differently than printed here. The fireplace was a solid affair, and was positioned extreme right. The two windows in the text became one good-sized window upstage centre, on the ledge of which Josey had his 'kitchen'; there was a niche here also for the fiddle, which allowed Josey to use it in the final moments of Act Two, playfully, as a gun; the window was attached to the stairs, going up a little way to nowhere. The scenes, marked in the text by gaps, were connected during rehearsals by movements that fitted the existing dialogue; there were few blackouts as a result. Also the window, stairs and fireplace were on stage from the start, and everything took place as it were in the house. In Act Two, page 47, the threshold was considered as downstage centre, and the horse crossing was indicated by sound only.

In Act One, page 22, the bed remained on stage, and was used for a horse, instead of one suggested by light. The dancers did not appear in Act Two, page 34.

Sebastian Barry
Dublin, 1989

Act One

Curtain.

Mick *sitting on the ground, slightly to left of centre, with a large purple sweep of light as of a mountain beyond him. He is a smallish figure, with a fishing hat on his head. He has his back to us, with his legs gripped in. It is evening, but early, and there is a full rich red in the sky above the mountain, which burns. The sky deepens and sweeps from right to left in a hurry. As a wind blows against his back he grips closer, keeping his head low, but watching the sunset. All around him is shadowy. The sky as it loses the sun gets deeper and deeper red, till it goes out. Then* **Mick** *is left in a dark blue light obscuring the stage.*

A tiny glimmer of light appears where the sun went and this increases to the dull glow of a turf fire. **Mick** *is in the same spot, but turned three-quarters to us, on a stool, staring into the fire. He is wearing the same black working trousers, an old nylon shirt, but without his hat. His face is hard and neat, shaven, his hair blackish, trained back, cropped close.*

Josey *comes into the light from the other side, the right, pulling up a backed kitchen chair.* **Josey**'s *hair is sandy-white, wavy but thinnish, a little too long. He wears brown working trousers, a whitish shirt, and a brown jacket. He has his cap in his hand, which he then settles on his head. He sits in his place, the fire between them.*

Josey I'd make tea for a halfpenny. Will I bring the horse down and put him closer to the house? I don't like the creature up there above the house in this rain.

Mick *stares with his own thoughts into the fire.*

Josey I was thinking today all day there was likely to be a deal of rain later, and now it has held off till night-time. There's something in the weather that it's always the same. You can predict it after a fashion. Well, Mick? So.

Mick (*not looking at him*) There's just wind.

Josey Is there no rain? Then the horse can talk to himself in peace. Will I call in the old dog so?

Mick (*looking up at him*) You old bastard. Can you not enjoy the fire?

Josey The old dog will be cold. He has no good bones left. Every one of them is a nuisance to him. But he is a very lovable dog.

Mick We've no dog now, Josey man. You buried him. He's up to his neck in soil, and I'm sorry for it. The sheep knew him well. It will trouble me to train a new one.

Josey It was lovely how he lay in the grass with the sheep. He was such a big mess of black. The sheep loved him.

Mick You fool. The sheep loved him? He never did lay down with the sheep.

Josey No, Mick. I meant when you were steering them. I meant when you told him to go down, when you had them going right. Just how he dropped down, the big black fellow. Collapsed at your word. You see I enjoyed that. The sheep loved him.

Mick The sheep didn't love him.

Josey Well. He was very black and he lay in the grass. In the summer he looked well enough in the grass, when the grass was drier. Will I shout from the door for him?

Mick Christ, man.

Josey You have great whistles.

Josey *stands, sticks his hands in his pockets, leans forwards. He gives a weak whistle, waves an arm. He gives two whistles, and laughs, and tries to whistle, calms, waves an arm.*

Mick Quiet yourself.

Josey I'm driving the sheep into the slope field, because the grass there is perfect, perfect. Listen to me.

Josey *whistles again, and calls.*

Shep! Shep! Shep! Gubb-a-bubb-em! Down, down!

He is nearly weeping.

Mick Ah, man. You've just driven the sheep away up across the hill. The dog's died from contradiction.

Josey (*laughing*) Bloody me! Aye, aye, aye.

He twirls himself, and makes a dance gesture, spreading out his hands, one foot out to the side, and holds it, and attempts a tap dance.

Mick You're feeling your oats.

Josey I am, heart. I am. Fred Astaire, man. I'm a great dancer. There will be a lady in a satin dress in here, if you don't stop me.

Mick (*savagely*) Sit down and shut up.

Josey *chastened, settles his cap, and sits again. They both stare at the fire.*

The same, but the fire is just a low ashen glow.

Josey (*leaning in*) We would never go to Killarney now for the pictures, I suppose. Groucho Marx is a great man. The head of the country that time. (*Sings.*) Hail Freedonia! Hail Freedonia! (*From the song in the Marx Brothers'* Duck Soup.) It was a lovely song. I loved the ducks in the pot, with the steam, but the ducks were all right. And that lovely woman with the big soft bosom. A soft night. A woman of a sort you won't see often in Bantry, unless she's a foreign woman staying in the big hotel. I would choose to marry ten women like that, and have them all in the loft stacked like big hayricks. We could lie on them and pray for help. The Yankee horses would come streaming up the track, with a pretty clatter, and rescue us.

Mick (*affectionately*) You old fool, you.

Josey Groucho, Harpo, Chico, and what's-his-name, and what was the name of the Frenchy man, the singer, on the boat with them that time?

Mick You old blasted fool.

Josey He was old in that picture, old but handsome, the perfect man for the bosomy lady.

Mick You know, I remember his name. It was Maurice Chevalier.

Josey What was his name, what was his name?

Mick *looks at him, blinks slowly.*

Josey It's like wringing the necks of hens.

Mick *is standing on a small wooden stairs, downstage right, shadowed. He is looking at* **Josey** *who is hunched over the embers of the fire.* **Josey** *has his hands outstretched to embrace the heat. There is a noise of waterdrops hissing in the embers.*

Josey The rain now. Coming in the same as October's rats from the cold. The horse will be a lonely man in the field. There'll be mud now on his hooves, and he has no fire or talk to protect him. Maybe I should have walked up in the cold and got him. He could stand outside the door here and listen to us. He could do so. It was like when Mick Collins was all the fashion, and Mick was away every night, and then every night away after that, when the old man was dead as a dog and the farm was ours in a way. It was our farm and no one came up the track to say otherwise. There were hens galore with brown eggs in them, there were two old pigs that wouldn't breed any more, there were more sheep, and a milking cow to boot. It is like that now, as if Mick were away all night at his game, and the country very silent in its manner around me. It is like that, with a bat coming in from the dark and losing his way in the firelight. Mick away, and the dark roof moving with the firelight. Mick away. Little heat from the fire in this state, the moon in her own house, Collins the same man that was buried afterwards. He was a big black man with a greasy face. Mick told me. He was the king of the country in his time. He was a lonely sort of man, I suppose. And he made me lonely. I'd make tea for a halfpenny.

Mick Josey, come to bed.

A marriage bed to the left, one side facing us. **Mick** *is lying on it on his side, with his face towards us, eyes open.* **Josey** *is vaguer behind him, his face turned up to the ceiling can be seen. They are covered in worn army blankets with a faded coverlet on top. The sheets are flannelette, brownish, the pillow is the one bolster.* **Mick** *has a finger in his mouth. There is a bit of a candle lighting his face, but the space beside the end of the bed, which is ample, is empty and pitch.* **Mick**'s *expression responds slightly to what* **Josey** *says.*

Josey A little bit of everything. A little bit of woe, a bit of mirth. A bit of bread, a bit of good butter. (*After a bit.*) Bless you, and bless us in return. Bless this small house and bless me and Mick. Bless the sheep and the dog and the horse. Go up and talk to the horse in his field in your overcoat. Bless the piece of money in the bank in Killarney, if it's still there.

Mick *throws his eyes quickly.*

Bless the trees and the whins, and the rowanberries and the berries on them. Bless the rain and the rare sun and the seasons four. Bless the mam in heaven and the length of time since we seen her. Bless the gate and the slope field, and the rocky land at the top of the farm, which is no good to us. Bless our jackets and the few trousers and the shoes and the leather laces Mick bought this year. Bless the potatoes and the swedes and keep them whole and hale in their pit when the time comes to bury them in. That will be October. Bless the dog.

He pauses. **Mick** *stares, waiting.*

Bless. Bless. Bless. Bless the old man. Bless the turf. Bountiful Mary, come into us this night and bless us. Take your old blue cloak off for us, and God bless you, and bless the cups and the spoons, and bless the old fiddle ruined with damp, that the old man cherished as his own bride, and that is propped in the niche of the window. Bless the postman should he come, and bless the Bantry road, both to the town and to the mountains. Good night to you.

Mick *wets his fingers and snuffs the candle.*

Josey Bless the darkness, come to that.

Mick'*s dream.*

The bed very dimly seen, with two masks in place of the two men's faces. To the right of this, in the clear space, is a table with four people playing cards. An oil-lamp behind them gives light. This, starting from nothing, is becoming brighter as the figures animate, then the scene darkens again. After a second or two the scene returns with the lamp fully lit, and exactly as the light is established, one of the two widows speaks. These are the widows of shopkeepers in Bantry. The other man is a widower, a shopkeeper himself.

Mrs Molloy What is it about cards that makes you thirsty? Is it the excitement?

She means this sarcastically. They are playing poker. **Mrs Swift** *can not make up her mind.*

Mrs Swift Hold up a minute, dear. Just let a girl think. There's a cabinet of alcohol behind you, if you want it.

Mrs Molloy I wouldn't dream, I wouldn't dream.

Mrs Swift You don't want me to get it for you?

Mrs Molloy Would you stop, and ask Mr Reagan for your cards. You're making a very long job of it.

Mr Reagan Two or three?

Mrs Swift I don't know. What do you think?

Mr Reagan Don't show me! This is a game for profit, Mrs Swift. Have a heart.

Mrs Molloy Mr Grady?

Mick (*surprised in his thoughts*) No.

Mrs Molloy What do you mean, no?

Mick Were you not asking me if I wanted a drink?

Mrs Molloy Man, you are worse than she is.

Mrs Swift There's whiskey behind you all in the cabinet. Dear me – two cards, please, Mr Reagan.

Mick I'll have the four. I can do nothing with these.

Mrs Molloy Keep your cards close to your chest, Mr Grady, and a poker face. I hope you have that ace.

Mick I need an ace?

Mrs Molloy To get four cards again you do.

Mick Well, I have it of course. (*Pleasantly.*) Do you want to examine it?

Mrs Molloy Examine it? Keep it to yourself. I am indifferent to it.

Mick What sort of whiskey, Mrs Swift? Irish?

Mrs Swift Not at all. Good Scotch.

Mick As I feared, as I feared.

Mrs Molloy (*standing*) As I feared, as I feared. A life of romance was the least a girl should expect. It was a good life in a way, but his shop was a mean shop, and there were too many items from

India. He took away every year I had to give a man, and then took away himself for good measure. He was a man after my own heart so I will not blame him. (*Sitting.*) This is a tedious game after a while. It is not really a lady's game.

Mr Reagan What is a lady's game in effect? Bridge?

Mrs Molloy That is a fine lady's game. But I can not play it.

Mrs Swift It needs brains. I can't play it either. It's a rich person's game.

Mrs Molloy There is often something very feeble and silly about you, Mrs Swift.

Mrs Swift Did you want that drink now, Mrs Molloy? I realise you want one.

Mrs Molloy (*standing, to herself*) I wanted one, I did want one. Curly things the same as bees. I think woods are glad of bees, the babies of woods. I wanted a little son I could watch all his first years, and hear talk, and he could have gone to school and come home, simply, richly. I wanted a head to stroke, a head of hair, black hair. There is something about a boy of nine that is preferable to a girl. He looks at the world with innocence, but is a creature to take his place in it all the same, a king. Whereas, alas, as I know myself, the life of a girl is just the dickens. Every man in the street will touch you or look at you, and in the lanes among the bread-and-cheese bushes, when the May is on the branches, and the bees idle like engines, and the big cars ease through the mid-morning, someone will come thrashing through the nettles and the docks over the ditch, and drag you into a quiet glade and yank up your skirt and murder his joke into you. A girl of nine should not go out walking in an Irish lane, when the May is out. (*Sits.*)

Mick Are you going to give me four, Eamon?

Mr Reagan Are you innocent of them? Sorry. (*He gives* **Mick** *four new cards.*) A bit of butter, a bit of bread. Fresh from Killarney. Comes in at six, you know, around the new coast road. We call it the new road because heretofore we were not in contact with the mainland, as we dubbed it, though we are not an island. My wife, usually a well woman, is buried some while since. We sell the *Press*, the *Independent* and the *Examiner*, but not the *Irish Times*. Though this is a planter town, which you might not expect so far south, we don't stock the *Irish Times* as a rule. There is very little reading in it, unless you are a Dublin man, or gentry. There are no gentry in this district, nor has been for many a long decade. We got rid of them quite. We burned them out. They were glad to leave and, indeed, we have baking powder, and custard, and even oats if you wanted them for your porridge. Every brand name you can think of lives in here a merry merry life.

Mrs Swift I have a right bellyache from that chicken. What can Dempsey's be thinking of, stocking chicken as tough as boots? I had to boil it for two days. Which included two nights. I heard it in the pantry, bubbling away in the heart of the old house. How very pretty my rooms look in the sunlight, in the night-time I often think they are a little tomblike, a little less than decent. My missal however keeps me going. There are some lovely prayers in the missal. Don't you often think that, Mrs Molloy? But I doubt if you would, with your roly-poly body and happy air and attraction to men. But if you asked my opinion, in a month of Sundays, your face is the visage of a horse, with a touch of hair where hair ought not to be on a woman. But never mind, have another piece of gâteau. This is fresh gâteau from Killarney and Mr Reagan's shopeen. It looks like the flesh of an old man's belly, my nice old man who never laid a hand on me without his mass-gloves on. I can not abide, or could not in the days when Declan was still living, the touch of a living man's hand on my person. It gave me the chills, such as was not to be countenanced. And yet, in the happy cinema in Killarney years ago, it was a different matter were a youth such as, well, whoever he might be, to just for a moment, just for a moment, well, fondle me. (*Clearing her throat.*) I wouldn't be seen dead in the street without my foundation and face-powder, though I understand from the younger set that powder has gone out of fashion. I like the puff and the case in my handbag always. I suppose they don't wear stays either. But some people are ill-advised not to

wear stays. The trees in the little square stay firm even in old
age, but we, well, really, it's obvious.

Mick I've nothing.

Mrs Molloy Everything comes to him who waits. Don't be a girl
ever in a boy's world. Last winter I went out in the yard with a
pan of cinders and threw them glowing on the snow.

Mr Reagan Are we playing cards or what? I don't mean to pry.
Tomorrow I may go out from the town for good and become a
countryman proper. Set up on a hill farm like Mick and his
brother, and be simple. I can then be in a position to walk to the
town from the farm and back again, through light rain, and will
be especially excited by the numerous murmurings of small
chaffinches and robins and sparrows. A light fiddle-music, giving
rise to the traditional music. I'd rather be done with it here than
endure another odd night above in Crow Street in my little
room.

Mrs Swift Well, come to that, I might put on every inch of good
stuff I have, and go out on the Killarney road and be taken in by
some traveller – commercial but not tinker. It really is a bonus
not having to submit to gentle entreaties. I much prefer the
greatness of our air, the famous Irish air that the foreigners love.
I am glad we can be so giving to the foreigners, with our air. The
foreigners are very fine people, very fine. They came from all
over.

Mick We appear to be stuck with this hand. Will we play
something else?

Mrs Molloy (*standing, putting her leg up on the table, showing a
garter*) We could play house. That's a good game.

Mick It's not a card game though, you know.

Mrs Molloy There's something I've always liked about you,
Mick Grady. You may be a small wizened little creature with a
square face and dark skin denoting I don't know what, but you
have an advantage, a steal on other men in these parts. I am a

very soft person, you know, that might be sunk into, with profit.
(*She sits.*)

Mick Rightyo, rightyo. Time to go home. Time to go home.
Josey will still be up.

Mr Reagan How is your brother, Mick? Is he in good fettle?

Mick He is. But he is also a man that feels loneliness very
keenly, and begins to pine if I'm away long. He forgets to make
tea for himself, or cannot do it if I am not at home. He is a very
peculiar, unnecessary brother that I have come to revere and
value by hook and by crook.

Mr Reagan Is your brother well, Mick?

Mick My brother is a well, deep, stony and dry. I throw stones
into the poor man that echo with a lost, deep sort of echo. I love
him, I love his idiocy.

Mick *turns about, and kneels on his chair, turned from the others, facing
upstage left. Two high columns of variously coloured light like stained-
glass windows appear, strengthen, displacing the other scene. Light falls
through the windows onto* **Mick.**

Mick Lord of the streams, the hills, the farms, of the farmers,
what's wrong with us, what's amiss with us? I'm a smallish man.
I would like a slightly larger acreage, with a deal of sunlight to
improve the grazing. I don't actually. (*To himself.*) I won't talk to
glass windows any more. I won't go along with them. Let the old
women do it. Old bastes, old cattle, I won't have a word for
them any more. It's idle little, idle little. On my knees in front of
windows. On my knees as if He was an English lord. If He met
me on the road in his car He would spit through the side window
at me. Long ago in his pony-and-trap He would have leant out
with His whip, and stroked me with it. Down on my knees.

He stretches out his arms.

Away up the road with you, you foreigner you!

Windows disappear, lamplight returns, **Mick** *sits as before.*

Mr Reagan We never see your brother in the town now. Is he well? We went to the same school and we never see him now. He was a great fellow for catching wrens. He had the knack. He could catch a wren nimbly with lime on a stick and he might weep for it after, but what can you do?

Mick With all my red heart I wish he might not survive me alone in the house. And yet I wish that I might not survive him. I will not live here with his shadow and our father's shadow, and I expect I will. They would certainly not leave him be, if they ever saw him do what I see him do. He is a brother that many people would be glad to know. A diverse brother but a comfortable one. He would never get in your way willingly or knowingly.

Mrs Molloy I suppose people say odd things about me. I am bothered by the thought. I always like to be liked where possible. Of course I am a dryish woman, an empty sort. There was a deal of love in me at one time. Someone to caress me.

Mick Well, there's my hand. (*Putting down the cards.*)

Mr Reagan Is there no more betting? I suppose not if you've shown. You have three kings and a pair of tens. That's enough to lick me.

Mrs Swift I had only a number of very different cards. I've no luck tonight.

Mr Reagan There's no real need to say what you had if you don't wish, I believe.

Mrs Swift I don't mind telling you. I wanted to. All through the game I felt a little foolish, holding such cards, and betting pennies on them.

Mrs Molloy (*looking at her, almost kindly*) You ought to have stopped, Mrs Swift. Don't you know you can stop?

Mrs Swift Of course.

Lamp fades.

Josey's dream.

The bed, as before. In the clear space on the right it is blueish, misty, with a sparkling of light from the ground to the extreme right, where the water is. A middle-sized, thick-set man with wavy white hair, in his sixties, dressed in workclothes, comes carefully from the left carrying a fishing-rod and a bundle of line whose hooks have cork stuck on the tips, a round float at the end. It is stormy.

Father It has to be a storm inside a mist.

Josey (*offstage left*) Dad! Have I lost my way? Am I right for the lake?

Father A curious thing that the storm takes his words and carries them to me. (*He puts down the line at the water's edge and arranges and then casts his fly-rod.*) If I catch a trout in this wind I will know a great deal. But it has to be a storm inside a mist.

Josey (*coming on muddily*) I never trust that path.

Father There is no path that I know of.

Josey I've crossed it a few times and I don't still believe it will take me.

Father (*nodding at the lake*) What do you think?

Josey There are crazy fish in there today.

Father They'd always be in there, Josey. It's a lake.

Josey Well, I can smell them, I can smell them!

Father Then you have a fine nose. I have only mist in mine. It's funny that we came up here, the only lake in Cork or Kerry that needs a storm, in a place that has no road after the mountain road, and where the trout are the wiliest buggers alive. You need to be a genius to catch these trout, and in a storm at that.

Josey The storm makes them hungry.

Father I expect so. It is called Hungry Hill.

Josey There are many big trout under the waves today, Dad. Are we to throw out the line?

Father If we catch one on the rod, we'll throw the line out. We'll try the line if we catch one now. (*Working the rod.*)

Josey There is something fierce about the fish up here. Isn't there a very wicked look to them, to their jaws? Do you remember when you brought me up here with the other men, and you made a line with fifty hooks, and stood both sides of the lake and walked its length? And you got as many as thirty fish, each one bigger and wickeder than the last.

Father I don't. I don't remember.

Josey There was a blue colour at the top of the sky, a strange blue colour like it was hot, and the fog was clothy and bright, and the edges of the grass tufts gleamed at the light. You and the men shouted across the water to each other, and it was a very bright storm with lights. It was very exciting.

Father No. I don't recall that.

Josey I was very young at the time. Perhaps that is why. It is hard to remember when you are very young.

Father There are no fish in here today I think.

Josey There must be. Fish away.

Father No, there are none. It's not likely you'll get one if you don't get one straight away.

Josey It is such a long walk. Fish away.

Father No, it will be better if we go down. We're wasting our time. Maybe the wind is in the worse direction.

Josey Stay, Dad. Fish!

Father (*turning to* **Josey**) Be quiet and silent, you cretin, can't you? There are no fish if I say so.

Josey Dad, be gentle with me. I am very excited and eager to see a fish.

Father Christ, do you not hear me? Will you not back away? Will you not go some distance there? Would you block my path?

Josey Fish away, Dad, fish away.

Father I'd rather crush you. I'd rather put my hands each side of your soft brain and pancake it. Do you think I want you running up here with me like a collie, a foolish collie that won't herd sheep without biting them? What class of a shitty boy are you? Will you not give me peace?

Josey We were up this morning at four, before even the night was gone. It was only morning by courtesy. You gave me bran and beer to drink, and we tied the rod and the line to your bicycle, and went off down the lane to the road. We have walked and ridden, me on the crossbar, for two hours, and now it is nearly daylight outside the storm. All night I was awake in the loft with Mick, breathing under the close wood, hot and shaking. I was going to fish with my father in the morning and we are here now. You did not take Mick.

Father I will kill you here. I have killed sheep in their flocks and flocks, and chickens' necks in their thousands, and I have swiped at rats in the sheds, and cut them in two with the spade. I have crushed more spiders in my time than a bird has cracked snail-shells. Do you think it would be a great thing for me to crush you? You are small and weak-headed.

Josey Dad, I am old and weak-headed. My hair is grey as yours. You lay on the threshold of the house like a flounder, staring up at Mick as he leaned over you in astonishment. You looked at him with your fish's eyes, and your heart stopped budging in your chest. And you never took Mick to fish, and he often asked me why was that.

Father You were my favourite, Josey. You were like a daughter to me. You were a lovely faithful daughter, as good as a dog. You honoured me. You were too stupid to look at me the way Mick did. You were too doltish to question. You were the half of me I preferred, you'd no brain to mar you. I wish I had been born like you, without a real thought in my head. You were the

best half of me, the half of me I killed in myself always. Mick
was the most familiar section of me. He could see me through
and through.

Light gathers and moves around the **Father.**

Josey (*hunched, quietly, speaking to the ground*) Fish away, Dad, fish
away.

*The bed, as before. The space to the extreme right has a bright hard
sunlight.* **Mick** *is standing extreme right, leaning into the fall of the light,
hands in trouser pockets, in his Sunday best: clean shirt, checked, with
green tie, good jacket, a newer fishing hat with a small feather, all his
clothes a little tight for him. He says nothing for the moment, while the
following lighting changes take place: the sunlight persists for some
seconds, then gradually a cloud goes over, shadowing the space inch by inch.
A wind gusts at* **Mick,** *the sunlight edges back, and a glittering light rain
falls in the same direction as the light falls.* **Mick** *does not move out of it.
He leans into the sun-shower.*

Mick (*in a quiet mumble, it is a line from the Marx Brothers' film*)
Room Service? Room Service? (*After a moment.*) Send me up a
room.

*His head dips an inch, and he cries with open eyes, not caring in the rain.
After some seconds he is able to stop crying.*

I was eager for them all, and at the same time didn't care much
for them. It was the way Collins looked, the way he stared about
him like a tiger, that I admired. Not the politics. Or it was the
politics. It was the politics, certainly, but I suspected it was
always going to be the spirit of the times that I and my like
would remain where we were and make do with that. In the rain
and the cow's muck, and the companionship of a soft-headed
brother. Whiskey with a glow, and the brother-warm bed. You
can strive, you can talk hard in a bar at night, and you want it to
mean something, you have a few ideas how things might go

when the business is done. What to set up and what to avoid, who to allow and who to resist, who is the mean man in the town and who the generous helper, the man with no thought for himself, who would lead best, and make decisions that would spruce up the farms and the feeling of the farmers. So there wouldn't be a burden ever again, or any loss, or any misdemeanour. That we wouldn't be fodder for books again, that we wouldn't be called peasants in a rural district, and be slipped into the role of joker by the foreigners from the cities. That we wouldn't have to stand on the roadside and watch the cars go by with creatures in them from outer space, plastic and cushions and clothes, another Ireland altogether, people who would mock our talk, and not see us, not talk to us except by way of favour. That we could be men of our country was all my wish, that we might have a country that would nurture us, a spirit to get us up the road and out of the rain. How is it that after every change and adjustment I still stand here in the same rain on the same mud, with the same sun laughing at me? And there's the time I stood in a bar with Mick Collins and told him we had the same name, and he said I seemed a very sound man, and thanked me for my part in the business. I said I would burn anything for him, shoot anyone, if we might have a nation after, a nation I would be a citizen of, an honoured ordinary man. And the world would hear of us, and wish to be near us. I said I would do the worst thing for him, if I might always wear my Sunday clothes and drive in a decent fashion over the roads, and get the damp out of my bones and he put his hands on my back as he was leaving and said he needed more men like me. Then he went off to his wars and I went back to the card-game in the little room and never said a word about him to the others. I was moved beyond telling them, I was aflame from my toes up my legs, it was a real feeling. I was going to walk across the fields with my legs on fire and walk over everything that was beating me down and set it aflame: my father would smile on the hearth and laugh at me in a different way than the sun: he would honour me. Then I would go out with his spade and a bit of cement and build up everything again, and put the good man in a big house, and leave the mean man to himself. There was a lot to be done.

Now the good man I had my eye on is a man on his own in the neighbouring farm, with a bicycle for vehicle and a mossy house, and his sole adventure is the shopping trip to Bantry on a Tuesday. I was to make everything watertight for Collins, and be a decent man in my own district. I was never, myself, to stand carelessly in the rain again. I was to be a dry man with responsibilities.

The bed gone. Outside the house. Dull overcast light for the main part, now and then a sweep of sunlight passes from right to left. **Mick** *is sorting tools in a toolbox, humming. The sound of hooves walking on clattering stones is heard, at which* **Mick** *stands straight and watches.* **Josey** *comes on from the right, leading a 'horse'. Aspects of the horse are suggested by light.* **Josey** *responds to its movements: his hands go up and he admonishes the horse when it chucks its head. It is a big animal.* **Josey** *stops and pulls on the unseen rope.*

Josey Hup, hup.

He walks, and brings up the animal to where **Mick** *is.* **Mick** *backs away when the horse pushes its flank against him.* **Mick** *smooths the horse's nose and the horse pushes against his hand, and* **Mick** *laughs.*

Josey Stand now, Charlie, stand.

Mick Go back there. (*Pushing his flank.*) Go back.

Josey Is he to stand or go back?

Mick Hold him steady by the halter.

Josey Is he looking well to you?

Mick He looks fine.

Josey He does too, the creature.

Mick How's the grass up there?

Josey Not great at that. A bit sparse. He has more mud made under the rowanberries than a herd of bullocks.

Mick Poor old fellow, poor old fellow.

He strokes the horse's big neck and slaps it. These sounds, the patting, the horse shifting his hooves on the rocky ground, are heard. The horse snorts heavily.

Josey Oh, the man. Would we be as well to do his mane? It's very knotted.

Mick He's a lovely big girl.

Josey A big girl? This great gelding?

Mick What was the farrier's name, that used to come?

Josey Driscoll. The songwriter.

Mick Hold him now, and I'll pare him.

He bends down at the near hind, and tries to pull up the hoof, facing away from the animal, aiming to draw the leg up between his own legs.

Mick Come on.

Josey Raise it up, raise it up. Charlie knows you're only a tailor.

Mick *struggles with the leg, and gets it resting on his thigh. With a pliers from the box he pulls the 'nails' of the loose 'shoe' and prises the 'shoe' off and throws the pliers (as if with the shoes and nails) back in the box with a clatter. He takes the parer and cuts some of the 'hoof'.*

Mick Do you want to give me that new shoe? Give me a mouth of nails.

Josey *hands him a shoe and some nails from a pocket of his jacket, and* **Mick** *puts the nails in his mouth, five, that jut out.* **Mick** *fits the shoe against the pared 'surface' (his hand holds the shoe the necessary distance from his thighs) and pares some more. The horse forces his leg down and moves forward a bit, going sideways.*

Mick Hold up, can't you.

Josey He's a devil for that.

Mick He's a rogue. Come on up now, Charlie.

Mick *bends again and takes up the hoof and leg and puts the shoe against the 'hoof'. He takes a nail from his mouth and takes up the hammer and beats in the first nail, and does this with the other nails with a rhythmical tapping. The horse snorts loudly.*

Mick Keep him steady now, Josey. (*Throwing the hammer in the box, dipping for a file, filing off the hoof. The sound of this is heard.*)

Josey Steady now, stand.

Mick Rightyo. (*Dropping the 'hoof' and stepping away, throwing the file in the box, with the shoe and its nails at the same time.*) Is the lower gate hasped?

Josey Aye.

Mick We can let him be here then. He'll be safe enough.

Josey *takes off the invisible halter with some effort, because the horse holds his head high. The sound of the horse walking away calmly, and snorting again.*

Mick Fine so. The other feet are fine?

Josey Ah sure yes.

Mick Sound. Tea, so. He has slain me.

Outside. More overcast, darker with the threat of rain, slatey. **Josey** *is standing left of centre, more downstage than* **Mick**, *who is standing idly.* **Josey** *is looking up at the sky, facing us.*

Mick (*singing vaguely and softly, suddenly*) Hoot en night en noot en night en noot en night en nyah.

Josey *shakes his head slowly at the sky.*

Mick (*suddenly again*) Hoot en night en noot en night en noot en nyah.

Josey (*suddenly, after a bit, looking up still*) It smells like vultures.

Mick (*turning away, walking upstage, light going*) Come on, Josey.

Josey *after a bit follows him. As they move upstage, curtain falls.*

Act Two

The kitchen. **Mick** *on his knees putting a match to the fire. The light increases slowly during the next few minutes of talk, finishing at the full glow of the fire. Noise of hard heavy rain falling outside.*

Mick That'll be it now for the whole of October, and November too maybe.

Josey (*right, in the shadows*) Cheese and bread I'm making.

Mick As long as you make tea I don't mind what I eat. I've no taste left much.

Josey I stood on the road this late evening and Brady talked to me. He said the boy in the top farm –

Mick What boy?

Josey Away up there where the waterfall is, and the mountain meadow – we were up there as lads. It is full of black pools. I remember it. There's a farm under the lot.

Mick Of course there is. (*Rising.*) You mean Jack Dillon's place.

Josey Well, he's dead.

Mick Jack?

Josey He died in the county hospital. He was in for a stomach complaint and got a pneumonia while he was there. Off he went.

Mick He was afraid of the hospital. He used to shovel stomach powders into himself. I saw as many as a score of empty tins in his parlour. (*Sitting on his stool, left.*) His mother was dead a long time.

Josey Brady said it was a sudden affair.

Mick He'd know.

Josey Will you go down to Killarney for the funeral?

Mick I won't.

Flash of lightning, illuminating the left window.

Josey They wouldn't be expecting you.

Mick Give me that bread, will you? He had no one.

Josey *comes to the fire, and hands him a saucer of sandwiches, and a cup.*

Mick Grub.

Thunder outside.

Josey I didn't see the flash.

Mick You were cutting cheese, man.

Josey Peeling it off, anyway. The wood will be soaked.

Mick It will be burned. I stacked it in. The turf's good though. We weren't cheated.

Josey Is that our turf?

Mick It's Carney's. I didn't dig a sod this year. My foot is banjaxed all summer.

Josey It's a poor thing when we burn someone else's turf. Did you pay money for it?

Mick I did not. He owed me many a favour. Don't you remember that great long week spent putting up his wire fencing?

Josey Was I with ye?

Mick (*laughing*) As far as I know.

Josey Well, there now.

Mick Sit, can't you?

Josey I'll call in the dog.

Mick (*quickly*) Don't start that.

Josey Is the father in?

Mick Don't start that either. I won't stand it. I'll have to go out.

Josey (*turning away to the shadows, right*) I suppose he's caught at the fair. Why did we bring no sheep to the fair this time?

Mick It's not fair day, is why. I have two ewes I want to sell on that day. I am sick of looking at them. There'll never be lambs in those ewes. They're only shadows of sheep. They're just grass-eaters.

Josey Would they stew?

Mick If you had a year spare to boil them.

Josey Well, so, I'd sell them quietly.

Mick Some of them half-wit farmers from Kenmare might go for them.

Josey Why not? They're grand sheep.

Mick Are you eating over there in the dark? The fire's warm now. (*After a bit.*) Bring your chair over here can't you, man dear.

Josey Where's that father at all? (*Coming over with his chair, and a cup.*)

Mick Did you eat?

Josey What's eating? I've no hunger. (*Looking into* **Mick***'s cup.*) You have cinders splashed on it.

Mick I raised the ashes when I swept. You need fuelling, man.

Josey Eat yourself. Go on.

Mick I will. (**Josey** *sits.*) That's a terrible rain. We'll be stuck with it now for a month. We'll be like fish in here now for a month.

Josey The wood will be very wet.

Mick I stacked it, heart. (**Josey** *gets up.*) What's troubling you?

Josey I'm going to piss.

A bright green light, and yellow light, as if a hedgerow, appears in front of **Josey**. *He stands in the midst of this light. A young* **Girl** *with very thin poor hair and ill-dressed, rickety and frail and scrawny as a hen, approaches.* **Josey** *ducks back. The girl looks morose, off-putting, and sick.* **Josey** *holds out his arms at her and smiles. Rook noises. The* **Girl** *does nothing, does not look at him.* **Josey** *jumps at her and flattens her on the ground, noiselessly, and rolls off. The* **Girl** *gets up and walks on. Lighting returns to kitchen as before.*

Mick What happened to you?

Josey I tripped on the linoleum.

Mick (*getting up and helping him*) You poor old sod. Have you pulled anything?

Josey I've not pulled the hernia anyway. I must be all right. I don't feel anything.

Mick It's not good for an old man to fall. You'll have arthritis on the bumps for Christmas. (*Laughs.*)

Josey I'm a very clumsy sort of man, I expect.

Mick You're not. You're a dancer. A real dancer. Catch your breath.

Josey God bless me, I've pissed.

Mick You shocked yourself. You confused yourself.

Josey I hate that. All wet. (*He shakes his trousers a little.*) Tch, a poor excuse.

Mick Wear your Sunday.

Josey (*astonished*) On a Monday? Are you ill? I'll put on the old brown jobs.

Mick Josey, boy, you have more holes in them than a cloth. They're a walking disgrace.

Josey They're dry though. I'll have a rash on me if I linger now.

Mick Take them off, take them off, I'll get my other pair for you.

Josey Oh, that will be grand. I like those trews. They have a kind of shine to them.

Mick From sitting on my arse by the heat.

Josey *laughs with his head back, very strangely.*

Mick *standing at the dark rectangle of the left window, suggested by grey-blue light. The window is quite big, a front window of a circa 1910 farmhouse.* **Josey** *is sitting by the glow of the fire, sunk into the heat.*

Mick It is in spate, the river. It is a dangerous thing for Brady's cattle. Fools of people. (*After a bit, shaking his head.*) Jack Dillon's waterfall, a wonder after rain. It was full of salmon once, that big stream. Pig farmers! (*After a bit.*) You sold them in scores to the Commercial Hotel, formerly. (*After a bit.*) You wouldn't know what a flood would raise. I can't eat a salmon. Why would I?

Josey (*vaguely, low as if it is a formula*) He has left us in our place, that man.

Mick I wonder now, I wonder.

Josey (*low*) I never touched a woman in my born days. I'll sit inside this downpour forever.

Mick (*not looking back, but addressing* **Josey**) Do you want to start marrying someone? Where would you seat her? This farm would not divide. It is already a scrap.

Whinny of the horse outside, and a fall of light as he passes the window. His shape can be made out.

The big soft girl.

Josey But I never touched a girl, unless you count the lass I knocked down in the lane.

Mick If you don't knock them down, they won't lie down at all.

Josey You never did it. It makes a man strange to himself. It is more breaking bones in a sack to add them to pigfeed, than any other thing.

Mick If you don't knock them down, they won't lie down at all. The people in this valley are very silent. Just as well, sometimes. (*After a bit.*) The roads will be streaming. (*After a bit.*) The people in this valley are as far away from each other as old ships in a fog in an old sea-story. There's a fog of rain that keeps them apart. Only the fiddles kept any sort of company going. (*After a bit.*) TV aerials.

Josey If he ever had any thought of vengeance, he has it now certainly.

Mick He has. (*After a bit.*) Except we are like married people. We sleep in the same bed like the wed. It is like a marriage. (*After a bit.*) Did he plan that, I wonder, him who seemed to despise Mam's company while she breathed? When she was dead, he mourned her, tilled her plot like a little field, sowed it with a harvest of snowdrops. You'd think she had been a fine film star –

Josey Hail Freedonia!

Mick A woman in ermine, stepping along in black and white, with a glister of moonlight on a Californian bay, and a dead man sunk under the jetty. Is that what he aimed at for us, a little marriage for her sake? Didn't I plot and plan to go to New York, where the tailoring would have been a good profession, instead of jobbing down there in the town for forty years, making jackets for the lunatics in the asylum, such jackets that hitched their arms, making them swing, putting a true mark of madness on the poor men. I made madmen mad-looking in my time. (*After a bit.*) I sleep in his dip.

Josey But why vengeance on myself? I was his favourite.

Mick Josey, it was vengeance on me only.

Josey You think I can sit here like an old gaslamp in peace?

Mick No other peace would've suited your temperament, man.

Josey I'd like to tell you, I had high hopes once, sitting in the flea-pit of Killarney, of going west myself in a train, feeding the carriages into the engine, and arriving in due time. I had no other hope in life than to be a Marx brother, a worthy ambition I should think.

Mick It was. You should have had your chance, Josey, instead of being stuck here on a hill-farm with me.

Josey Aye.

Mick (*quietly*) That I might find the big scissors that would cut this farm in two. That I might eat my way through the sheep, and go to some glittery big city, with long cars in it.

Josey Aye, and injuns, and wagons, and those big open farms with grass waving on them for days.

Mick And drink at a distant bar, after work, and go home with a confident step, and put meat on the table in a brown parcel for my wife, who would be old now but pretty with make-up, like Mrs Molloy. To think that the girl I would have met, in some park or in some street, is now an old one like myself, and it was someone else she met and kissed, and was nervous talking to, and then grew stronger with. And all these years of seasons and floods, of greenery and streams and mud and whiskey nights, she has cleaned her American home, and looked out at the brisk sunlight without me.

Josey I always wanted one of them furcoats, the sort that makes the head look like a lost moon, Mick, and a pair of them shining socks. I'd look like a scarecrow in them, but I could be happy in such attire. I might walk the length of the towns, and print my footstep in concrete like Charlie Chaplin, laughing with a jerk at me in the cinema. Now how did he know I was there to see him, to give me that laugh?

Mick He gave it to us both.

Josey I was always very like that boy that roomed with Charlie Chaplin. I might have been the boy.

Mick You were the boy. You were always the boy. And you always wore a fur coat too, in effect.

Josey (*after a bit*) He foxed us for fillies, God's truth.

Rain as before. **Josey** *in the chair still.* **Mick** *is warming his hands and back at the fire near him. When he speaks he almost hisses.*

Mick Strange black hair, long red face, hard hands, good at shelling peas, soft lap enough, not a local woman. TB – Mam.

Josey Rightyo . . . Mam.

Mick Is that how you recall it?

Josey I don't recall anything about it at all.

Mick She kept hens there, in that very yard, such hens as few wouldn't want to own for themselves. She had three dresses, Mam, one black for deaths, one blue with white dots for wear, and a grey one for music. There were no bought clothes then, not up here.

Josey Was she fair?

Mick Listen to me. She was red-faced, black-haired. She couldn't speak a word of English or any other tongue.

Josey Was that the way?

Mick She kept her own counsel to the last degree. (*After a bit.*) Silent all her life, except for peculiar grunts. She waved her arms a deal. When she shelled peas, she used a tin dish for them, and had a flick in her wrist that sent each row of peas in hard, with a kind of pattern. She could do it with my head on her lap. I watched the sky, and ting, ting, ting, went the peas behind my ears. I could hear her smiling. You have to get on with things.

(*After a bit.*) Thirty years old. If I saw her on the road now she'd look like a child. She was a great beauty, I should imagine. (*After a bit.*) No. (*After a bit.*) She could walk of course, and listen. She could hear the rain begin to fall over Bantry, seven miles away. She'd have the sheets in off the bushes in a twinkle, you wouldn't know why. The rain would be along presently. That's a talent.

Josey *rises, and goes to the smaller window on the right, where the old fiddle is.*

She scolded us with her hand. She seemed to make a favourite of me, I think. I appreciated it. But she didn't scorn you, nor neglected to tend to you, Josey. You were a wild boy often. You could throw a fit quicker than a rook in a tree of rooks. You were often a very wild rook, boy.

Rook noises. **Josey** *comes back with the fiddle and its bow.*

Josey Listen to me now. I'll make it talk anyhow.

He plays the untuned strings, a scraping with the occasional note.

Mick (*in a gap in the playing*) Good. Lamentable but good. (*After a bit.*) Good man, Josey.

Stage darkens. Four figures dance slightly, with their backs to us from the right, in a line. They are wearing cloaks at the back. **Josey** *has his eyes closed in the murk. He plays on. The dancers turn briefly, with the same step in unison that* **Josey** *did earlier, splaying one hand, putting forward one foot. On this side they are wearing the costumes of chorus line dancers, glittery. They are large women. This happens briefly, then they turn their backs again, and dance off. Light as before.*

Mick (*after* **Josey** *stops*) I don't know what the hell the tune was, but it put me in mind of something. How she was always very mouselike when he played. A great big woman like that.

Josey I don't have the name of the tune.

Mick It was a great pity.

Josey I never had it.

Mick No, that she was dumb. She was the kind of person you wanted to apply to for answers on certain matters. She had an awful clever look to her often.

Josey I expect.

Josey *is now asleep on the chair.* **Mick** *is over to the right, where a smaller smudge of windowlight is, the dark glimmer of a small window on the weather side of the farmhouse, where the fiddle is kept. He holds the fiddle in his hands, looking at it.*

Mick If you can play this you can do a lot. It has strings like Charlie's tail, very wisps of music, a music that has died in my hands and Josey's. There were tunes in this fox-coloured thing that would . . . When our legs were spindles in the school trousers we danced to his tunes, like fools of lambs. What's this silent tune we dance to now, the rain's hammers?

Mick *stays quiet in the shadows. A patch of light shows the* **Mother** *in a blue and white dress, with a bowl and a few pods of peas. She is sitting downstage left. As she shells each pod deftly, she aims the peas into the bowl, where they rattle. She hums a tune silently, almost angrily. She gathers herself and gets up and carries the bowl and the empty pods over to the right, the light going with her as if a private atmosphere, to where* **Mick** *stood before in the rain.* **Mick** *is visible in shadow some way upstage of her. A further light beams down on her, falling from right to left. She holds out her arms slightly, pods in one hand, bowl in the other, and turns her face to the light, eyes closed, begins to smile, and holds herself there. After a while the light thickens, and rain falls lightly at a slant to her. She laughs lightly for a little, silently.* **Mother** *goes off right, previous lighting returns.* **Mick** *smooths the body of the fiddle, looks at the dust on his fingers.*

Mick There's varnish on her still, under the cake of mildew and paw-prints there's a shine on the old creature. You could play this and be young. Young and be still in your heart's kindness, young as a white potato in the drill, a new spud for the pot or the pit, for to give a man and his brother life. Now they kill brothers in policemen's quarters, they bring them out into a yard among the back buildings. I've heard this as clearly as a badly bowed tune, as clear as an ill dream or a clatter of rain. They ask the brothers in for questions, clean out their pockets and their toothbrushes, brought in in expectation of a long night of asking and telling, strip them down gently, picture them, and beat them. The brothers are old enough, one belly a bit fat, sagging under the ugly lights. They are beating the brothers under the lamps, the older one, the heavy old one buckling, what distance those legs have traipsed, buckling, at the belt of a whittled stick, a stick to answer promptly. Buckling in the light, in a hard time, to make you stop and think – 'Sweet life' you are thinking, 'Sweet life', everything of value is your brother, your tobaccos and papers and talks, your dreams, your hope held up as a poor cloth for protection and secrecy. So the old brother goes down to the gravel ground, a thing to watch with a bloody look, his blood in your eyes. The brother goes down, buried in his own messes, and you return to the gates of the prison alone. Nothing, no fiddle full of early days and boys' legs cavorting like goats, can bring him back. I think then, thanks for my old sleeping brother, unbeaten, as quiet as an owl in our house here on a hill above a new flood. Let me stand between him and all harms, all human harms, if no one better's to be found.

As before, but **Mick** *is now centrestage. The bright green and yellow bush lights, as with* **Josey** *and the* **Girl** *before, form around him. The* **Girl** *approaches, not looking at* **Mick**. **Mick** *steps into her path, and stoops towards her. The* **Girl** *is staring, not seeing, at his chin, stalled.*

Mick Did you ever see a brown trout in a deep, muddy hole? You did not. But he is there. (*Getting more and more severe.*) Did you ever see a chick turn in his egg, in the liquid? You did not. Did you ever see the bladder of a mare, as she stalls in the fields, hindlegs splayed, and thrashes a pillar of piss on the grass? You could not have.

Girl Out of my path and let me home.

Mick Did you ever admire the look of a white slug on a fresh young cabbage, plucked from the leaf and set down on the wooden draining board, did you ever come out in the morning and find the world of your farm stitched and corded with trails, snails' journeys that have no rhyme or reason? Did you never play foot-the-ball as a child and step on a snail, and hear the wet crunch, and curse yourself? Did you never see your father take up a tiny pup, and put its tail in his mouth, and bite it off, blood trailing down his chin?

Girl Out of my path and let me home.

Mick Did you ever rise to the bait of a corner-girl, get confused in a town by cries and accounts and askings, did you never feel the trouble of a girl as she walked in front of you, agitating her skirts, making her bottom stick? Did you not, indeed? Were you never mocked, giggled at and ruffled, did you never carry your shame into an alleyway, and cry for yourself, hugging your jacket? Did you never sweat in the summer dark, did you never lie in dirty sheets, gripping yourself like a lever you could use to drive out along ploughland, did you never hear a priesteen tell you that girls had no yen for anything, no moisture, no need, no cry, no thoughts? You did not. Did you never have to stop in the street crippled by your own blood, your poker jammed in your trouserleg, in such a manner as was plain to the every passer? You could not have. Did you never pray under soaking leaves, and wipe warm, white seeds in a cloth of jelly off your gansey? Did you never smell your own stinking perfumes, feel your body constrict in a queer mess, did you never ask the sky for a girl to hold your shoulders, stroke your forehead, say something to you you could store up for a hundred times? Did you never look in your pantry of sweet remarks and find it ever bare – bare in boyhood, barer in manhood, barest in first old age? You did not.

Girl Out of my path and let me home.

Mick Do you think we are not princes, Josey and me on the hill? Do you think he could not honour you? Do you think he would always knock you on the track? Do you think he has been taught anything? Do you not see the gentle cogs in him? Do you not hear his engine whirring gently? Do you not see a moon in each of his eyes, brown eyes without whites or pupils? Do you not see a creature that would care for you? He would walk over every townland telling farmers of you, if he only knew how to do it. Do you think all the talk he has heard in his school, in the roads, in the lanes, on the gates of farms, has anything to do with him? Do you not think it is just a crust, a dirt on him, that you could wipe off if you knew the trick of it, and discover under it the house of the cleanest snail? Do you not see that, if he was unsuitable, I would do, as much for you as himself, if you were generous, and could see me in this matter?

Girl Out of my path and let me home.

Then, in her own light, her face turned away from **Mick.**

His mother was a bad speaker. A rat stole her tongue. She was hard to work. She was a slave. She bore a tailor's goose, an idiot-man. The river is the better man, good for clothes, and for drowning. Here goes nothing. There were lights, there were lights to find me.

The same, **Girl** *gone. The rain has stopped.* **Josey** *is still asleep.* **Mick** *is standing where he was with the* **Girl**. *Now and then* **Josey** *whimpers in his sleep, like a dog.*

Mick (*to wake him*) Josey.

Josey *whimpers again.*

Mick (*walking to the stool*) Josey. You sound like Shep.

The **Father** *comes on from the left, stands between them in front of the fire.*

Father (*looking at* **Josey**) The old cretin. What use is he to you?

Mick (*not looking at* **Father** *but at* **Josey**) He is every use to me. He is the thing I know.

Father (*putting out his left hand and taking a toothbrush from* **Mick**'s *breast pocket*) What do you carry this for?

Mick In case someone might think us uncivilised.

Father And do you use the item much?

Mick (*thinking, then after a bit*) A great deal.

Josey (*waking, at which* **Father** *goes off left*) Warm. My heavens on earth.

Mick What is it?

Josey I dreamt something.

Mick You'll toss all night in the bed, sleeping down here like that.

Josey Old men may dream.

Mick What class of a dream was it?

Josey I have not the least remembrance of it. It was water though. There were lamps. Lamps of a pony-and-trap, not a car. The old high lamps, brass lamps, stuck up on poles that pony-and-traps had. If there was ever a beautiful contraption in this valley, it was a pony-and-trap. (*He wipes his face in his hands.*) Well.

Mick It's a dark night. Do you want to go up?

To the left, a circle of light around the **Mother**, *where she was sitting before, kneading the clay around the roots of a geranium in a clay pot.* **Mick** *steps back towards her light, and settles on the ground a little away from her, watching what she is doing.*

Mick Mam.

The **Mother** *looks up briefly.*

Mick How's Mam?

The **Mother** *nods at him, pressing the clay still.*

Mick There's a very strange trick in the town now.

She looks at him.

Mick No, there is, there is. I'll tell you. I was down there after school. A few of the lads were talking about the new contraption they've set up for the sake of Moran's Meeting Rooms. So I went in myself for the mischief. It was a most unusual thing. It's like a beer mug with a lid, but it's big and white, and under the lid there's a seat for your backside.

The **Mother** *stops kneading and raises her fist to him, smiling.*

Mick Well, there is. I can't help that.

The **Mother** *encourages him with her forehead.*

A big thing enough. I was marvelling at it. It was filled with water, you'd think it was for drinking out of, or washing your paws, the water was so clean.

Mother *laughs silently.*

You see, Mam, you're to regard this contraption as a sort of quiet spot, like a clay pit.

Mother *looks at flowerpot, nods.*

It was a marvel, the clearness of the water, and what they expected you to do in it. I wouldn't have pissed in it for the world.

Mother *shushes him briefly, laughs.*

Mick *walks back to where he was, while* **Mother** *goes off left. Previous lighting.*

Josey Give us a time here still with ourselves. We've not much on, have we? Will you bury the spuds tomorrow?

Mick They're in.

Josey Fair dues.

Mick I don't know. I went through the leg of the dog doing it.

Josey Where? Over by the whitethorn?

Mick You shouldn't bury animals in good earth. You'd no marker nor other stone to tell me. You put him in there because the soil was soft from last year's pit. It was less work for you. But a potato pit is not a grave, man.

Josey He'll salt the spuds for us.

Mick I filled him in again and dug afresh.

Josey Fair dues. (*He strokes back his hair.*) I was tired and dry earlier.

Mick Jesus Christ.

Josey How, Jesus Christ? A lovely man he was, with a skirt.

Mick I'm stymied. I'm like a bullock stuck in a bog. I feel that if I move again, I'll never be contented.

Josey What do you mean? On the floor there, stymied, do you mean?

Mick Stymied.

Josey You were always stymied, weren't you? Stymied was your tune.

Mick Aye. There's no sense in me.

Josey There's only very little. You are almost a halfwit.

Mick The pot and the kettle.

Josey Are you asleep? You have the room troubled.

Mick I should have gone down to the town tonight. I'm not myself.

Josey Well, you should have suited yourself. I was asleep completely. I might have slept till you came home. It's always home here.

Mick I'll go out and walk. I'll go up to the top field a little way and look down on our roof. That helps me. I am shivering like a lamb. I must have been born in the snow.

Josey Go on out. Talk to the horse for a minute. Don't fall over.

Mick I'll go out for a little while. The starlight will do me good. I'll look at the boulders going up the back of the farm, or talk to the horse. I'll be able to see the old dun if there's a moon, or imagine it.

Josey It will be muddy after the rain. Don't fall on a loose bit of ground.

Mick If everything is dripping, I'll be content again. It is a lovely sound, the dripping bushes.

Call of stranded cattle below.

Josey Sheep on a hill are best, poorer but best.

Mick That must be some water now, in the channel.

Josey Go out and see it.

*Outside. Dark, rush of river below. A patch of daylight grows on the threshold, showing the heap of the **Father**, lying on his side, his face turned upwards. **Mick** leans into the circle of daylight, bending over the figure.*

Father (*softly*) What's this putty in me?

Mick How will I help you?

Father When I breathe, I can feel putty moving in me, with hardship.

Mick Will I pillow some part of you?

Father It is an uncomfortable thing, being full of hard putty.

Mick Will I warm it in my fingers?

Father Go away out from me, I am not used to you.

Mick Should I fetch something? Some other person?

Father Pray for me.

Mick (*unhappily*) What did you say?

Father I said, pray for me, are you hard of hearing?

Mick Our father who art in Heaven, let me talk to this man before it is impossible. Amen.

Father That is a bad, ill-sounding prayer.

Mick It is my prayer.

Father I suppose you'd like to stamp on me?

Mick That isn't what I want.

Father Ah, go away with yourself somewhere, and let me lie.

Mick (*trying again*) Father most wayward, pray for –

Father Pray for me properly, you fool!

Mick Accept this most beautiful, most wayward father among the other fathers.

Father *closes his eyes*.

Old fisher, goodbye.

Josey, *alone in the kitchen. He stands centrestage, facing the 'door'. When he talks, he talks conversationally, but with stilted gestures.*

Josey You might miss the travelling forge, Driscoll's, the songwriter, but there's no horses left for it. Charlie's the last man, the rare boy. You won't get a farrier to come up here now. There was a horse on every farm, sometimes two for a plough. Charlie is the last man. It will be a queer drop of water in the waterfall, I have seen that. I have seen that waterfall. There's a

thing about a flood that's rarely said – it is greedy for the fields.
It is a bull for them. You can't prevent it. Mick can not eat a
salmon! He could not touch one. There are none now, there are
none. The pigs ate them. The slurry, you know. You would want
to bring the cows up here when they call. They wish it. Once a
year in the flood they wish it heartily, to come up here with the
two dark men. (*Laughing.*) We will hold Charlie to the house the
winter, we will nurture him. We will bolster him, like our
bolster, on the bed above. Mick sleeps in his dip! She left none.
We could not have bolstered her. She died in blood, like a sheep,
she was a stick, a small stick. He was ever a pleasing horse! Even
from the furthest field he will come when I shout for him, he
wouldn't budge for a foreigner. He has no interest in sugar. Do
you want sugar in that, Mick? Don't poison it, he says!
(*Laughing.*) He is a wise old horse, but very old. Let him stick by
the house, certainly. He can pull the cart still, he enjoys himself
in the shafts. I saw the loose shoe when he brought up the wood,
I spotted it. (*Laughs.*) I can see, I can see. I saw that. He has
plenty of go in him still. But he's troubled by age. Princelike.
Holy. The very best. Isn't he? Brady's mare foaled him. Best.
God now. He has pulled, he has pulled a host of loads, turfloads,
timberloads, big sacks of grain and feed, bundles of firesticks like
farmers in coats. He is too old. We must guard him. The friend.

*He goes off left, the stage is empty. The length of the downstage section
begins to light more brightly, putting the upstage region generally in
shadow. The* **Mother** *comes on from the left with a bowl of henseed.
Clucking noises off. As she walks she flings the seed, but silently. When the
'hens', suggested by red brushstrokes of light, rush in, she seems to want to
drive them back with stamps of her right foot. She is wearing a black
dress. The seed that she casts is pierced and lit by sunlight, in beams from
low upstage. When she reaches centrestage,* **Josey** *comes on after her. He
is holding a dead rat by the tail.*

Josey (*holding himself in*) Mam, Mam.

The **Mother** *glances back and then goes on casting the seed, the sunlight
washing it till it falls.*

Josey Mam!

She turns properly and looks at him, and he raises up the rat for her inspection. She steps back a pace, and mimes for him to throw the rat away downstage. **Josey** *looks at her blankly. She mimes again. He flings the rat away into the dark of the stage. She sweeps forward and places her palm on his cheek softly enough, but with almost a blow, straightens his jacket, pushes him away by the shoulder gently, turns and walks off right, casting the seed. This time no light falls through it.* **Josey** *looks after her. He walks a little way after her. At centrestage he lies on the ground, curls somewhat, sleeps. Darkness for a space. Light of the kitchen fire returns, and when it does,* **Josey** *is still on the ground, but his feet are facing us, his legs and arms spread as if he is fastened at the ankles and wrists. As he says the first word, the room darkens and a clear yellow light falls on him.*

Josey (*quickly*) Mick!

He pulls on his invisible bonds.

Mick!

His head goes back and he rests. He jerks suddenly at the bonds, straining his face up to look in front and to each side of him.

Ghost of God! Mick!

The **Girl** *comes on, as odd and dirty as before. She walks on her knees.*

What is it?

She does not answer. She stops near him.

Where have you me? Am I far? Who has me tied?

Girl Did you ever put a buttercup under your chin and see the yellow?

Josey What has me tied-up? Are you going to sell me? Is it fair day now?

Girl Yellow, yellow. A bad colour all told.

Josey Would you loosen me? I would pray for you if you could. I've no money.

Girl Did you ever notice how much improved the countryside is in a good summer – how the place looks very much another place? And gives you different hopes.

Josey Mick has the money, you see. I don't even see my pension. The post office gives it to him. Of course it is an ideal arrangement. I would lose it on the road back.

Girl It is very difficult though to understand the most of it. How you are to have hope, and then no hope, for the rest of the stint.

Josey Loosen me, please. I have a great crick in my neck from this.

Girl Rain falling on the mass – that's what I thought. We are all here, all of us, the sinners and the saints and the mixtures, inside the wooden church, and the rain is falling on us. On the mass.

Josey Can't you hear me? I was asking you many questions. Already you have answered none of them.

Girl We huddle in the porch. The whole townland almost in the one porch. Not much of a place if we are all there is to it. We've bred no one of any repute that I know of. It is not a world.

Josey Where am I here?

The **Girl** *turns on her knees and starts back.*

Wait now, wait now.

The **Girl** *stops.*

Girl (*not looking back*) Yellow, yellow. Bitter, bitter.

Josey That's a nice song.

Girl *starts to go again, and goes off.*

Josey Wait! What has me here? (*Quietly to himself.*) Tell me what keeps me.

Outside, noise of dripping and the rush of the swollen river below. There is a clear, dark, rinsed light, with high darkblue clouds crossing an otherwise lustrous night sky. The larger kitchen window is a rectangle of brighter light, illuminated by the fire inside. **Mick** *stands with his back to us, arms at his sides, staring at the house, silent. The figure of the horse goes slowly, quietly, head down, from left to right, passing some way in front of* **Mick**'s *back. After a time,* **Josey** *comes into the area of the 'door'. He looks at* **Mick**, *pauses on the threshold. He comes forward, places a hand on* **Mick**'s *shoulder, and brings him in.*

Inside the kitchen. The stairs are again visible on the right. **Mick** *and* **Josey** *stand a few feet inside the 'door'. The fire is low.*

Mick (*needing help*) Josey.

Josey Christ in His Heaven.

Mick What, Josey?

Josey Mick, I dreamed I was a girl. I fell asleep on the floor.

Mick What were you like?

Josey I was miserable.

Mick Much the same then.

Josey Oh, but I was very miserable, I wanted to go in the river quick.

Mick Dreaming. You'll have strange pains from the damp in that floor.

Josey I didn't want to be miserable. I was making a great effort. I was like a slave. (*Crying.*) I know nothing. I am a cretin.

Mick Do you know this fire? (**Josey** *nods.*) You're my brother. If you were ever a cretin I was one too. You were dreaming.

Josey *goes a few steps up the stairs.* **Mick** *is behind him, still on the floor.*

Mick There will be more rain. Of course there will be. (*Laughing.*) We're surrounded. The Indians. You never see them, they shoot from behind boulders. It is very much as they say. I think I'm done for. I don't think I can wait for those cavalry horses. (*Touching* **Josey**'s *knee at the back.*) You hold out without me. You take my bullets. Don't waste your water on me. Don't let the Indians creep up on you. Keep your eyes peeled, Josey. Take my bullets. (*Taking his hand back, talking to no one.*) Is there no sign of them bloody horses?

They remain like that for a moment.

Josey There is. There is every sign.

Curtain.

Prayers of Sherkin

For Barney, Maureen, Henry and Barbara,
the four friends.

Characters

Fanny Hawke, *thirty, plain.*
John Hawke, *her father, sixties.*
Hannah Hawke, *her aunt,* **John***'s sister, bowed back.*
Sarah Purdy, *sister of* **Fanny***'s mother. Arc of white hair.*
Jesse Hawke, **Fanny***'s brother, thin.*

Mr Moore, *the ferryman, fit, seventies.*
Eoghan O'Drisceoil, *fisherman, from Cape Clear.*

Patrick Kirwin, *lithographer, forty.*
Meg Pearse, *shopkeeper, handsome.*
Stephen Pearse, *her husband, considerably older.*
Singer, *impoverished woman, twenty.*

Matt Purdy, *the founder of the sect, in the form of an angel.*

Setting: Sherkin Island and Baltimore, County Cork. 1890s.

Prayers of Sherkin was first performed at the Abbey Theatre (Peacock stage), Dublin, on 20 November 1990 with the following cast:

Fanny	Alison Deegan
John	Alan Barry
Hannah	Doreen Hepburn
Sarah	Joan O'Hara
Jesse	Phelim Drew
Mr Moore	Eamon Kelly
Eoghan	Owen Roe
Patrick	Brendan Gleeson
Meg	Ruth McCabe
Stephen	Wesley Murphy
Singer	Gina Moxley
Matt Purdy	Donal O'Kelly

Directed by Caroline FitzGerald
Designed by Bronwen Casson
Lighting by Tony Wakefield
Music by Shaun Davey

Act One

Curtain. A shadowy stage, except for **John**'s *workshop. Dusty late sunlight through a high window. Ten candles hanging from their rack, partly formed by ladling.* **Jesse** *with a simple basin. The broom in its place on pegs. They wear plain trim workclothes with natural-coloured aprons. Their accent is Sherkin with a tint of Manchester.*

Jesse Will you clean off your own hands now?

John (*looking at light*) I think I must. (*At candles.*) Another while of care for these characters. (*Washing his hands.*) But not this day, Jesse. Did you douse the wax-fire?

Jesse I did douse it, softly, Father.

John Give it another douse with this water now.

Jesse *goes off. He casts the water into a small stove. It hisses and steams.* **John** *takes the long-footed brush and begins to sweep in a careful style. Dust stirs.*

Does it build again?

No answer. **Jesse** *has headed home.* **John** *sweeps.*

A chandler must know his dirt. It is to be kept out of the yellow candles. And much the same caution for a baker. It is to be kept out of the bakery of his life. (*Light failing.*)

Outside. The whitethorn with its September berries. A low fresh moon in a late daylight sky. **Jesse** *comes on alone, without apron, a few candles in his hand. He sits in under whitethorn as is his practice. Scratches at the roots vaguely. Hugs his knees. The moon freshening, the face and form of* **Matt Purdy** *in the moon's gentle light. He is small and ordinary, he* *wears the 1790s clothes of an artisan from Manchester, and his accent is the same, strong and sincere.* **Jesse** *does not see him.*

Matt Purdy We embarked from the dark port of England and sailed to Cork in the whitest ship. There were storms in the purple sea and there were fruitful fishes, and the three families clung to the rails and found their haven. We followed the message that came to me in the dark of Manchester, under the chimneys and the black moon, the bright words ran over the rainy roofs and over the tumultuous graveyards of that city and over the factories where the children sweated and over the heads of the government officers and the policemen marching in the squares and the purple soldiers. And I, Matt Purdy, had my vision that was like unto the vision of John of Patmos, and it came to me in my dreams to go to Ireland for to find an island where we could abide. And we sailed out of the city of suffering to Cork, and found out this little island of Sherkin where we could wait for the city of light. Remember Thou the faith of the Purdys, the Smiths, and the Hawkes.

Distantly off, **Fanny** *is calling* **Jesse***'s name from the house. He scuffs away out from under the tree, only the moon in place of* **Matt Purdy.**

The darkening main room of the **Hawke** *house. Very plain and Quakerish, wooden, items on pegs. Two square windows, an unlit wood-stove, a bench and two high-backed wooden chairs, one still hung on its pegs. The other, brought over to the door,* **Fanny** *sits on, looking out. The light from outside moves through like water. She wears the entirely unadorned skirt and bodice of a Quakerlike sect of the 1890s, and an evening headcloth. She is watching for* **Jesse** *and her father. The table is set for five, with very simple bowls, white.* **Sarah** *comes in from kitchen with a lit taper, worriedly guarding it, lights the five candles in the room.* **Fanny***'s face brightens, she sits back a little, she sees someone coming.* **Hannah** *comes in from the kitchen more abruptly, carrying a bowl of steaming food.* **John** *steps in with* **Jesse** *on his heels.*

John Here is the nest of birds.

Fanny *gets up and kisses him, he rubs the kiss.*

If I had no kiss I might never come home.

Hannah (*looking at her work*) What a good plain table now.

They sit in their places, **John** *with* **Hannah** *and* **Sarah** *on the bench,* **Fanny** *and* **Jesse** *each side of them. They listen intently to* **John**.

John If you do please, Lord, this is our night prayer. We do ask you for the peace of this family. We do ask you for the silence and the storm of Sherkin. Once there were three families, Lord, that Matt Purdy led from Manchester. There were black chimneys there and the rotted streets, and they came for to wait for the new city. Lord, we do abide, even unto this third generation. There are no others. Lord, you have taken my wife Charity. Bring in your own time a plain husband from Manchester for this our daughter Fanny, and a plain wife for Jesse. Lord, we are not lonely but we are few. Send us your help. Lord, we pray that you have not forgotten us, your five remaining. Send us increase. May you not leave one of us alone here since all around are the darknesses of the Catholics and the strangenesses of the higher Protestants.

Sarah, *despite herself, sneaks out a hand to judge the warmth of the bowl.* **Hannah** *checks her.*

Lord, we trust in your promise to the poor and the revelation of your servant, John of Patmos, the blessed islander. Since he has shown that for us surely the New Jerusalem is by. Keep us ready for to be the tribe you mention, and let there be others still in Manchester though we have heard nothing of them for many a year. Lord, thank you for the prosperity of the candle manufactory and the ease of this plain house. Oh Lord, we do abide.

All We do abide.

They set to in silence. **Fanny** *looks back out through a window.*

Fanny The evening star, Jesse.

A simple music. The night deepens around them, the candlelight brighter. **Jesse** *takes a last careless spoon of food. He starts to choke.*

Hannah Oh, Jesse, you are too idle with food.

She pats his back.

Sarah Oh, Hannah, save his life.

Hannah I am saving his life now.

Jesse *better*.

Fanny His poor throat is crooked.

John He put it the wrong way. Bless you, child.

Hannah Now, Sarah, will we cross tomorrow to the yard? I have heaps of honeysuckle for the graves.

Sarah We could wait another week. I would have some selling butter then, in a week. I could hardly manage a batch tonight and tomorrow, dear.

Hannah I was thinking of the honeysuckle. I have never seen such good blooms. They would look well on the beds, now, would they not, Sarah?

John Moore would row you anyway, with or without butter.

Hannah Baltimore has butter enough without yours. (*After a bit.*) Though it is good butter. The best.

Sarah I do not like to cross without purpose.

Hannah Flowers is purpose enough.

Fanny And we would love to come, me and Jesse.

John (*to* **Sarah**) Now.

Sarah Well. The wicked thing is I love to cross. I dream of crossing. I am too attached to the town. I dream about that material in Pearse's. Wicked.

John Who is to mind a dream?

Sarah There is a ribbon-box too, Lord forgive me.

John Mr Moore will row you. I will give him a hand of candles as usual and he will row the lot of you and an angel to boot.

Sarah (*simply*) Matt Purdy saw five angels on the bridge crossing the great river. He saw them walking among the crowd of mortals, plain bright people with feathered wings.

John (*as a fact*) I never did see one. (*Rising, gathering bowls.*) Now, let us please the pig. You do not mind if I cast the remnant to the pig?

A little delay as **Hannah** *realises he is talking to her.*

Hannah He will be very cross if you do not.

They laugh. **John** *and* **Jesse** *go out with everything. The remaining three listen.*

Fanny He is serenading. I can hear him.

Hannah As near to a person as makes no odds, a pig.

John *and* **Jesse** *returning in good spirits.*

John A very fierce companionable pig.

Jesse The skeleton of a pig is similar to a man's.

John There is an observation. That boy has things in his head that only an angel would think of.

Hannah (*vaguely*) Oh, angels.

A simple music. **Sarah** *and* **Hannah** *alone.* **Hannah** *shakes out the white bedspread they are working on, some tiny sand-flowers already embroidered on it.* **Sarah** *brings to the table two more of the candles. The light is more theirs. She slips in under the cloth, the two of them begin to sew, together on the bench.*

Hannah Some peace now.

She winds her thread around thumb and forefinger on each hand with a quick practised movement, and snaps it.

At least the storm is not blowing again.

Sarah Or Fanny and Jesse could not have gone out.

Hannah It rattled the island. The lanes this morning were full of green branches.

Sarah Think of it far out at sea now, with all its froth and turmoil in the waves. Pleasant enough.

Hannah You would not say that if you were a sailor, like Mr Moore was once, or indeed a mere fish. I saw no big fish beached on the sand this morning this time. I did not see a blessed soul, only a man bringing his cart down, for weed.

Sarah Did you know him?

Hannah I think it was the hotel-keeper's cart. He has a little field of potatoes behind him. He would want the weed for that.

Sarah He has rights there to weed.

Hannah No doubt.

Sarah How many ships that were set for America, and foundered by Sherkin, no man knows.

Hannah I do believe you.

John *comes in from kitchen, peaceful with his book.* **Hannah** *and* **Sarah** *give him a smile. He takes down a chair and sits under a dark window.*

John May it not rain on the children.

Hannah Amen.

He settles, starts to read, almost immediately begins to daydream instead, flicking the clasp of the book.

(*The cloth is caught under something.*) Can you lift it from under your foot?

Sarah (*looking down*) It is not under any of my feet.

Hannah Ah, it is my own.

John Tell me, Hannah, what would be the best flowers to grow for bees?

Hannah Oh? Oh?

John There is no reason why we could not keep bees, I was thinking. It would save me buying in the wax from our little nuns. There would be no nuns' fees. There would be a great use in that. And I think it would give me a great pleasure, tending the bees. I understand there is a particular outfit for them, with a veil indeed. Something like a swordsman's outfit.

Hannah *smiles*.

Hannah Now, I imagine it would be the flowers with the best pollen.

Looks to **John** *for confirmation. He thinks, nods.*

Flowers with the best blooms. I imagine honeysuckle itself is a bee-attracting plant. I would be happy to grow more honeysuckle.

John Naturally, I could make the little houses myself. Jesse could do the designs. If I sent for a handbook, I think he might find it easy enough.

Sarah I cannot see it being too difficult for Jesse.

Hannah Mrs Pearse discussed a new flower with me, called the rhododendron. But I often saw bees on the gooseberries when they are flowering. Do you know, John, I feel the winds might be a bit rascally for bees here.

John (*accepting this*) Of course, we light the town already. A seaboard town. It is very good to stand on the pier and look over at Baltimore in the night and see the lights.

Sarah It is a great thing to light a town, I think.

John (*pleased*) The other day, when I was over in Baltimore, I had a most pleasant talk with Mr Pearse. How likeable I find him. He said there were never such candles in the world before the Hawkes, the Purdys and the Smiths came to Sherkin. And you know (*Laughing*.), he said his grandfather used to say that.

Hannah They are both very likeable, him and his wife.

John They are.

Sarah He is your special friend. And why not? You have every right to be loved by any friend.

John You know, Sarah, it is often said that the heron is the messenger. Sometimes you tell me a thing, and it has the force of the message the heron holds for the privileged stranger.

A short gap.

Do you remember, Hannah, when you heaped Moore's boat with honeysuckle, when we were bringing Charity over to the yard? It is an egregious plant. It is something for the donning of a corpse. Charity lying there. It was a kindness of Mr Moore's, to carry her so in state. Hah, he is a man of excellence, Michael Moore. Of the Catholic men on this island he is the paradigm. There is always something to learn from Mr Moore. He has been to very many places, in contrast to ourselves. There is a man that can sing the song of Valparaiso and he knows he has been there. He can see the streets of Valparaiso in his old head when he sings his song. It is not just a name. He carried Charity over to the yard heaped in honeysuckle. He rowed I think with a special pride.

Sarah Well, now.

John (*almost to himself*) Of course, Moore has a hearth, and has his hearth-lore. But we make do with our English stove.

The women shake out the cloth.

A sky of stars. The high moon. **Jesse** *and* **Fanny**.

Fanny Do you not feel that this island is moored only lightly to the sea-bed, and might be off for the Americas at any moment? Jesse?

Jesse *surveying the heavens.*

The pig would come with us, and never know, but that the weather might change, and he would freckle. We would line up with the Bahaman Islands and no one notice us, though I would be sad to lose Clear Island out there with its people and wandering lights. Oh, Jesse, we are not from here and I have such a sense of home. I am always thankful that the holy couples came here. They might have ended anywhere. I think it is the site of our New Jerusalem, which is to come from the heavens, right down from those stars.

Jesse *looks at her.*

You need not frown at me, I know you are not watching just tonight for any holy city. (*To herself.*) It would frighten a lion such a thought. (*To* **Jesse**.) You are careful of the stars for their own sake. A technical brother, dear. And, Jesse, you are a brother to excite something in my own head. There is a little stage there, and the dancers appear. Lord, Jess, they are can-can dancers like in the posters, and they are not speaking English. Your stars set off the dancers, and they are lovely big women with mad dresses, and whup, when they all kick their legs up, may you have mercy, but they are wearing nothing beneath.

Jesse (*not heeding her*) But all very tussocky grass for a scientist to lean his paper on.

Draws a pencil stub and a scrap of paper from a pocket. **Fanny** *lies on the ground, stomach down.*

Fanny You can make me your table, Jesse.

Jesse *looks up at the stars again, and starts to mark their positions.*

The grass has a lovely smell. It smells of tiny flowers.

Jesse The stars are as small as flowers to us. That is because of their great distance from our concerns.

Fanny (*turning onto an elbow*) Is that why you care to draw them?

Jesse No, this is science, Fanny. It is to see their relative positions. Ursa Major, Ursa Minor. The names are best given in Latin.

Fanny Oh, do not give any more of them in Latin. (*Getting up.*) Do you see, Jesse, how the beacon on Cape Clear, and our own house there, like a star fallen to the fields, and your own evening star, mark such a big triangle in the sky?

Jesse Ursa Major, Ursa Minor.

Fanny I think we had better not stay here longer. I can feel the breath of the grass rising into me. We will be sitting at home creaking like creels with damp.

Jesse I have the work now. (*Stuffing the paper in his pocket.*) August is a month of wonders. Any man like me lives for August and its moon. But I do not scorn September, between storms.

The candles bring back the room again. **Hannah** *and* **Sarah** *have cleared away their work.* **John** *hangs up his chair and waits by the open door.*

Hannah We will go over to Baltimore tomorrow, John, me and Sarah and the children, to put honeysuckle on the families' graves, and to get whatever scientific purchases for Jesse as can be found in a little place like Pearse's.

Sarah (*taking a candle for bed*) Oh, my dear, Pearse's. A dangerous spot for an old lady like myself.

Hannah We might look over a few linens. (*To* **John**.) A few sober-dyed linens.

John *nods, peacefully.* **Fanny** *and* **Jesse** *appear out of the dark.*

John Oh. Why, you both smell of rain.

Sarah (*going out with her candle into kitchen*) In Pearse's tomorrow I will pass by the ribbons. I will not put my hand in the ribbon-box.

John (*taking a candle, showing book to* **John**) I did not see much of this.

Fanny *smiles, kisses him, kisses* **Jesse**. **Hannah** *is preparing the bench as a bed for* **Fanny**. **John** *puts his hand on* **Jesse**'s *shoulder and leads him over to the kitchen door.*

Hannah (*to* **John**) I have a jug of milk in the drip-press for your morning.

John (*smiling, looking down at* **Jesse** *as he says it*) That will suit me.

They go out.

Hannah This is a fresh bed, dear.

Fanny (*starting to take off her clothes*) It is very inviting.

Hannah (*taking up a candle from a window, seeing that there are also two more*) How are there three candles left?

She sets the candle with the other one on the table.

Fanny (*working at the buttons on her underclothes*) Jesse took no candle for his book. He must be very sleepy.

Hannah *holds a big nightdress for* **Fanny**, *standing in front of her.* **Fanny** *takes off the last of her things and over her head goes the nightdress.*

Hannah There, now.

Fanny *into bed.* **Hannah** *draws the clothes up over her, covering her arms.*

When you were little I used to sing to you now, did I not? If I was let. I have no voice and Charity was always jealous for your rest. And quite right.

Hannah *leans over* **Fanny**, *taking the pins out of the headcloth.* **Fanny** *sneaks her arms out and puts them around* **Hannah***'s neck.* **Fanny** *seems both upset and happy.* **Hannah** *hugs her.*

Hannah Well. What is that story about? Now.

She disentangles herself and puts the headcloth with the other clothes, pats them.

Now. Put in your arms.

Fanny Do I look like her at all?

Hannah In this light, you could be her. Put in your arms.

Fanny Oh. (*Does so.*)

Hannah (*snuffs a candle, takes her own up*) I am glad there is no storm tonight. You will be asleep before I reach my own bed. Sleep well, child. God bless you.

Fanny And you, Aunty.

Hannah *goes off. A thickening of moonlight. The moon is big above the roof.* **Fanny** *takes her arms out again. Thinking. Stirs herself. Her prayer.*

The hour for a mother to come and kiss her child asleep. An hour darkened and sunken. Mine own hour that I cannot fear because of Jesse's concerns. There is a father asleep in his goose bed, there are two aunts in the same wooden room where they often slept as girls. There is a brother in his niche under the wooden stairs. There is a sleep over the islands. Cape Clear is low and dark on its own piece of dark sea, the lost glass lobster-floats bang in the deep sea-ravines, the dogs of the sea bark at each other on the bleak slabs. Peace to the Ganges, my God, the Amazon and the Shannon. Peace to the darting fishes and the crushed fishes of the very deep. Peace, my deepest Lord, to the great fold of shadow that the earth must draw around her in the night.

She sleeps. A simple music. The moon sets quicker than it could in real time. Light clears the ragged sky. A foot of sunlight creeps in over the windowsill. Enter **John**, *from kitchen, freshly shaved, clean, eager, simple, spick and span in his workclothes.*

John (*putting on his hat*) As long as there is dark there must be candles.

Fanny *wakes abruptly.*

Fanny Drowning!

John Drowning?

Fanny I was fighting in a waterfall of the Orinoco.

John Oh. Very good.

Sarah *comes in, already dressed for the town.*

Goodbye, Sarah.

Sarah Oh, goodbye, John. Do you have your cheese?

John *pats a pocket. He goes out.*

(*To herself.*) What a morning for creation. Fanny, go up to Hannah for your town dress. What a morning.

Fanny What a tremendous relief. You are dressed already?

Sarah What do you say, child? You should not rub your eyes, Fanny. The sleep will scratch them.

Sarah *puts one hand on a hip, and* **Fanny** *drifts out, still thinking of the Orinoco.*

Well, oh, well. That sunlight is a prayer in itself.

She busies herself with her bonnet.

John *in his workshop. He is humming a tune, very content. He likes the mornings. He puts on his ladling gloves, takes the wax-ladle off its peg. Approaches the wax-fire, holding the ladle out in front of him like a weapon.*

John (*amusing himself*) Nor shall my sword sleep in my hand. (*Goes off. A little clatter of tin. Reappears with a smoking ladle.*) To every saint his wickedness. (*Positions himself for ladling the candles, lets the wax flow down the first wick.*) This coat for Sarah. (*The next.*) This for Hannah. (*The next.*) This for Fanny. (*The next.*) This for Jess. (*The next, hesitates.*) Well, this for Charity. (*Looking at remaining candles.*) Who these others are I do not know. (*Addressing them.*) I do not suppose you do know yourselves? I will give you coats anyhow. For it is such weather.

Bright early morning, the pier. A long white-wooden rowing-boat, **Mr Moore***'s.* **Fanny** *and* **Jesse** *in the bow seat,* **Mr Moore** *centre with oars. Their good town coats,* **Mr Moore** *more anciently dressed.* **Hannah** *and* **Sarah** *on the pier.* **Hannah** *holds a big armful of her honeysuckle.*

Sarah Mr Moore, you are sure there will be no sudden gustiness?

Mr Moore Very likely.

Sarah Very likely yea, or very likely nay?

Fanny Mr Moore is an expert at this crossing, Aunty, do enter the boat. Me and Jesse are like two shifting horses here. There is a whole morning in the town if you will just please get in, Aunty.

Hannah Mr Moore, where shall I put my flowers, of your kindness?

Mr Moore (*rising*) Well (*Holding out his arms.*), I will give them to Mr Jesse Hawke.

Hannah *steps forward with the flowers.*

Sarah If you please, Hannah, do not go trusting there. The pier has a little coat of greenness. It is only waiting for you to surrender your balance.

Hannah Well, hold my coat at the rear. (**Sarah** *does, unnecessarily.*) It is all right, Mr Moore (*He has shown no worry.*), I do not intend to bury you in flowers. I have a string about them.

Mr Moore Ah, good for you, Miss Hawke.

He takes them, sets them in front of **Jesse** *and* **Fanny**. *He assists* **Hannah** *into the stern seat.*

Sarah (*hopelessly, to* **Fanny** *and* **Jesse**) She is very efficient. Since I have no butter this time, I will be better staying.

Hannah Sarah. Do not let me wander about Baltimore alone. I do not want to be taken by pirates, do I, Jesse? The sea is perfectly courteous and flat today, is it not, Mr Moore?

Mr Moore Very likely.

Hannah Sarah, dear, behold. See for thyself. Between here and the town is a gentleman's dinnerplate.

Sarah Naturally I will come. (*Stamps her foot.*) I will come, (*Stamps.*) I will come.

Fanny Think of Pearse's, Aunty.

Sarah *launches herself.* **Mr Moore** *and* **Hannah** *help her to her place beside* **Hannah**.

Sarah Oh, my world.

She adjusts her bonnet, looks very pleased now.

A silly old woman.

Matt Purdy *appears above, shaking a light sunlight across them.*

Matt Purdy It was best to bring them away out of Manchester, in that white ship, upon the hilly sea. Our friend was the full of time, our foe the slight nature of our numbers. What was to be if ever there were none to marry? That was the dark figure in my dream. Oh lend us endurance, thou, Mount Gabriel. Lend us long strength, thou, Bay of Roaringwater. And, ye, little gathered islands, lend us the future of children.

He mingles back into the general light. Creak of boat. **Mr Moore** *is slowly rowing them, across the channel. The mingle and plates of water.* **Sarah** *jubilant.*

Hannah Is it not lovely now, Sarah, love?

Sarah Oh, a very special treat for an old dame.

Hannah Mr Moore is a famous rower, are you not?

Mr Moore (*smiling*) Very likely.

Fanny Mr Moore was given the prize of a ticking-clock at the Cape Clear rowing races.

Mr Moore Oh.

Hannah And did you have to accept it in Erse, Mr Moore?

Mr Moore I had to row in Erse, let me tell you.

Streaming light and water. **Jesse** *trails his hand.*

Hannah (*to* **Sarah**) I do not like to leave the people long without flowers.

Sarah Oh, I agree. Um, hum, hum.

Hannah I do hope you will bring such flowers to my resting-spot, Fanny?

Fanny I would not leave a gardener without her flowers. (*To* **Jesse**.) Do you see the curtain of light hanging there? It seems to travel along.

Jesse There is a phenomenon similar to this, under the North Pole. It is called the Aurora Borealis.

Mr Moore The Northern Lights. And I saw them.

Jesse Ah, to measure such a thing.

Mr Moore You don't care to measure them, Mr Hawke. You are leaning on the ship's rail. Your coat sticks to it with a glue of pure ice. It is the dark of the night, when the world is a whale and you are Jonah. Overhead, clear through the black spars, that wonderful sheeting of strange light. You think of your God.

Hannah And quite correctly. (*Nods at* **Sarah**.)

Sarah Oh, yes.

Hannah There are many points of similarity between us, Mr Moore, as between this, this light that Fanny saw, and that, that Aura you mention. I have always said it.

Sarah You are an excellent rower, Michael Moore.

Mr Moore I thank you. In Mayo they call that (*Indicating light.*) veins. (**Hannah** *showing polite interest.*) Yes, veins.

The curtain of light falls around **Mr Moore**.

(*As if alone.*) In particular if I could have the crow at my command I would be most thankful. In particular if I could have the robin. In particular if I could have the whistler at my command, and the warbler and the croaker, and the cryer and the caller, and the weak-throated, I would show my gratitude. Oh, yes. In particular, the shallow-rooted bush, the wind-haggard, the frost-nipped, the fluent sea-grass, the ruckled dunes, the stranded fish, in particular the long-beaked sandbird, in particular these at my command would cause in me gratitude. Oh who is the farmer of these acres, who is the farmer of these acres?

Everything as before, the light moving on.

I thank you, I thank you.

Baltimore. The town goes up above the wharf. Long blocks of shadows from the half-risen sun. **Mr Moore** *helps out* **Sarah** *and* **Hannah**, *who wait on the wharf with a certain public air. He hands up honeysuckle,* **Fanny** *and* **Jesse** *climb out. There is a quietness about them all, below* *the town. They would prefer to whisper.* **Mr Moore** *ties his rope to a ring on the wharf.*

Hannah We will go up soon to the upper street. We will make the briefest of pilgrimages now.

Mr Moore *returns to his boat, tends a clay pipe.* **Sarah** *catches* **Hannah**'s *eye.*

We will have our good time in Pearse's, never you fear. (*Leading* **Sarah** *away a little.*) Let us examine a few examples at the greatest leisure possible.

Sarah (*hushed*) If we saw a linen that we liked. Sober-dyed, mind you.

Hannah It will be our adventure.

Mr Moore (*to himself*) A pipe is as tender as a bird's leg. Tap not thy pipe.

Hannah The old must have adventures. Old maids in particular.

Sarah Oh!

Hannah (*coming back a little*) Michael, if you wished to wait for us in the hotel? You might find that cold waiting.

Mr Moore Ah, I'm much the happiest here by myself. I'll puzzle out my own concerns. Partly by philosophy, partly by daydream.

A yew-coloured light. The graveyard. **Fanny** *and* **Jesse** *wait for them.*

Hannah The holy couples.

Sarah They are always here.

Hannah They have found some peace for themselves by this sea.

Sarah (*attentive*) They have.

Hannah (*quietly, to* **Sarah**) Charity. (*Laying some of the honeysuckle.*) Sherkin has not its Charity now. She is with her wains there. That is what she wanted. My, do you recall the commotion when Fanny was born living, after these two damp boys?

Sarah *takes some honeysuckle and kneels at another spot.*

Sarah I must give old Matt Purdy a good dose of these. (*Finding something.*) Why, Hannah, a feather. I should think a starling's feather. Or a corncrake. But that needs corn. It hides itself away, in the harvest, and crakes before night.

Hannah Indeed.

Sarah (*risen*) I have greened my knees.

Hannah Look at this long root here, growing in my mother's grave. (*It is* **Mr Moore**'s *rope.*) What tree is it from?

Sarah One of the yews. A yew will walk yards from its place.

Hannah I must pull it out.

Sarah You will not pull that root out.

Hannah (*hauling*) How hard they hold.

Sarah Have a care for your back.

She puts a hand on **Hannah**'s *back.*

Around them gathers Pearse's general shop. Materials, rolls and lengths, Hawke's candles, tins, boxes, cliffs of buckets, axes, coats, boots, marked wooden drawers, bottles. The two women rise up in wonder, taking it all in. **Fanny** *and* **Jesse** *smile at them.* **Hannah** *goes forward to the counter. There is a round box there, ribbons of all sorts spill from it.*

Hannah Even this old bell I like. Will we bang a bell?

Sarah Wonders. It is all girlhood here.

Sarah *creeps to the middle of the floor vigorously.* **Meg** *comes out to them, putting up her gold hair in a loose tie.*

Meg A best of days to you all. Isn't that sunlight now, for September?

Hannah Why, it is, Meg. It is.

Meg You would make a mighty bellringer, Hannah. If there's ever a vacancy in the tower.

Hannah (*laughing*) I know! (*Turning.*) Approach, Sarah, approach. Never be timid near linens. (**Sarah** *comes up beside her, by the ribbons.*) What would you like Meg Pearse to show you?

Sarah Dark cotton! That good stuff with a hint of oats in it, of the Carolinas.

She lays a hand on the counter, not looking at it, her fingers mingle with the ribbons. **Fanny** *and* **Jesse** *find a dark corner of the shop where they poke about.* **Fanny** *draws* **Jesse**'s *notice to* **Sarah**'s *hand.* **Meg** *lands a roll of cloth on the counter.*

Meg Do you think a fisherman would give me a job? Landing fish like that?

Hannah I cannot see why he would not.

Sarah *inches in, feels the cloth.*

Meg That's what my mother used to call an easy cloth. I made a funeral dress out of that myself.

Hannah (*making a doubtful face*) Oh.

Sarah English.

Meg (*impressed*) How did you tell?

Sarah It is lighter and yet stronger than an American.

Meg Towh, Sarah, you are an expert.

Hannah She is a wonder at cloths, yes.

Sarah London-milled.

Meg *turns again.*

Meg (*pulling down roll*) Here is my dark blue. (*Landing the cloth.*) I have rarely had a cloth so rich, and it isn't-pricy. I sell this to the nuns also. They make the laundry dresses from it, for the poor girls. But it's a superlative cloth just the same. American as you can wish. Those Americans know how to pack their goods. The cloths don't seem to know they've passed the wild Azores. The cloths think this is New York here.

Sarah (*feeling it*) It has a slight lustre that is agreeable.

Hannah Very fine. Of course, I am no expert like Sarah. It is extravagant for laundry girls, no? Will you show us something of that dark red?

Fanny *has found a roll of tin. She shows it to* **Jesse** *and they pretend it is a spyglass, looking through it magnificently.* **Meg** *lands the last cloth.*

Meg You don't have John with you? Or I'd call Stephen in. He's away up the top of the scallion yard.

Hannah Not this time.

Sarah *is again half at the ribbons.* **Meg** *and* **Hannah** *wait for her to say something. A bit of a gap.*

Meg And will you select a ribbon?

Sarah (*taking her hand away, laughing*) No, no! Oh, Hannah, save a friend.

Hannah You could take a black one.

Meg Look at this quality. This is a pinnacle of fashion. A stranger would speak French to you, if you wore this on your head.

Sarah Oh, no, no!

Hannah (*laughing*) Oh, Sarah, take one short ribbon in your pocket.

Sarah (*looks to* **Fanny**, *a hand one side of her mouth*) Oh, they are tormenting me, Fanny.

Meg Fanny, come over here into the light of the door and let me see you.

Fanny *hurries over.* **Meg** *grips her shoulders and looks her up and down.*

What a perfect person you are. (**Fanny** *laughing with* **Hannah**.) I am all the better for seeing you. Now give me a hug. Well, Jesse,

I won't embrace you, because you are a gentleman these last
years.

Stephen Pearse *puts his head in.*

Stephen Where's that bear?

Jesse *looks about for a bear.* **Hannah** *and* **Sarah** *look at* **Stephen**,
arrested.

Ah. Is there no John with you? (**Hannah** *shakes head.*) Ah.
There's Jesse Hawke. I had something for you, Jess, I have it
deep in my pockets here. (*Takes out newspaper item.*) Have yourself
a cool look at that, sir. (**Jesse** *reads.*) Isn't that the most unlikely
thing, Mr Jesse? I should think so.

Meg (*very kindly*) We've a little bit to do here, Stephen, you don't
mind?

Stephen I'm out away again. I'm out away. I'm hoeing like the
devil's own maid. But I'm halving worms mostly and I suppose
this will bring us more worms. Let us hope they're decent
earthworms and not chaps to eat my scallions. (**Jesse** *hands back
the item.*) What do you make of that?

Jesse A deep curiosity. How do you say that, Armagh?

Stephen You have it, Armagh, Armagh.

Fanny What was in that little paper, Jesse?

Jesse They have telescopes in Armagh, Armagh, at the house of
a gentleman called Johnson, and they've been digging for to
make a new tower there, for a fine new Holland instrument.

Stephen That's the cold fact of it. The magic they've found
there, under the old foundations, is the bones of an old animal,
maybe there your million years, and they are the poor
withershins and arms of an old bear.

Jesse There were bears that walked in Ireland once, Fanny. One
time you might have met a bear, in Ireland.

Stephen There you have it. Well, let me extract myself. It was a
joy to see you all so shipshape in my shop. God keep you.

Sarah Is that John you call a bear?

Stephen Yes, indeed, Sarah Purdy, in compliment only.

Sarah Oh, of course. Yes, yes, a bear is apt.

Stephen Be sending him now Stephen Pearse's wishes.

Sarah *smiles.*

Scallions!

He's gone.

Fanny Meg, we are looking for some sheets of paper, for Jesse, for his drawing.

Meg Paper. Paper. Why, two doors down, Fanny, my dove. Why, we have a new printer now in Baltimore. That's style for you. He'll have paper, dotey.

Jesse Who is the new man, Meg?

Meg Excuse me, Jesse?

Jesse The new man. He is not too fierce?

Meg Ah, no.

Hannah Bring Jesse down, Fanny. Here is a few coppers.

They go to door.

Meg He's a big gentle fellow. Tell him I sent you. Ah, fierce, no, no. It's Patrick Kirwin his name is.

They are gone.

(*To* **Hannah** *instead.*) From Cork City.

Hannah *responds vaguely. She looks to make sure* **Fanny** *and* **Jesse** *are gone. She beckons* **Sarah** *closer. The three heads.* **Meg** *expectant.*

Hannah Buttons!

Outside the lithographer's shop. A young woman singing. **Fanny** *and* **Jesse** *listening simply.*

Singer (*with a poor voice, but strongly*)

Are you Aurora, or the beauteous Flora, Euterpasia, or Venus
bright?
Or Helen fair, beyond compare, that Paris stole from her
Grecian's sight?

Fanny *gives her one of the coins.*

Singer (*proudly*) May God bless you.

Fanny Yes.

The lithographer's shop. A table with a lithographic stone. A high window. Dusty, familiar. **Patrick** *is busy smoothing the stone. His hand is white with dust.* **Fanny** *and* **Jesse** *peacefully watch him. He nods at them. He smiles.*

Patrick First stone in the new place!

Jesse (*after a moment*) That is wonderful.

Patrick Aye, aye. It is. See the holes in my hands? (*Shows them.*) What do you think did that?

Jesse I do not know, sir.

Patrick (*indicating walls*) Whitewash!

Noise of bee coming in through the high window. **Patrick** *fixes on it.*

Tell me, friends, what is it about Baltimore that has it plagued with bees? That's the ninth bee this good morning.

Fanny Oh, it is the nuns at the back of the town. They keep bees for wax and honey.

Patrick Ah. Good Catholic bees.

Fanny (*awkward*) Yes.

Jesse (*pointing at stone*) What is your work there?

Patrick Lithography. I suppose, rural lithography now. In Cork City I was lithographer to a newspaper. The Examiner. You read that, I'm sure.

Jesse We never see newspapers.

Fanny We never have news.

Patrick Ah, you're right. There's no good use to them. This is for a land notice. Rural, you see.

Jesse Are there no land notices in a city?

Patrick Oh, maybe, maybe. But I was at other things, from city gatherings to murders.

Jesse *intrigued*.

Well, when a man is murdered, an artist is sent out to draw the corpse. The corpse, in an attitude of terror. You see? The artist brings back the document, I smooth my stone, a stone like this one here, and I do it out for him. I do it out. (*Marking the imaginary picture.*) A hundred, a thousand impressions of the murder can be made in this way. The world sees it, the world understands the look of murder. By means of such a stone. It isn't a gentle craft, that newspaper craft. (*Brightening.*) A stone like this comes from but the one quarry in the whole world. It's in Germany, the quarry. Think of that. Well, I was mightily tired of murders. Here, around Baltimore, land notices, nice black letters, and a rare ship's notice. Much better, much. (*Lays his hand almost on the stone.*) It would be soft like a dream stone if I touched it. But I mustn't grease it. It is devious, devious. There can be a score of drawings made from this stone, if I will only smooth it, smooth it. Ah, it is a pleasure. Let me tell you (**Fanny** and **Jesse** *drawing close*.), there are little creatures held forever in this stone. Sea creatures the size of your nails, little fishes. In the quarry, on big stones, they sometimes find an old dogfish!

Fossils, fossils. When I come to a fossil, I tell it the world misses it greatly. You see, I have fled the murders!

*The **Singer** begins again.*

Do you hear that? She has been at it all morning.

Fanny That is a dance, I think. I know the steps to it.

Patrick Oh, dance it. I will be up on these local dances then. I'll be a terror at a dance by surprising everyone.

Fanny It is not a dance like that. It is only a religious dance.

Patrick I'd be honoured to see a religious dance. It'll be a blessing for my new life here in this shop.

Jesse *encourages her.* **Fanny** *dances, a stiff circular walking dance. The* **Singer** *stops.* **Fanny** *holds motionless.*

Singer (*outside*) Sir, thanking you. Sir, thanking you.

Singer *takes up song,* **Fanny** *goes into dance again.* **Patrick** *and* **Jesse** *encouraging. The song finishes.*

Fanny Now I am damp as a pony.

Jesse *puts a hand on her back.*

Patrick (*fanning the bee away from himself*) We've stirred up that wild lad of the nuns.

The bee goes to **Jesse**.

Jesse If you stand perfectly still you are safe.

Bee goes to **Fanny**. *She cannot help shooing it away. It stings her hand.*

Fanny Now, look at that. What a biter he is, that little bee.

Patrick (*coming around to her*) The savage.

Fanny But it will die now. It was my doing.

Patrick *peers at her hand.*

I am sorry for the Catholic bee.

Patrick (*to* **Jesse**) My room in the back there, my kitchen. Will you fetch me the bottle of vinegar there?

Jesse *hurries away.*

I'm sorry to touch your hand.

Fanny *smiles.*

Patrick I have to draw out the sting, you see. Would you look at my own paw. (*He means the white dust on it. Some of it transfers to hers.*) Alas, I have no instrument for this.

He works to get the sting out with his nails, close to her hand. **Fanny** *watches his crown. He goes down on one knee. They are silent. He draws out the sting. He looks up at her to speak. Sees her watching. A moment together.* **Jesse** *returns.*

Jesse What is vinegar?

Fanny *laughs.*

Patrick Ho, mercy. Well, of course, vinegar is a mystery to some. My mother was a Lisbon woman, a Jewish woman, that my father brought home to marry. (*Realises his own proposing position, rises, confused.*) She spoke three tongues, the Portuguese, the Hebrew, and the Cork. She was the sort of person that likes vinegar in her supper. And so do I.

Fanny Where is your mother?

Patrick My mother? She has a stone house. You understand me? The star of David and the cross of Jesus are cut there on it. I did that, though it isn't my trade.

Fanny (*rubbing her hand*) Thank you.

Patrick Yes, yes.

Fanny Do you have some nice paper, it would be for Jesse, he charts out the travels of the stars there in the sky above our Sherkin, and he needs a good plain paper without wax.

Patrick I can manage that. (*To* **Jesse**.) I suppose you have a good spyglass British-made for your observances?

Jesse (*regretful*) No.

Patrick No matter. I have paper with a little English watermark. It is the best paper in this world. I hope that will suit you!

Fanny *and* **Jesse** *laughing.* **Patrick** *winks.*

Aye.

Mr Moore, *alone with his boat. He sings a few lines of a marriage song in Irish.*

Mr Moore (*musing*) Valparaiso. To think of all the sailors that have whispered a prayer passing Cape Clear, the last of Europe's land. And they were never on it once. And yet I've seen its fine lighthouse, talked to that keeper, a man who knows how dark and gold his sea may be. There is a barracks there full of Lancashire boys. And some weighty houses, and a school by a stony beach where the children murmur their new words. And a fine harbour, and green roads and brave sorts of figures in those houses, men that fear fathoms too. It's odd to think of all those heartfelt prayers directed there, by sailors growing lonely. And all unknowing the people in the houses. Such tenderness. Valparaiso. (*After a moment.*) Ah, dear sailors. How simple the heart becomes at the head of a long voyage, a cargo of coals out of Cardiff maybe, to go round Cape Horn to San Francisco. Through lightning that melts the little weather-cock on the high mast. Molten stars strike the deck! The men in the yards find the ends of their fingers charred. Dear sailors, simple, leaving aft the prayers of Cape Clear. Ah, human men. I know the words myself. (*Mouths a half-silent prayer, with a gesture of goodbye.*) Go dtugadh Dia slán abhaile sinn.[1] I suppose in their time a few prayers have missed Cape Clear and washed against Sherkin.

[1] May God bring us safely home.

The prayers of Sherkin would be firewood of that sort.
Valparaiso. Tháinig long ó Bhalparésó.[2] And so on. Valparaiso.

Hannah, **Sarah** *with a little parcel,* **Fanny** *and* **Jesse** *with his roll of paper, descend towards him.* **Sarah** *and* **Jesse** *tip their purchases against each other.* **Mr Moore** *bestirs himself.*

Ah, here they come, my stormy petrels.

A simple music. A scattering.

Evening, the same day. **John** *is struggling in his workshop to set up a separate candle-making frame. He attaches to it one long wick. He is ready. He takes the ladle.* **Fanny** *comes in. He brightens.*

Fanny Father, we are home again.

He gets the glove on his free hand by sticking it under his oxter. He touches her face.

John Were you away someplace, child?

Fanny We were in the shining capital of Baltimore.

John (*going off, clatter of stove and ladle*) Is it an object of envy, this head?

Fanny Sarah has her three-day soup.

John (*returning with filled ladle*) Ho, that three-day soup.

Fanny It is your time to come home, if you wished. (*Touches his arm.*)

John *winks and nods. He stands on his stool, lets the first wax flow down the wick.*

John This is the blessed candle for the nuns. It is the Easter candle. There will be true gold bound to it, and they will set in

[2] A ship came from Valparaiso.

blue lines made from a store of lapis lazuli. And they will hoard it nicely till April and even then it will only burn in the bowel of their mansion. They will watch over it zealously. It will be their candle.

Fanny They are always happy with their candle.

John And it is a tricky thing to make a nun happy, I think.

Fanny They are reasonable little women.

John Oh, they are wonders. There is an ancientness about them that in a light way appeals. That dress of theirs with the blackened cloth and the hoops of cowls like big lilies, you know what that is, Fanny?

Fanny I think I might, Father.

John It is something from a medieval world. Among nuns you may be in the twelfth century still. They are the opposite of women of fashion. And yet they are highly fashionable among the scattered people.

Fanny They have a stronger world.

John I do not mind nuns. No. I think they are waiting also over there, the back of the lighted town. It might be that we would meet them in any New Jerusalem, since they are happy nuns.

Fanny They will look strange in the bright new streets.

John Strange women enough, but an adornment.

Fanny It is not just we three families then always? And extra brothers, if whatever, from Manchester?

John Who will say that? Not I.

Considers his work.

Fanny It is a famished-looking candle at this moment.

John Oh, I have yards and months of ladling to do. I will do it piecemeal when the spirit takes me. It is a special task for me, because of course we depend on them for wax, year by year. I could not quarrel with a nun here. The next site of wax is by Cork City I believe, and that is a lengthy way. You would be heaped up in a cart five days to Cork City, and be thoroughly rained on. And it is a decent sort of wax, the nuns' wax. If we did not live on an island of winds, we might manage our own.

Fanny Father, in your prayer, when you prayed for a husband –

John Yes, Fanny? (*Stepping down, setting aside ladle. Off with his gloves.*) Did I not pray correctly?

Fanny You did, Father. I understand you. Oh, Father, I am lost in my feeling for Matt Purdy. I wish that I had met him.

John (*putting his hands each side of her face. His hands are a little gritty from the gloves*) Charity and I were late with our work, my heart's child. Old Purdy was terribly elderly, even when I was young. He stepped in his own time, and was not for you, it seems. But he was a man of splendid eyes. His face was as soft as yours all his life, his hair rose up in a pleasant mass of flames. He was a curious seer. Our perfect father.

Fanny He led the families here, Father.

John He did, Fanny.

Fanny Father, let me tell you. In the town today there was a man, he was a pleasant, a pleasant-tongued man, from Cork City. He is the lithographer, the new figure in the town. (**John** *shows he may have heard of him.*) Father, as I watched him, my cold body stirred, I was moved towards him.

John Easy, easy, child. You may be easy. You are a clear person. It is wished by God that a person makes her children. You are a savage little mother, you, Fanny. Yes. It is far older than nuns. But all present cities and towns are dark things, which light cannot alter. It is often with an uneasy hand (*Showing right hand.*) that I mete out my candles to Baltimore. Am I not bringing little bundles of light to a place that light cannot feed? But contrariwise, the town needs light, and my poor trickle of it, maybe, can help the widow in her long night, the child in his beforesleep. And, Fanny, a child is light.

Fanny The lithographer touched my heart, Father.

John Yes, yes, child. And he is from Cork City? Does he have his manners? Did you see what he was?

Fanny He spoke of his old life there. Some of it went hard by me. He had I think a pride for his trade, as you have, and as I have for Sherkin. He seemed to put his stony work against the difficulties of a life. He was buoyant. He had no malice, but he liked to play, with Jesse and me, in words. He thought we were donkeys, I am sure, and so we were. He rescued me, look, from a bee-sting. Oh, he was dressed in the world. He was not like us. But I knew him.

John A good man, a good man. He is a rare man. But there will come certainly a brother from England if Matt Purdy wishes it, or his abiding spirit. In good polished boots, will come that man, for you.

Fanny (*simply*) I do know, Father.

John It is an article, Fanny, that we must abide. There will be no city for us without it. Were you to go from the families, how could you return? There would be a tearing in you. To marry such a foreign sort, you would need to embrace more than him, you would need to loosen us from your arms, and embrace his beliefs.

Fanny It was a moment, Father. It is certain that he had no notion of me as a person there.

John I will tell you this, Fanny, because you are my own. I have no true hope for Jesse, no true hope. He is a kind of wonderful boy, I imagine in my soul that he is a kind of visionary, but clipped down to the earth. There is a great deal of Matt Purdy in us all, but in him greatly again. Ah, in my dreams I see no wife for Jesse. My little child, there is not anything fearful in what I say. But my prayers are that, in spite of all, a brother will come from Manchester, though we have heard nothing from there for so many years. I see him arriving, like a veritable planet, when I am asleep in the goose-bed. He is just an ordinary man, and tired from his voyage. But he comes to us plainly. And if it is unto the fourth generation that we are to abide here for the city of light, then he will come surely. I can say nothing else to you. But I know what has leaped in you. It is the gazelles of life. It is the spirit of your children, and they are as eager as you for the earth of Sherkin.

Fanny Father, I will abide.

John Dear, dear Fanny. Here in my workroom, here together in secret, in this moment of our hours, I bless you with a father's word. There is nothing to keep you with us, Fanny Hawke. The four doors of the island are open. Walk away out if you wish or must. Ah, you could not return from such a voyage, but it would be a true voyage and your own. Whatever your star is, morning or evening, you will know best. There would be a long and tedious mourning in my heart if you were to go. But I would have my own light daughter stay only in her freedom. Fanny, you are the heart's tincture and the candle of this Sherkin. When your father sees you he is proud and easy. When Hannah and Sarah and Jesse see you, they are proud and easy. Fanny Hawke is our familiar light. Every creature knows the lighthouse of Sherkin.

Fanny Father, I will abide.

Act Two

A simple music. Late evening in the town. **Meg** *in her shop, with all the quietness of the end of the day.* **Patrick** *has come in to her. He is awkward, trying to be casual. She sweeps the shop floor methodically.*

Patrick Mrs Pearse, you know me now a handful of months, less maybe, while I've been (*Smiles.*) setting up here, and to-ing and fro-ing between this paradise and the city. I have never talked to you.

Meg But you have, Mr Kirwin, in a fashion. If you think you haven't, that's since you're a very awkward man, Mr Kirwin. And I mean that in kindness, I do.

Patrick Aye. Kindness. My very theme. I could write out a school attempt at that. Kindness. I don't want to shock you with vocabulary, but kindness means in the original use, matters of family. Did you know that?

Meg I'm not a scholar, dear Mr Kirwin. I went to the Presbyterian Institute till I was ten. And then no more. Let me tell you, Mr Kirwin, it was a release. I can count and read, I cannot spell, but I'm happier now so. There was a very dreary master with a lively stick. He never beat me, but, oh, the very waving of it over your head. I never did see the point of all that conning and scholarship.

Patrick Aye. Well, look. I am a plain man. Truly, from a place like this, set within the supposed glories of Cork City. I was reared there poorly. There is nothing to recommend me to anyone. Yet I worked hard and long at my trade, and I'm fit for it. I must be the most passionate tradesman ever put his name above a lithographer's shop. That recommends me, if little else.

Meg Now, Mr Kirwin.

Patrick You are a very, a very complete person, Mrs Pearse. You are my own age and I can speak to you, at least.

Meg My God, Mr Kirwin, you must be forty, by the most diminished account. What kind of compliments are you offering me?

Patrick Ah.

Meg Never mind, I'm not so empty. What are you wanting to tell me?

Patrick Ah, you're kind, Mrs Pearse. And merciful. It is this. Here is my speech in a nutshell. I am poorly born, I am – I am awkward, as you say. To tell you all the truth, I didn't have the stomach for my work in Cork City. Too many murders, a surfeit. I was happy to lithograph the horse races, the buntings for the royal visit, the fine bits of carpentry done in the streets for it, the men elected to councils, the women that astonished the city with their feathers and their gowns. But murders, young women killed, great rows of young men and bodies after, knifings, and then, Mrs Pearse, the poor creatures down in the prisons, the women that robbed and the rope around them, the men that lost their eyes in debt and the rope around them, such things are gristly and discommoding, believe you me. A famine of charity.

Meg Credo, credo.

Patrick Look at me, Mrs Pearse. Am I company for anyone? I have got wild there in my shop. I should have linked myself to friends here. Well, I intend staying here not so long more. Certainly murders withered me, but Baltimore is driving me from what wits I had.

Meg Another astute compliment. And this is no nutshell, Mr Kirwin.

Patrick (*a touch fiercely*) There were two in my shop these few mornings past. A strange boy with a crooked throat and a resplendent girl. Well, she was more woman than girl. They are from that close island.

Meg Fanny Hawke and her brother Jesse? She is my own age, Mr Kirwin, though she didn't school with me, being what she is.

Patrick But what is she? That is the point. What is she? She was very, well, skimming, on the matter of Catholic bees, and I was frightened to ask her. They are not your own allegiance?

Meg No, not hardly. They are some of those people that in English cities concocted new religions. I suppose they were types of the times. Previous times, since the heart is gone out of their movement. I have heard them described variously. Prelapsarians, Millenarians. All such names.

Patrick Millenarians? Hat-makers?

Meg No, no, that's milliners, Mr Kirwin.

Patrick Long names for such a girl. Quakers?

Meg Something in that yard of things. Visionaries. (*Taking down a packet.*) That's them there too. Hawke's Ideal Candles. Sixpence.

Patrick Here, give me them. (*Fetches out sixpence.*) It is beyond me. Beyond me. You are no bigot, Mrs Pearse, or I've got madder than I think. The truth is, she came in on me, she washed in on me. Of course, of course, she didn't notice her effect. She is an angel maybe, and sees no desire.

Meg Oh, I doubt that. I do. Mr Kirwin, you are telling me in your own way that you're smitten by her?

Patrick Well, that's it.

Meg They don't marry the likes of you, or of me either. They are tribalists – that is to say, they keep all as it was before cities and such. I must say, they would make an outcast of Fanny Hawke if she turned herself to you. Now, that's all I know. Believe you me, it's a dark and difficult faith they have, and there's no real amplitude in it. The tribes of Israel were never so odd.

Patrick Israel, Israel, yes. (*About to say something, changes his* *mind*.) You make me sweat. This isn't good. Let me introduce you to my wife, the visionary.

Meg Aren't you a sort of tribalist yourself, Mr Kirwin?

Patrick Aye, aye, so I suppose. If I let myself.

Meg Mr Kirwin, you're trembling. We like you, Mr Kirwin, because you are clear. You make a good field notice. You are pleasant and an addition to the town. But you are a little dishonest here. For wouldn't Fanny Hawke have to make another thing of herself for you, and how would that please anyone? You have wild bishops now, that wouldn't let you touch her till you'd made a pleasant little changeling of her. And what is this, but a girl you saw in the morning?

Patrick Aye. But I don't care for bishops. Bishops are just government. And I don't care for that either.

Meg Well, a very great rebel. Still, you might just let her go past you. (*Rubbing an arm, as if cold.*) Her father is very mad, I think. They seem to me all mad, in their way. Though I admit that Fanny is a good likeable person. Extremely. In fact, such an extreme is likely a poor tying for you. To balance it she is bright and funny. I'm always glad to see her. I doubt if you're the first man to feel her force. Maybe. But it's only a great mire you'd be treading into – a great mire. She has two aunts like sentinel hounds. Miss Hannah Hawke is just as her name suggests. You could hunt mice and hares with her, if you could find a hood for her head and a glove for your own hand.

Patrick I don't seem to mind any of that. I think I'd risk the murder. And someone else could draw me on a stone. Mrs Pearse, I'm in a quandary now. You've talked a yard of sense. I'll try to let it go past, as you say. I will try. A wind in the bushes.

Meg You were good to come and talk to me, Mr Kirwin. You don't need to hesitate again. We like you. Mr Pearse likes you, though we hie to different churches on a Sunday.

Patrick Aye.

A brief wave with the hand holding the candles. He goes out looking at the packet. **Stephen Pearse** *comes in from the house. He carries with him a hand of scallions.*

Stephen Am I too late for him, Meg?

Meg For who is that, darling?

Stephen Wasn't that my big bear of a friend, John Hawke? He's going away there in the darkness. That's certainly himself. Let me call him back for a little parley.

Meg That's only the poor lithographer. Let him be, with his new thoughts.

Stephen Haven't they the same back, the very selfsame cut to them, those two?

Meg Oh, a miracle. But Patrick Kirwin might steal from John Hawke, for all that their backs are the same.

Stephen How so, Meg, how so?

Meg Ah, he's in talking, talking. One of those Hawke women has him spinning. Men in love are mules.

Stephen Not Hannah. Not Sarah!

Meg Fanny, dear, Fanny.

Stephen Fanny Hawke is a child.

Meg She isn't, dear. (*Smiling.*) She is my own age.

Stephen By God. (*After a bit.*) There's no marrying outside for them, is there, Meg?

Meg No more than ourselves.

Stephen That's true, that's true. (*Knocking the scallions on the counter vaguely.*) He's a nice old person, John, I wouldn't care to see him troubled. By such a mere city man too. But no danger of that, no danger of that, not in our close world.

Meg *makes her face show otherwise.*

Perhaps I will hint to him when I go out ordering candles.
Perhaps I will do that, now. A few choice words, to John.

Meg Perhaps you'll leave it alone. I told seven white lies and put
Patrick Kirwin out of his frenzies. He isn't such a terrible city
man. He's a bit of a honey, now, like your own honeyed self.
Look at you, with those poor scallions.

Stephen I think our friends the worms have got the best half of
these jobs. Those worms are just wild characters, aren't they,
and eager for their unjust share. Every poor hanged villain
comes back into the world as a worm, and they're all up there in
that yard, yarning away about the old killing days, and taking
bites out of these between speeches. By God. Are they no good to
you, sweety?

Meg Well, I'll give them a good chop with a knife, and kill off
any wormy remains in a fierce stew.

Stephen Ah, you will, you will, and why wouldn't you? They
showed no mercy themselves when they were murdering men. I
was three months of a summer growing those.

Meg My dear old gardener, sure.

Stephen I am, come here to me.

Meg (*going to him*) Is that my name now, come-here-to-me?

Stephen Isn't it a lovely perfect name? Lean there on my breast,
Meg.

Meg Ah, I will for a minute. I'm fond of this breast.

Stephen It's an old breast.

Meg It would look fine enough in a goose-bed. I have just such a
bed upstairs, here, in my husband's shop.

Stephen Is it just up there? I seem to know the way.

Patrick *juts in.* **Stephen** *would pull away but* **Meg** *holds him.*

Patrick Mercy me, friends. But the sixpence.

He spins it, bright and new, across the shadows of the shop. **Meg** *catches it.* **Patrick** *is gone again.*

A simple music. The moon over Sherkin, a sickle. It grows to fullness. It's three weeks later. Dawn, a clear spread light. The whitethorn a little barer. **Mr Moore** *leaning, smoking, enjoying the morning, a little way off the pier. The thin smoke drifts upward. (In the shadows of* **John**'s *workshop, the Easter candle is somewhat fatter.)* **Eoghan O Drisceoil** *rises from his currach, with a thick net over his shoulder.*

Eoghan A land with a little hotel. There is no high path to the farms, no green road to the middle farms, no metalled road to the school. There is no beach of large round stones with ragged children. There is no brace of soldiers walking redly. There is no kirk, (*Playing with the word.*) kirk. But it's a simple yellow land with some peace attached to it. I can love my Clear Island. Sherkin I can love too.

Takes out his bone-needle and squats on pier to work. **Mr Moore** *taking cognisance of him.*

(*To* **Mr Moore**. *He speaks English with almost a Scandinavian accent.*) You're early here.

Mr Moore I brought a man over early. I didn't know him. From the city maybe. O Drisceoil is your name, is it not?

Eoghan It is. I am taking advantage of this fine flat surface on your new pier, and the lack of crowds.

Mr Moore Oh.

Silent for a bit. Peaceful.

Any sharks this year out at your island?

Eoghan Not this year.

Mr Moore I saw a shark myself in the summer sea by the Rock of Filth. Another man caught one under Fastnet. You've fewer in October. Shark meat. Did you ever eat that?

No response.

It's the same as eating courage.

Eoghan Who was it caught that shark?

Mr Moore A man out of Bantry.

Eoghan Is that it?

Mr Moore Very likely.

Eoghan (*spotting* **Fanny** *coming down the track*) Here is a little monk.

Mr Moore *looks, waits for her to reach him.*

Mr Moore Good morning, Fanny Hawke.

Fanny Good morning, Mr Moore.

Eoghan Dia is Muire dhuit.[1]

Fanny I would like to greet you in your proper language, sir, but I do not have it. My brother has it, a little.

Eoghan Ah, there isn't anything in it. It is just an old tongue. It isn't so great in the world as your own babble. It's a creaking tongue, spoken by a rusty people. (**Mr Moore** *laughing.*) We're much rained on, out there, on the sea. We're gatherers of rain. So you needn't mind it.

Fanny You are very generous about it. I know well from Jesse what it is. He says it is a language of voyages, and of fighting.

Eoghan Jesse, is that his handle? Lord God. And he should know about fighting, a thief of his renown.

Fanny *doesn't understand him.* **Eoghan** *shakes his head, laughs a little oddly.*

[1] God and Mary be with you. (common greeting)

Hah. I leave all fighting to the English soldiers. It is easier, and they like that better. They get the potatoes with the black eyes from us. They're blind potatoes. It isn't any good to feed such potatoes to a woman with child. She may bear a bat.

Fanny You are not a fighter but a fisherman.

Eoghan There are fish too that are fighters, and fish that are not. A mackerel is a pugilist, whereas a pollack makes a weight of himself but never stirs a muscle in his own defence.

Mr Moore I often noted that.

Eoghan That's it. What protects him best is that he's not the best eating. The mackerel is an oily fellow but he puts flesh on the devourer. But pollack in a pie is my dish, and my mother's dish.

Fanny Is that how you have it over there? You are as wise as Jesse on the fishes.

Eoghan Your Jesse has a deal to say and it's all sense. And we thought he was in Mexico! But I like a man that can talk to a foreigner with his own few words.

Fanny You are not a foreigner.

Eoghan I am a foreigner on Sherkin. That's why I like it.

Fanny And myself?

Eoghan You are a foreign woman at home here.

Fanny *laughs*.

Fanny I am informed.

Eoghan Aye. Don't mind me.

Fanny *moves away again*.

Tell your outlaw his secret is safe with me.

Fanny *looks to* **Mr Moore** *for clarity*. **Mr Moore** *shrugs*.

There's something Sherkin has that we don't. (*Working his net.*)
An outlaw.

Mr Moore How do you mean that, an outlaw?

Eoghan Ah, I got a little book off a soldier. The Only True
History of Frank James, by Himself. There was good reading in
it. He was robbing railroads there, with his brother, Jesse, in
America.

Mr Moore (*after a moment*) And what happened to them?

Eoghan Ah, some say they're in Mexico, and some others say
they're in South America. The main thing is, according to my
book, they're alive. They got away.

Mr Moore Valparaiso.

Eoghan (*after a moment*) Maybe so, maybe so.

Patrick *arriving at the whitethorn. Previous scene gone. He seems to hang
about, very uncertain. Looks around him, then puts himself in against the
whitethorn and unbuttons his flies.*

Patrick You'd think I'd be spared the tyranny of the bladder for
once.

Waits, looks down, nothing happening.

Christ, the reluctant suitor.

Jesse *passes the other side of the tree, carrying the broom to work. He
spots the unexpected figure, brandishes broom,* **Patrick** *hurries to fasten
his flies.*

Jesse Leave away, man in the bush!

Patrick *raises a hand to calm him, but finds he needs it more for his flies.*

Patrick Mister, mister, you know me.

Jesse What evil are you bringing to my tree?

Patrick The little crossing in the boat has put the tea through me.

Jesse Oh, step away back from that innocent whitethorn!

Patrick I'm clear, I'm clear. Do you see who it is? I am Patrick Kirwin, that sold you paper.

Jesse (*calmer*) I suppose it is. Yes, I know you.

Patrick I've hurried over between storms.

Jesse You had better hurry back. There is a long black storm preparing.

Patrick I have the last room of the year at the hotel. I tell you, it's an hotel for rats.

Jesse So we hear. (*Leaning on broom.*) I have never been.

Patrick The sheets are like the yellow leaves off the big plants in the Botanical Gardens in Glasgow. Do you think I haven't seen them? I have, like elephants' ears, sir.

Jesse (*letting the broom swing in his hand like a pendulum*) I am sorry for your comfort. This is not a holidaying island. The hotel is a night-house for whatever travelling persons come to see us, to sell us stuff, as may be, or glories that do break in a day. Gentlemen that do hail from the East and hurry back there, I tell you, when their goods are tested by this island. I suppose we put a bend in most things. The odd stray bird stays there in that hotel, and even they in a morning look dishevelled and tormented on the pier, as if they had slept with lions like Daniels. Your owner there is properly a seaweed collector. That is his yearly work.

Patrick It's no matter. I've no interest in comfort for now. We've met very awkwardly here, Jesse, but, have charity, and take a word for me to Fanny.

Jesse (*holding the broom steady*) For what use, stranger?

Patrick I want you to take a word to her, for to meet me, under that hotel when she wishes, by the blank blind wall. (*Tentatively.*)

I will wait there, Jesse, it is where my present window looks out on a waste of scrubby rock. Mr Hawke, dear, even I can see winter out there, the sea is blackening, it has an army out there in those waves. There are white waves like a stand of bitter trees, God help us, there is smoke and wild white leaves mixed wildly. Will you carry that word for me, boy?

Jesse (*brandishing the broom*) I may. I may.

Patrick To your sister, Jesse.

Jesse (*angry*) I know to who. My sister is my own. She is our own. (*Shakes his head like a sweating boxer.*)

Patrick Your father I know has a tongue of terror, (**Jesse** *puzzled by this, lets it go by.*) – I know, or I would ask him. Did Mrs Pearse tell me right?

Jesse (*threatening with the broom*) She is not your kind, man.

Patrick I haven't so much to say. I haven't a speech. Will you have her come?

Jesse (*giving up*) You do not understand me. Did you never see an ant stepped on? It is a very slight death.

Patrick I won't stay beyond a night.

Jesse I wonder what you will make of one of our island nights.

Jesse *goes on with the broom. The bare, poor hotel room gathers about* **Patrick**, *at first darkly, then a thin light of early morning. He has not slept. The bed.*

Patrick There are fish in the mortar of this wall and they are not fossils. It is that damp, they're swimming around in it. I have been in Glasgow, where they have many cheap hotels for cheap travellers. Pity, pity to the man who must spend his life in such a room as this. (*Rubbing his face, scratching his thigh.*) I thought I'd had my allotment of fleabites in this life. I was brother to many generations of fleas in my youth. Well, that's how we lived. There isn't any need for nobility. I will never keep a cat. That's the most vicious fleas. I think Fanny Hawke has a clear head. I think she is much the best, much the best. Still, I never saw one like her, so I don't know. Maybe she's a ghost. A sort of vision, in her terms. I think maybe Baltimore is a vision too. A hellish one. Of course it is myself that is the vision. Of misery. The fleas are taking great nourishment from a vision none the less. Christ, (*Trapping a flea.*) that's not a flea, that's the whole dog. Maybe it is wrong of me to take a visionary child away from her island, or seek to. But I can do no other thing. If I require to be forgiven, forgive me. I'm following only before a thing that's far wickeder and blinder than myself. Not so wicked, no, not so wicked. In this fashion I would say, I love her. Was there ever love more foolish or more forceful? I have a fire under my arse, and it isn't only made by the mouths of fleas. My head even is just a hearth. You could leave spuds in it at night and take them to school in the morning, in the frost. Christ, I am lost for this bright woman. I have to submit. (*Strikes palm on bed like a wrestler.*) I submit. Take that twist off my arm. And I will not be put away from her. I'll be greater than I am. I'll be subtle, I'll be a real dancer. No one will know me. I'll get a shock in mirrors. Ah, I'll weep wicked tears if she'll even hear me. I swear it. I'll lose my legs as well as my heart. She'll slay me. And I'll rejoice. I'll send penny cards to all my acquaintance, saying, Fanny Hawke killed me. That is the better sort of murder. And may God give me good words for her, give me words.

A few small black pebbles are thrown into the room, which at first he doesn't see. He is itchy in his legs. He leans forward and pulls up a trouserleg carefully, to see if he can spot a flea.

Oh, you have me devoured alive, you subtle devils.

Now he is a better position to see the next sequence of pebbles.

Christ, them are fleas.

He creeps over, catches a flea as it were, examines it, realises what it must be, strikes his forehead, hurries to window, looks down.

Merciful Christ.

He goes quickly from the room. Outside, **Fanny** *is throwing pebbles.*

Gulls screeching. It is a cold dank wall. She tries to see up into the window. It's too high. She has her arm reared to throw again. **Patrick** *comes up behind her, touches her raised hand briefly. She turns, dropping the pebbles. She is a little angry.*

Fanny What is it then?

Patrick (*confused*) Aye.

Fanny Mr Kirwin.

Patrick Aye, I know. I have only half of a notion now. Well, look at you, here. I feel myself to be a very awkward being. Well, what is a hero? I am a lithographer, from Cork City, and a fool. I feel like a mouse, scratching at a parlour door, and there is only big cats inside, if he knew.

Fanny (*laughing*) A mouse?

Patrick I have been peering out my whole life for the familiar face. (*Stops, because* **Fanny** *is puzzled.*) I have this to say to you. Think of me now as you see me, think of me, store me in your warm head till the spring, and I will come then and ask you to come away with me. I know all your particular difficulties. Now, I leave you with that. And if you are wiser, and won't come, it'll be hard news, but I won't trouble you after.

Fanny There would not be any purpose rowing out here in the spring, Mr Kirwin.

Patrick Yes, yes.

Fanny I am not a woman to go. We are very established religious people here. (*Laughing.*) You cannot imagine what holds me here. It is my life but also other lives. I am bound to this place by family willingly.

Patrick Oh, that talk is your talk. That's what has me shivering by this wall. There's something in you that shocks me, but only as a piece of lightning shocks a chimney. (*A gust of wind.*) Oh, a foolish speech. And I wonder, listening to you, if I would be worthy of you.

A darkening over.

Fanny I like you and your mouse, Mr Kirwin. It is just that you are speaking to a woman quite given over to this other existence. It is not a life as you follow it, (*A sudden rain falling.*) I think.

Patrick And could I ever lead this life? Could I bring myself here? (*Hunching in the chill.*)

Fanny There are only three families for this place, unless you are a Manchester brother. I do not think you are.

Patrick (*mouthing*) Manchester brother. Is that something in particular? What is such a thing? (*Gives up.*) Nevertheless, you'll find me in the spring, a sort of seed-sower at the door. You will watch out for me, you think?

Rain lifts. A patch of sunlight crosses them.

Fanny Keep where you abide, Patrick Kirwin. Hold to your shop. Do not waste a sixpence for Mr Moore on me.

Patrick Aye, but he's only the thruppence.

Fanny *leaves him, heads away. She is stopped by* **Eoghan** *coming to her from the pier. He carries a frame with larger-sized shells attached to it. He holds it out to her.* **Patrick** *sunk in thought, darkening by the wall.*

Eoghan I've made for you a shell-toy. (*He hands it to her.*) If you set it right in your window, a change of wind will sound in it among the ears. (*The ground steaming after the rain, birds, scents.*) A fisherman would use it to foretell a fishing wind. But you could use it for a pleasing toy, as any Clear Island child might.

Fanny *takes it gratefully, nods her thanks, turns and carries it into the house. She places the shell-toy in a window. A simple music. By the stove are empty baskets, one full of driftwood. It is deep winter, late afternoon, the five candles are lit. The remote glow of the stove.* **John** *stands by it, with his book, intending to read to them. The whitethorn tree is bare, frosted.* **Sarah**, **Hannah**, *and* **Jesse** *ranged to hear him,* **Fanny** *sits down, just a little apart from them, thinking. A flash of lightning.*

Sarah Too bitter for me, and dark, this weather. (*Rubs her eyes.*) Dark!

The crash of the thunder overhead. **John** *stares up.*

Hannah Sarah. Nonsense.

John (*hesitant*) I have selected, I have underscored (*More confidently.*) with my black pencil, these passages following out of John of (*Flash of lightning.*) Patmos (*Fierce rain.* **John** *looks up again, silenced, waiting. Crash of thunder overhead. He goes on listening,* **Hannah** *and* **Sarah** *looking at him.*)

John *strikes away out through the storm to his workshop. His candle is further advanced.* **Stephen** *arrives in, heavily coated, shaking the rain off himself, pulling a big hat off to reveal himself.*

Stephen I've brought myself over! Good gracious, John, what a wild day. See, (*Drying his hands off, delicately taking from an inner pocket a slip of paper.*) to give you this order.

John Ah, ah.

Stephen We were going to endure a scarcity otherwise. And that wouldn't do, this closing-in weather.

Sets paper on grid. **John** *grasps his hand.*

John Stephen Pearse, too long since we met! I am full of remorse. I have made you a fresh store of candles as usual for the lighting of the town of Baltimore, and I hope that you may forgive me my not bringing them over before this late date!

Stephen *just a trifle taken aback by the force of this.*

Stephen Lay them by for us, John, and get them over when you can arrange it with Moore, and, the God of this weather.

John (*brightly*) I will do that for you, Stephen.

They shake.

Stephen I lay some store by you, John Hawke, and not just for candles.

John I know, Stephen, and it is a mutual liking. It would be hard for me in the sense of money not to bring you my candles, but even leaving that aside, and were I to find another shop, I would not be happy with it. Friendship inspires. There is a sense in which I make them for you. Hawke's candles are sold there in Pearse's, and that seems to me the fitting arrangement. It has been so for two, three generations, eh?

Stephen Yes.

They relax.

John You will abide here a little while, and dry out your nice coat?

Stephen Thank you, thank you. (*He peels off his coat, drapes it to dry.*)

John Just a second, Stephen.

He goes off to the wax-fire and comes back with two bowls of **Sarah**'s *soup.*

There is the thing now for us in this extremity.

They sit on whatever available perches. Eat.

Stephen That's a very strange affair now, in Mafeking, out beyond there, in Africa.

John *blank.*

I'll tell you something now, which I mightn't have told you, if you weren't of especial importance to me and Meg. Do you know the lithographer, Patrick Kirwin?

John No, I have never been in his shop. He is a Cork City man, I believe.

Stephen Look, John, he is a good man but he was in talking to Meg some while since, very keenly. He is taken in some manner with Fanny, and I think he would ask you for her as a wife.

John Yes, I do know. Did she tell him, Meg, what we were?

Stephen She did. He went off in the end very disappointed. She told him that Fanny was only for marrying of her kind. That you are a very strict people in your way.

John It is beginning to be a difficulty for us. It was fine just as long as we had our own husbands and wives here on the island. Poor Fanny. I cannot tell what to do for her, Stephen. But how can there be a question of permission? I have no permission to give. It was Matthew Purdy's most profound article. And he was a soft man enough. 'He that leaves the families must be outcast and outlaw, and shunned of the tribe.' It is part of his pre-Satanic vision. She must abide on the island or else she is not a daughter of our families. It perhaps sounds harsh and ill to you, Stephen?

Stephen What was done in old cases, when they went?

John Why, no one has ever left, but to the graveyard.

Stephen Things are set as they are set. I know the long vigil you've kept on Sherkin and what your business is here. So, I think Meg has thoroughly frightened off Patrick Kirwin. You might have sounded like a strange affair to him. I saw him go away very dark.

John Fanny is not fixed, nor are any of us. We are not imprisoned, why that would be the opposite of what Matt Purdy wished. But we have our own doing of things. We were only three families that fled. We are terribly reduced. It would be a terrible hurt still to lose her. She could not go in that normal fashion that people know.

Stephen He is a Catholic to boot, of course.

John Ah. It is hopeless. Why, your own son even, if he had existence, could not marry her without the same loss. Even he could not be one of us. As little, Mr Kirwin, he is not a brother. She would have to suffer a change to have him. She would cross from one condition to another. I am not the father for Patrick Kirwin. I cannot be Patrick Kirwin's father.

Stephen Well, he knows that now.

John Often I trouble myself that ours is a bitter creed. And yet it is based on kindness, on family and hope. It has been such a long waiting. I thank you for your mercy, Stephen, in seeking to discuss this with me.

Stephen Well, I revere you.

John *silenced.* **Stephen** *clothes himself. Takes* **John***'s hand.*

Good evening to you, John.

John May Mr Moore row you carefully home.

Stephen He is a careful man.

The easy fall of waves. **Fanny** *alone, out on the edge of the strand.*

Fanny The tide of this island is a fierce tide, it could carry you. The Atlantic here is a huge muscle, a huge bearer, it could carry a person to America with ease, but not living. This is the strange marge of everything here. I would stay here only if I were a sea-bird or a creature like an otter, the dog of the sea, fit for these strands. The fit land of America is far. Sherkin my home is near, where the pollen flits, where each plant talks to the next with pollen, and the webs and the messages of lives run over the night lanes, and across fields under curious clouds. We are people for this place now right enough, we are caught in its purpose, a small manufactory that makes and unmakes, a bare stone cautiously marked with green life that is our blood and our dream.

Matt Purdy *shines out across the strand, he is yellow with light and has his heap of wings.*

Who art thou, my life?

Matt Purdy I am thy grand old man, Matt Purdy, an artisan of Manchester. This is our strand, yours and mine. I know you, the little fire that walks through the house, hearth of your father, the warm woman of my blood that is not afeared to walk out here where the wind bothers with no trifles and all is big and worse.

Fanny Thou art a first vision, Matt Purdy. Never have I seen thee before this.

Matt Purdy I am not a vision for thee, but out of my dead heart I bear for thee a kindly speech. It is something I must give thee, that I cannot give without this form. I did not live enough for thee. For I would give thee a lithographer out of Baltimore, a gentle man of little account who has borne his trouble. Moreover, I have given him a dream of thee, that he may come to fetch thee. For that he is a gentle heart. For Fanny, I would not have thee curious and alone here. Your heart beats up to me a message almost violent. Listen now, Fanny Hawke, and hear these calls.

Her name is called distantly by young voices. (Curlews, kittiwakes, gulls.)

Fanny Who is this calling me, Matt Purdy?

Matt Purdy They are the voices of thy children. They wait for you up the years, and you must go. All about them lies a cruel century of disasters and wars that I did not foresee. I steer you back into the mess of life because I was blinder than I knew. I saw a vision in time, that will not serve me outside time. I give you back to the coming century, Fanny, and your children are calling you. There are lives that are waiting to be made in a black century, and though they will see suffering, yet they will value their lives. Oh, in darkest heart they will cherish them. They can be nothing without Fanny Hawke. I, Matt Purdy, awkward artisan of the black city of Manchester, that fled from those streets of murder and loves too bleak to bear, give you a lithographer out of Baltimore to be thy husband and abide by thy side. Your children use the winds for their voices, (**Fanny** *raises a hand.*) and it is their happiness you must go to give. Hear this in place of my love that I could not give thee. I, Matt Purdy, battered angel, wanderer, simple founder, put you under promise of present love, that you may take your life from my words. I would kiss thee but that I am a tattered angel. Go, little

Fanny Hawke, into that Catholic darkness, into a century of unlucky stars. So words in future time may be said of thee, that thou did well to go, and said you would, and did, and rose greatly to go.

Fanny *silent. A wide cloth of stars falls over* **Matt Purdy***.*

John*, in mid channel, in the bow of* **Mr Moore***'s rowing boat,* **Mr Moore** *rowing strongly, both their faces twisted towards their destination of Baltimore.* **John** *eager and drawn. The big Easter candle sticks up, pointing forward,* **John***'s arm guarding it. Gun-grey wind. They strive forward.*

The bulk of the town in spring. **Patrick** *and* **Meg** *on the wharf, he wrapped to the chin, she with a handsome coat gathered about her.*

Patrick There it is coming over now. Wouldn't you be hoarse shouting for that boat? Give me a wish for a good journey, though it's just a minute in a local boat.

Meg I won't say that it's not a good thing you are trying to do.

Patrick Give me your wish before it's tried, because after you may not choose to speak to me.

Meg I? Not speak to the hero? I think I will speak to you.

Patrick Not in this town, I think – I hope she and I will be March hares by then, or April, be deer by then, be wilder creatures all wrapped and sitting up in a rough dogcart.

Meg I give you my wish, Patrick.

Patrick That's the whole matter that I needed. Thank you.

Meg Be careful, Patrick Kirwin, that you leave her a place to slumber, in the upshot.

Patrick I understand that. I intend to. Even if it's a long dry hedge of flowers stretched somewhere in the lost lands of this Ireland.

Meg A city bed will suit her. Here is my wish.

She touches his shoulder.

Patrick It's the smallest foolishest thing that holds the promise.

Mr Moore *brings in his boat.* **Patrick** *sees* **John** *struggling with the candle and he goes quickly to help. He draws it up.* **John** *climbs out.* **Patrick** *puts the candle in* **John***'s arms, nodding and smiling.* **John** *nodding and smiling.* **Meg** *gives him a slightly embarrassed wave of her hand.* **John** *heads up the town.* **Patrick** *into the boat.*

Patrick Am I all right for a crossing, sir?

Mr Moore (*looking after* **John**) You may be, if I lean in to these old oars.

The sweep of the bare sea. A sea music. A full burning light on the whitethorn, which is in first flower.

The room of the **Hawke** *house. Baskets gone, stove cold. Between the windows, a bowl of big spring flowers.* **Sarah** *and* **Hannah** *on their bench.* **Hannah** *biting off the last thread on new backing to an old dark dress. She pushes it up on the back of the bench, where it lies stiffly, like a third person almost. She has a folded cloth on her lap, which she shakes out and spreads on their knees.* **Sarah** *feels it.*

Sarah What have I stitched here with you, Hannah?

Hannah Why, Sarah, none. It is a clear cloth. A clear.

Sarah (*laughing*) Are you certain? I feel some little workings here.

Hannah That's the little snags. Gatherings of the weaver. It will make an adequate bed cloth. But best cloth would be the wrong praise for it.

Sarah (*touching her head*) There is sun on my crown.

Hannah It is a perfect freshened spring morning. I will go and bring joy to that pig's stomach in a moment. That present three-day soup has reached its fifth day. Into our pig it must go. It is very wicked of us to be stitching at this hour, but the light is better for you.

Sarah Oh, yes. Far better. Thank you, dear.

Patrick, *his arms full of flowers, steps in carefully.*

(*Staring over, sniffing.*) Who is this person with the spring?

Hannah *is flustered to see a stranger.*

Patrick How do you do, ma'am? I am looking for Miss Fanny Hawke. My name is Patrick Kirwin, ma'am. From the town there, over.

Sarah (*to* **Hannah**, *frightened*) Who is this man?

Hannah *looks at* **Patrick**, *trying to know him.*

Hannah (*at last*) How did you get out here so early, Mr, Mr – ?

Patrick I shouted across to a figure on the pier. I shouted my poor head away. And Mr Moore came over and got me.

Hannah What a wonderful pair of ears Moore has.

Patrick It was terribly still. It is golden water there this morning, but glass-clear. A better man than me might have just walked across.

Sarah (*to* **Hannah**) Was that a low remark?

Patrick He had a big, dark-suited sort of a fellow in the boat with him, that carried a great giant of a candle, so I suppose he was heading over anyway.

Hannah Fanny is out there somewhere searching for our hens' eggs.

Sarah (*in a friendly fashion, finally*) You never had hens like ours. They would lay in your ear and not tell you. You could search for a week, and be deaf the whole time. You have never had mad hens, sir?

Patrick I have met a few. In people's yards, you know.

Hannah Go out to her loudly. Do not make her jump by creeping about. Although it is unlikely, she may have just a few eggs in her dress, and we would rather you did not cause her to break them.

Patrick *nods. Goes away out.*

Half the island's flowers in his arms, that man had. (*Shakes her head.*)

Sarah Heh, Hannah, do you think our little hens would ever reach heaven?

Hannah They get in everywhere else. Why not heaven too?

Patrick, *awkwardly, in the area of the whitethorn. He is cold, with his flowers. He sees the sheltered place in against the whitethorn and sits there, still holding the flowers. He grows comfortable, sleepy, topples slightly, wakes, stirs himself a little, but sleeps again. After a short while,* **Fanny** *appears, holding a front pocket lightly, where she has stored a few eggs. She pokes about in places that she knows, with no luck. She gets to the other side of the whitethorn, carefully rolling up the sleeve of one arm, and reaches in amid the scrubby grass, and with some triumph finds two eggs, which she happily looks at, one in each palm. She hears a slight snore, steps around the whitethorn. She takes him in.*

Fanny Oh. The loved one.

Patrick *wakes. He jumps in half-sleep, sees her, tries to get up, is hampered by the flowers, but he makes it,* **Fanny** *stepping back to give him room. She is still holding out the eggs.* **Patrick** *grips the flowers tightly.*

Patrick My speech, my speech. (*As if by rote.*) I did spend such a winter. (**Fanny** *silent.*) That's to say, a happy one. A happy winter. A change of things. The house was different. (*Differently.*) You know why I've come out here? (**Fanny** *nods.*) Since you know. (*Abruptly.*) I dreamt of something. (*Workmanlike.*) I've purchased a new premises in Cork City, it is beside the new theatre hall. If you don't mind comedians and risky dancers too much, we might stick our sign beside such light and splendour.

Fanny (*in wonder*) The theatre hall?

Patrick Over the shop are two entire floors, for a house of children. A spring-cleaning. A new start. Well. Dear Lord.

Fanny *gathers words to speak, opens her mouth, but only gabbles.*

Is this the desert of the world, this island? No. I did try to get away, I went away from Baltimore, you see, but you see, I brought you with me, you know, in the noggin. It was just like having the sun on my head all winter. Heh. (*He smiles.*) My friend, if you will, you will come with me to Cork City.

She makes her leap of faith.

Fanny (*finding her words*) Go yourself to Baltimore now, Patrick. Wait there a last while. I will come to you before dark.

Patrick There's no doubt? You'll deliver yourself from your place?

Fanny Yes. I will go from my family like a dreamer, and wake in the new world.

Patrick It's my joy.

Fanny It is mine. (*Putting the eggs quickly and carefully into her pocket with the others.*) Let me touch your face. (*She does.*) Go on away out.

He goes, still clutching the flowers. **Fanny** *remains a moment, holding the pocket of eggs gently, she heads slowly towards the house.*

The **Hawke** *house.* **Hannah** *cleans the shell-toy with flicks of a duster of goose feathers.* **Sarah** *by the bench, holding the mended dress to herself, gauging it.*

Sarah Will that fellow take some three-day soup, do you think?

Hannah (*looking out of window, watching* **Patrick** *go by*) I think he will take no three-day soup here.

Sarah Well, he will not get soup like mine in his own place.

Hannah A creature like that has no place, maybe.

Sarah There is a leaf on this island that does something to soup.

Hannah Wild mint. It is miraculous soup. It is plain soup.

Fanny *comes in. Stops, seems to think about speaking. Goes on through to the kitchen, past* **Sarah**. **Hannah** *follows slowly to the door.*

Sarah Is that the child? I smelled eggs.

Hannah How can you smell eggs, Sarah?

She looks in at **Fanny**.

Sarah I do not know. I hope I cannot smell the rear end of a hen now. I would not care for that.

Hannah (*to* **Fanny**) You found a few handy?

No answer.

Patrick *alone. He throws the flowers from him, they spread about. He brushes off stray blossoms.* **Jesse** *approaches, with a long twig.*

Jesse (*very friendly*) What is this mysterious custom, (*Meaning the flowers.*) Patrick Kirwin?

Patrick Ah, Jesse. (*Acknowledging flowers.*) Ah, they weren't needed in the upshot. How's Jesse, anyway?

Jesse Jesse? (*Puts the twig in his teeth.*) Nesting, nesting!

Patrick Why wouldn't you, Jess, (*Patting his shoulder briefly.*) why wouldn't you?

Jesse You have been a while away from us.

Patrick I was in the city. There was a host of things there you'd care for. I saw a mariner's telescope, but to be honest, there was a terrible price on it. I suppose it's the brass in it, Jesse. Look now, I'll be away. Are you fine? (*Moves away. Comes back to shake Jesse's hand vigorously.*)

The **Hawke** *house.* **Sarah**'s *black dress on the bench, light glimmering along it.* **Fanny** *just inside the room,* **Hannah** *by her.* **Sarah** *close by.* **Fanny** *bewildered.*

Hannah A marriage? A marriage?

Jesse *comes in.*

A going-away, Fanny?

Hannah *cries.*

Is that Father back from Baltimore, Jesse?

Jesse Oh, yes. Just in. I did see him, mid-channel, from the yellow hill.

Hannah Please do run for him, Jesse, please do run.

Jesse *turns and runs through switches and twigs of light to* **John**, *in his workroom unpacking a new store of nuns' wax.*

John No piece of something for us, child?

Jesse, *panting, thinks, looks in his trouser pockets.*

Jesse No bread. No bread. There is someone come. (*Holding* **John**'s *sleeve*.) He said there is only the one quarry in the whole world. One, Father!

John Who is come?

Jesse *knocks his knuckles on his head.*

Is it someone then maybe from Manchester?

Jesse No, no, a man that was tired of murders. He is Fanny's own man.

John (*knowing who it must be*) Do you see this for wax? The nuns were besotted with that lovely big candle. I will never get over the enthusiasm of nuns. (*Differently.*) And is he still on Sherkin, your man, Jesse?

Jesse He is not my man. It is Fanny's man. (*Suddenly.*) I hope I did not cause it!

John Jesse. (*Holding his shoulders.*) My excellent son. You are a scientific person. I know the man, and the history, and have spoken with Fanny. Beloved boy.

Jesse I ran like a rabbit, Father. I have forgot the bread to revive you. I have given you this news as fast as I was able.

John My sweet son. We will go and see. (*Touching the wax.*) A work is enough to hold our world.

The **Hawke** *house,* **Fanny**, **Hannah** *and* **Sarah** *barely moved.* **Jesse** *and* **John** *come in,* **John** *stays at the door. He looks at* **Fanny**, *knows.* **Fanny** *returns his look. He sinks his head a little.*

Towards twilight, slow deepening of light. A simple music. The table is set with their dishes, **John**, **Jesse** *and* **Fanny** *in their places.* **Hannah** *comes in from kitchen with a bowl of food, sits. They wait for* **Sarah**. **John** *looks at* **Hannah**. **Sarah** *comes in with lighted taper. A gust of early evening wind comes in the windows, makes the shell-toy murmur, and blows out* **Sarah***'s taper. She doesn't realise it. She locates the candle on the windowsill by her, feels the wick, thinks she is lighting it.*

Hannah Do not bother with the candles now, Sarah.

Hannah *lets her go on to the other candles. After 'lighting' the candles on the table,* **Sarah** *'blows out' the taper.*

Sarah (*standing near* **Fanny**, *the taper crossed on her hands*) When I was a girl with Charity, we walked often on the strand beyond the last dunes, where the tide ticks, does it not? And sometimes we were shocked by freshwater ducks that stood out there maybe resting between flying. How little envy we had for those ducks, stout creatures though they were, since we were bright in the fold of the families. And those small shells, that we could see through to the great sky with, she used to strew about, and she said they were like fingernails, that any Hawke or Smith or Purdy had on their fingers, that showed they were of Sherkin. And she said, all those years after, that I wasn't to let her go off Sherkin without a handful of those shells somewhere put in with her, and I did that, yes.

Sarah *crosses to the door leading outside.*

Hannah Where are you heading now, Sarah, dear? Our meal is here for us.

Sarah I have no need of the meal just now.

She goes to step out.

Hannah You cannot go walking about out there now, Sarah. It will be quite dark in just a little.

Sarah I am afraid it is of no import to me now, the failing light.

She goes out.

(*Off.*) On this island anyhow I need nothing so extravagant as eyes.

Hannah (*getting up*) I am not that ready for eating now, myself. I will go up to the cupboards with myself.

She goes out by kitchen.

John You can walk around this island in a fifth of a day. You may see the part ruined by the great force of the Atlantic, and by the channel sheltered you may see the hopeful farms. The strand is peaceful this evening, but the Atlantic is broiling far out. Nothing breaks the wild surface of the storm there but dolphins and angels.

Fanny *looks at him.*

Jesse Do you go easily? You do not at all. You go like our father's dolphins, breaking into the stormy air. You will need all your muscles.

Fanny *smiles at him.*

John (*arranged for his prayer*) If you do please, Lord, this is our night prayer. We do ask you for the peace of this family. We do ask you for the silence and the storm of Sherkin. Once there were three families, Lord, that – (*He looks forward, shakes his head, in difficulties.*)

Hannah *comes back, carrying an old wooden case.* **Fanny** *stands up.*

Hannah This is one of the old Manchester cases, can you credit that? You would think the worms would have long devoured it. But there are still four of them above on the byre rafters. Look at this label. There is a picture of a sailing ship, but I cannot read the names. This is your proper hope-chest, Fanny, with tansy and heart's-ease to freshen the clothes.

Fanny I do thank thee.

Hannah (*at the label again*) It must say the name of the ship. It must give the place of destination. Is it not a queer old case?

They called this a sea box, the old women. (*Patting her chest, pointing at herself.*) The old women! Think of the women of this house. I gather them all together in my mind, as no doubt they will gather on the splendid day. Why, we will abide and there will be the day when all the women of this house rise up from the yard and we will have a holiday rowing them with honeysuckle to the twelve gates. Oh, I do not doubt it. See, (*Opening the lid of the case.*) see under there, what I have slipped in for you.

Fanny *comes closer to see. She lifts out a framed mirror, looks in puzzlement at* **Hannah**.

Now, child, whose mirror is that, would you say? (*Laughing.*) Oh, child, child, do you think no one ever owned a mirror? There is not such a terrible strictness on every side. The river of light flows despite many a curiosity. That is your mother's mirror, Charity's mirror, and it is a plain thing enough for a vade-mecum. (*Puts her hands over* **Fanny**'s *holding the mirror.*) We will hold gently.

Fanny Will you kiss me?

Hannah *kisses her. They refasten the case.*

Hannah I have forgotten your coat and bonnet.

Hannah *goes again to fetch them.* **John** *gets up, comes round to* **Fanny**.

John When you were born I was out in the first field digging, and I dug the better because you were nearing. I pleased myself to watch a flight of land-birds going away over to America and having no cognisance of my luck. Sarah Purdy was standing in the frame of that window. She flung up the casement and called out to me to run in. I burst through this room and flew up the stairs. Charity was a thing of sweat, and our bed was a wild splash of blood and matter. Out of our human earth had risen a strange red-skinned girl, that Hannah held fast in her arms, and poor Sarah was still calling at the window, as if I had not heard, though I had run right past her. Why, I kissed my Charity and my bawling child, and sick with joy, walked out onto the bare strands. There was a singing in the wind all full of your name,

Fanny Hawke, Fanny Hawke, and I that never could dance
could dance that day, and I danced, and shook out my legs.
(*After a moment.*) Remember these things, Fanny.

He embraces her.

Fanny I will, Father. I will remember everything.

John Child, I love thee.

Hannah *back with the coat and bonnet. Helps her with it.* **Fanny** *is
ready to go. She stops by* **Jesse** *and with her free hand touches his cheek.*

Fanny Goodbye, little brother, with your long face.

Outside, **Sarah** *in the yard. She has sand on her shoes and her lower skirts
are damp. She has small shells in one hand, she is making them grind
lightly against each other. It is quite twilight now.*

Fanny Sarah. You are nearly home again.

Sarah Oh, I am relieved, Fanny, I thought I might have taken
the wrong path and be among the yard of the hotel buildings.

Fanny No, you are by me here. You need walk only a few steps
further. Our house is near.

Sarah (*gripping* **Fanny**'s *hands, giving her shells*) Hannah says I
have a cold hand, for a bed companion. Do I have a cold hand,
Fanny?

Fanny Yes.

Sarah Here is a little question, for I see, or imagine, that you are
going. If I wished it to go with you, would you take me, with
even these eyes?

Fanny Oh yes, come if you wish. I wish it. I will buy you such
spectacles.

Sarah No. That is all that I wished. I can stay here easier if I know you would have taken me. I am for this place mostly, I think, Fanny.

Fanny Let me take you back into the house, Sarah, dear.

Sarah No. This is my path here. (*Going purposefully forward.*) Now I will go along it. (*Turning to her.*) May thy own journey be as safe and bright, my love.

Fanny *walks between the darkening hedges.*

The pier. **Eoghan**'s *currach. He is readying to row out home. He has lit a lamp, that is fixed on a pole at the bow. It is a candle in a square glass. It sheds its light on the water.* **Fanny** *with her sea-box.*

Fanny Fisherman?

Eoghan (*surprised*) Yes?

Fanny Fisherman, will you take me over?

Eoghan In this falling dark?

Fanny Yes.

Eoghan To Baltimore?

Fanny Yes. Will you take me across?

Eoghan I will, I will take you.

Out on the water. **Fanny** *in the stern seat, her sea-box held firmly.* **Eoghan** *rows. The darkening sea spreads all around. Plash of oars in still air. The lamp shedding light. A quiet moon, above. In his own bright light,* **John** *comes to the end of the pier.* **Eoghan** *rows,* **John**'s *light diminishes plash by plash. He can barely see his daughter. He gives a* *slight wave to her. His light extinguishes. Slowly, the other side, from the darkest shadow, on the wharf at Baltimore, light grows on* **Patrick**, *looking out, worriedly waiting. Plash by plash his light increases.*

Curtain.

White Woman Street

For Jim

Characters

Trooper O'Hara, *in his fifties, left Sligo in his youth, a red-headed man, narrow-faced, dark*
Blakely, *from Lincolnshire originally, now in his fifties, dark-haired, round-faced, lined, reddened*
Mo Mason, *from an Amish community in Ohio, in his seventies, a full man, still has his hair, not tall*
Nathaniel Yeshov, *from Brooklyn, Russian father, Chinese mother, the appearance of an eastern Russian, small, in his thirties*
James Miranda, *from Tennessee, black, about thirty or younger, the nearest to handsome of any of them, bright*
Clarke, *native American, from Virginia, in his seventies*

The play is set in Ohio, and in the small town of White Woman Street, in 1916.

White Woman Street was first performed at the Bush Theatre, London, on 23 April 1992, with the following cast:

Trooper	Jim Norton
Blakely	George Irving
Mo	Roy Hanlon
Nathaniel	David Yip
James	Patrick Miller
Clarke	Kevork Malikyan

Director Caroline Fitzgerald
Designer Kendra Ullyart
Lighting Tina MacHugh
Music Shaun Davey

Act One

*Deep shadow downstage, five rough bed-sites ranged about a wood
fire, burned down to a redness. A shaky set-up across the fire, a coffee
can at the side, cups knocked together. Four of the men are asleep in
their blankets, their possessions by them, leathers, guns, hats. The other
blanket, red-dyed, is pulled aside, empty. Five 'horses' are tethered
upstage. A local music, quietly. First light. Gold and red edges freshen
the shadows near the 'horses', where* **Trooper** *stands with his rifle.
The light colours* **Trooper**, *dressed in old army clothes and other
items. He's watching the sun rising in a scoop of land beyond the trees.*

Trooper (*alone to himself*)   You could stand on the back step
of an April morning and watch the men go up with lights to
fire the gorse. That was how gorse could be managed. You
could stand there watching as a boy and hear the hot sound
start in the distance there and the deep red fires begin to
mark the hills, scraps of it, as if hares were sitting up in the
gorse, all aflame from the sun rising behind their fur. You
could hear the cock crowing in the deep valley, and you
could hear the farmer there stirring up his horse to lead it
out into the yard to be hitched to the yard-arm of the butter
churn. Then round and round that horse would walk till the
wife tapped on the window of the dairy when the butter
came at last, and the farmer wouldn't hear but the horse
always did, and stopped. And up behind him would come
the following yard-arm and knock him in the hocks, and the
farmer cursing then. And when that farmer was ploughing in
the autumn he would bring his horse to his neighbour's horse
for the yoke. That selfsame gorse they cut then with the
stubbing-axe and fed the crushed root to the horse for to
make him strong to plough. And if the neighbour's horse
hadn't had the whins, why it would smell the whins off the
breath of the farmer's horse, and wouldn't work in the trace.
For you had to give them both the whins. And then in the
winter we were back in Sligo town for my father's business
and my schooling, and we left the cock to crow in the

growing cold till Easter following, when the gorse would be lit again. And by evening of that spring day, when the butter of the world came, and the yard-arm of the world followed round and knocked my legs, the half of the hills would be burning, and you could see something, maybe the shape of America all deep yellow with high flames and a fume of smoke.

The long lights creeping into the camp, ropes of sunlight approaching the sleeping men.

They were things I left when I myself began to fume with youth and had the silver for a ticket to Cork, and for the ship of sails to New York. And I traded my gorse and my father and my Sligo for an army horse whose saddle became my home, and I was out among the Indian wars. And when too weary to do that work I looked about me but was good for nothing. So one day and the darkest of my life I rode into a young town of those days called White Woman Street, where the canal workers and the troopers went to visit the famous whore, the only white woman for five hundred miles. And I was keen to see her and my heart was sore and I was needing a hint of home. And in I went to her.

A wind blows in further light.

So thirty years ago not far from here I saw the worst sight of all my days and I hit the roads of America as a simple outlaw and followed that trade. And I was a different man from that time on, and my heart was a kind of hidden hill where at the last hour of the night men got up and climbed it with fires and fired the rampant gorse. So now with memories of home I aim to head for home again and rest a local man in Sligo. But I can't go till peace is made, till I stand again in White Woman Street, and beg a certain ghost for her good word. In this filthied land of thinning trees, to send Trooper home. At Easter here, in Ohio.

*The wind heaps in shadow across **Trooper**. A blade of gold sunlight touches **Mo**'s face. He rubs at it, grunts, locates his old hat without looking, sets it across his eyes. **Blakely** wakes abruptly, fumbles for his rifle, looks about, hits the side of his head to get it working.*

Blakely How's that now, Mo? – You waked, Mo? – I could feel fellas creeping up.

Mo (*from under his hat*) Who, brother?

Blakely Blackfoot, Crowfoot, some class of foot – Redmen.

Mo (*peering out*) Not none of them running around Ohio these times. Redmen drinking and praying in Ohio now. You'd fear more from bears. Preachers couldn't convince *them* to leave off their wild habits.

Blakely Don't I like to drink and pray myself – when I can. Where does Trooper be?

Nathaniel *throws off his blanket.*

Nathaniel (*stretching*) Sorry to leave paradise. Dreamed I was there. Loose women – lovely, lovely loose women all about me. Silk drawers, gents.

Mo I'n't he there in his nest?

Blakely No, sir. My guess he be up in a tree stealing honey, or a-running after some varmint for his breakfast. Maybe your bears sneaked up and dragged him away, Mo.

Mo No, he be crushing daisies and such, most like, finding a quiet spot for himself.

Trooper *comes downstage, fixing the braces on his old trousers.*

Blakely Morning, Trooper. Any luck?

Trooper Why do I lick that rock sugar when I know what it does? (*He sits himself down near* **Mo**.)

Mo That human nature.

Blakely (*seeing* **James** *still asleep*) Someone wake that poor sleeping man. Nathaniel, wake that bosom pal of yours.

Trooper When you wake him, we can be talking. I got something fixed now.

Mo He maybe weary still, Blakely.

Blakely Weary – but he know where the coffee-grinds is.

Mo Wake him up, Nathaniel. (*To* **Trooper**.) If you feeling poorly, brother, I can be boiling hogweed for that.

Trooper (*shaking his head*) No . . .

Nathaniel (*shaking* **James**) Rising up now, Jim, why don't you? (*Shakes some more.*)

Blakely That man thinks he got the right to freeze up every morning of his life now. We got to wake a man from the living dead to get a cup of coffee.

Nathaniel *works at* **James**.

Trooper He got a government bullet in his back somewhere.

Blakely West Virginia. But that three year ago now. His black nose twitched.

Mo Log in a little river can work the same mischief.

James's *eyes open*.

Blakely Hallelujah. (*Waving a hand.*) You there, Jim? Where the coffee?

James (*to* **Blakely**) Good morning, Mr Whisky.

Blakely That a nice thing to call me, Jim, and me sworn off liquor. I'm going to fill me now all right, with that coffee. Where is that coffee?

James *rises stiffly and starts to ready the coffee.*

Mo That thoughtful God made us a sweet morning.

Trooper Southern Ohio weather, can't best it. I watched the mist lift off the valley. Where it goes no creature knows. The woods get gold when the old sun starts his rising. This be bare country, but a fella can gaze happy at dawn.

Mo Come May, you seeing that shining dogwood, blossom of home – Ohio i'n't so bare then. Right honest weather for

an old man, and from Ohio in his early days at that.
Familiar to me, this springing weather.

Blakely   Mo, Mo, you the chicken of spring.

Trooper   Well, boys, you may be wondering these last days
why I bringing you through these empty lands. Why we
setting our horses over fields without a harvest sown. Why
we wandering through these thin woods.

Nathaniel   Just most of the world strange to us, Trooper.
None of this more special.

Mo   You fixing something, Trooper?

Trooper   I fixing something. I know a gold train . . .

Nathaniel   You know a gold train?

Trooper   I know one, passes through a town two days from
here.

Nathaniel (*to* **James**)   A gold train.

Mo   You been at this town, Trooper?

Trooper   I been. Maybe thirty years ago.

Nathaniel   That so?

Mo   Mightn't be running there these times. You know if it
is?

Trooper   No. But I believe it does. I hoping it does. Army
train, and army train tends to run regular enough through
the years.

Blakely   Worth a look-see.

Trooper   I got to look-see, anyways.

Mo   I can hope too in this train of hope, Trooper.

Trooper   You all want to go and check?

Blakely   Sure. (*Looking around at the others.*)

Trooper   Jim?

James   Gold train? I don't mind being a rich man. You got James Miranda.

Trooper   All right then. Two days.

The light fuller now. **James** *hands round the cups. The men nod to him in turn, glad to get it. A small ritual.* **Blakely** *stirs himself.*

Blakely   Black hot coffee suits this man. What you say to another month, and summer?

Mo   Optimistic, like the fella said.

Trooper   Some dark grievous winter anyhow.

Blakely   A dark winter for poor robbermen without no homes. Blackest rain all through. Never saw such dribbling and weeping of the skies. Need a gold train . . .

Mo   God listening, Blakely. Luck in silence.

Blakely   I know. Just rambling.

James (*sitting down with his cup*)   Water in winter, sweat in summer, two useless thing that everyone got.

Blakely   That some of your southern lore, Jim?

Trooper   Whaling man I knew once, in Nantucket, wore the best skins I ever saw. There weren't any rain of earth could drench him, he were so wrapped in those skins. He had a hat just as steep as a mountain, a black thing. Gold man he was, in his yellow skins, in the prow of a storming ship. Could take any weight of sea on his head and just shake the sea off. A gold man.

Blakely (*as if putting up an umbrella over himself, and pursing his lips*)   Make rain-umbrellas from whale-ribs, they do. Maybe be raining in the night – see any whale spouts out on these green seas lately? There, there she breaches!

Nathaniel (*rising up laughing*)   Making corsets too out of them ribs. See any corsets?

Laughter.

(*Sinking down again.*)   See the same scarcity, women and whales, out here.

Trooper (*a little excited*)   You'll see women now in White Woman Street. You'll see plenty good women. I know. You'll see those Indian women waiting for you, in those high-stockinged dresses. That's what you'll see there.

Mo *looking at* **Trooper**, **Blakely** *at* **Mo**.

Blakely (*after a little*)   Hate to rob a nice town like that.

Trooper   Not robbing it. That train i'n't the possession of that town. That a through-going train, Blakely. We can be moral men there in that town, believe me.

James (*poking about in a leather sack*)   Best buy some stores afore we chance the train. Going to be stewing up hickory in the mornings otherwise.

Blakely   You want to go and store-shop elegantwise before you take all that glistening gold off of that good through-going train?

James   You care for that Jim's coffee, don't you? We got three spoons left of it to sprinkle now.

Blakely   Sure, sure, Jim.

James   That's it.

Trooper   Don't be saying again we be robbing that town, you hear, Blakely?

Blakely (*attacked from another direction*)   Sure, sure, Trooper.

Nathaniel   You try them nice Indian girls, Trooper?

Blakely (*generally*)   Anyone else care to grizzle me?

Trooper   I didn't have no money then – not for wild women. That's thirty years gone by and I'm as short now for them grinning eagles.

Blakely (*making up*)   I thinking too, you don't got no money now, Trooper.

Trooper   That don't matter to me.

Nathaniel   We got enough for girls, Blakely?

Blakely   I'n't you a robberman, Nathaniel?

Nathaniel   I should think so.

Mo   They have a bath-house in White Woman Street there, Trooper?

Trooper   Not those thirty years ago. Maybe it's a big, upjumped, civilised place now.

Mo   Could steep for a Monday. I believe, I believe I got the dirt of last fall under the dirt of winter just gone by, and now here's the dirt of this spring weather, dust and birdshit and such devilment.

Blakely   That's all as good as a raincoat, Mo.

Mo   Rain touches this, just lightly, Mo Mason turns into a quagmire. That the word, i'n't it, Trooper? You the scholar.

Trooper   Why, Mo, certainly is.

Mo   A quagmire.

Nathaniel   You doubtless is a funny old man, Mo.

Mo   I doubtless am.

Blakely   Doubtless!

He directs the grit of his coffee into the fire and the others expertly follow suit. **Trooper** *drifts left alone, the others take up their gear and ready the horses. They move slowly, fixing their guns, their hats.* **Blakely** *dons his long travelling coat.* **Trooper** *seems apart, in another light, of new green shadows. A local music.*

Trooper   Berry-gathering. One day she comes in with red gloves, as she might say, the next blue. Maybe purple, maybe the strange stain of the elderberry. All them things would turn up later in bottles – local wine. I don't know if she lives. People in Sligo who knew her said she could make a good wine out of haws – a thing rarely done. Or better, yewberries, the killer of cows. Maybe the ma done that. Maybe her arms smelled so good because she was forever scrubbing them – scrubbing off the juices – in that white tin basin with burning soap. Sometimes her arms were just rainbows. She smelled of the fires of soap. A young woman making wine for her husband's friends. Making all them wines. And scrubbing. I don't know if she lives.

The light spreading about the others. **Trooper** *fixing his stuff.*

Blakely   What time of the clock is it, Trooper? For a man who i'n't hurrying.

Trooper (*looking at his fob-watch*)   What time of the blessed clock? 'Tis now ten good minutes past the hour.

Blakely   Which hour is that, Trooper?

Trooper (*pocketing his watch, mounting*)   The seventh hour, Blakely.

Time shifting, a local music, the wild meadowlight around them, walking slowly, the blow of birds, the dart of things, bright flies, beams, sparkling. The men settled, easy, in the little heave of the horses.

Blakely   Man such as me likes to travel through such bleak districts, through these old ash woods and broken pine. Gladdens a Lincolnshire boy. What day now we likely to gain White Woman Street, Trooper?

Trooper (*to himself*)   To beg a certain ghost . . .

Blakely *rests back in his 'saddle'.*

Blakely   Huh?

Trooper *stirs himself.*

Trooper   One more night with the owls. (**Blakely** *cheered, responding.*) And tomorrow, gents, we see that town below us. Little place bunched in against a yellowed plain like a pile of Texas tumbleweed. There'll be the black spike of the railroad running north-east, and a canal they got that men like to me built forty and more years ago. It kind of trickles in from the strict north.

Blakely   You saying army built it?

Trooper   Saying Irish built it. Irish toiled to dig it and many killed. Not much more than a ditch, not much more than a grave.

Blakely (*cheerfully*)   That be the ghost you mentioned?

Trooper (*blackly*)   How so, ghost?

Mo   That be how they be making a canal. With a tally of deaths, usual.

James   Railroad better than any water-road. I come north in America to see these marvels, and I see few enough of them – so far, so far. Give me gold, boys, and I might forsake them.

Nathaniel   I'll say a word for bridges, I did like the bridges of that Eastern coast. Looking like seagulls writ large, them good bridges sometimes – in the morning maybe. Bridge of Brooklyn. Mist rising around it, men blowing about with paint pots and new bolts up high in the summer.

James   But I'm finding – there be a pile of something better than bridges. Or them railroads or even glistening automobiles! Something I never went to find. Beauty somehow now and then. Here, North. Something easy in the airs. Aren't I better for being here? Maybe you don't know the days of Tennessee. Things there you finding. In a ditch out on a farmer's road, in yellow fields, in that half-done time of day. You might find a friend of your, the blood out on his face – I was thinking, you stay, James Miranda, and you be like that other James quite shortly, that had his head severed off, that was John's poor brother, in the fine, high days of the black book of Jesus. You best not stay so, James Miranda, were my words then.

Trooper *kicks his horse on. They all move into a bright clattering canter.*

Blakely   What you want to do, Trooper? You want to skirt that wooded place?

Mo   I thinking, you could catch a deer in that cover.

Blakely   We a-deer hunting, Trooper?

A good local drumming music.

Trooper (*happily*)   I am happy to hunt a deer there, quick.

Mo   That be a silent serious animal – but I know her marks.

Nathaniel   Wild boar more likely! Don't you understand Ohio? My pa's wild pigs – he got them on his Central Plains. That in Russia, boys!

Trooper   Take our road through the wood!

Nathaniel   Wild boar not rare in Brooklyn neither, gents!

Dark running green of trees. Sudden blind shadowiness. They duck the branches. Music.

Blakely   Whoop! Man got to say, whoop! When he loving!

Nathaniel   Pigs of Brooklyn, pigs of Brooklyn!

Trooper   Fellas running! See them, Mo? Cross them, cross them, wedge them, boys!

Mo *slowly raises his rifle. A fresh light, a music. The others stilled. He rides with his head down, his body down. Up comes the gun. With a bleak dart of redness he fires the old gun. There's an earthly squeal. Mo stops his horse. The others surge down from their mounts and off to retrieve the boar. Mo watching on stage alone. Alert, sad. The others then bring on the dead boar – big, bristling.*

Blakely   Heroes! That hunting!

Mo *pleased, quiet.*

Nathaniel   Pretty bit of hunting, Blakely – that's true.

Trooper   Maybe we give up the trains and go businesslike for this. Jingo – don't they bleed? (*Trying to clean himself off.*)

They stop, just looking. Then **Nathaniel** *opens the neck-vein.*

Nathaniel   A fair-looker of a sow. A nice shapely girl.

James   Handsomest sow I ever saw. You see her on the beer sticker at home. Sow Brand Beer. Some things were wholesome!

Nathaniel   Sure was a fair-looker – considering . . .

Mo *rests his gun against himself with a certain air.*

Trooper (*putting a hand on* **Mo**'s *back lightly*)   Shooting, Mo.

Mo   Not so bad!

Trooper (*generally*)   I don't suppose any men ever had such a shooter in their midst.

Blakely   Speaking truth. That were (*searching for a good word*) a shot, Mo, a shot indeed. Looking like no one can shoot as sharp as an Amish boy of Ohio.

Nathaniel (*drawing his knife along the belly*)   Skinning, boys.

He sets to. **Blakely** *and* **James** *fix the fire. They put a pole through the boar and set her up across the fire.* **Blakely** *turns it about and about. Meanwhile* **Mo** *alone, looking at the work, rifle in hand. His own light. Music.*

Mo   A fly was sitting on his nose and it buzzing there and we were waking up in the bright room and Ezekiel looks down his nose at the fly and says, 'You go buzzing there, little fly, no harm to you.' And I was saying in my own sheets that he could do well to raise a hand to that daft creature and show the creation of flies that it weren't good to be sitting on the noses even of Amish folk and buzzing like that in the heat of the morning, and all the day of work before. And Papa drifting by outside in his black suit of linen with his beard as shapely as a spade, drifting the way he did, kind of disturbing the solid heat. And Ezekiel says that I was for roaming, since my thinking wasn't the likes of Papa's. And it wasn't. So in the morning a week following I shook Papa's hand and left him in the house. My brother came out on the track with me and gave me a blessing. He were an older man than me and he had a strong face and his hands and feet were big. He holds out his big hands and he says, 'Moses, you seem to be fixed on this going.' And I say, 'Zeke, it i'n't right for me to stay,' and he says, 'I think in all you're right there,' and he looks at me. Because he knew, once gone, he wouldn't see me again, since I couldn't return, no matter what befell me, according to our law. And that sun of morning was gold kind of like in his eyes, and I says, 'Zeke, it's a long road,' and he says, 'If ever you have a yearning for to scythe a sea of wheat, or to catch a roaming swarm and get that gold out of it, you know the place to come.' Well, he was lying then in his teeth. 'Zeke,' I says, 'thanks for the fresh pair of drawers and the Sunday hat,' I says, touching the rim of the hat as I spoke, and the gold just vanished out of his eyes because he turned away then. Zeke. It was the difference between wanting to kill that fly, and not killing it. And that was nigh on fifty year ago, in the brittle fields of North Ohio. I just weren't gentle like a proper Amish.

Blakely   Come on, Mo Mason, and get your grub!

Mo *goes over and sits with them.*

Nathaniel (*holding something out in his fingers*)   There you go, *Mr* Mason. (*Hands it to* **Mo**.)

Trooper   That the killing bullet?

Nathaniel   That's the one.

Mo *looking at it in his hand. Everything still. Light deepening to a clear burning sunset. A local music.* **Blakely** *slowly leans forward and turns the boar a last time. It's eaten away on the shown side. The light goes, the fire illuminates them now. They're replete with boar meat.* **Mo**'s *sitting with the rest.*

Nathaniel (*poking at his teeth with a twig, smelling his own breath*)   Guess that sow was a garlic-eater.

Mo   So a cook will say – a pig eats clean.

Nathaniel   We won't see witches at this fire.

Blakely   You think? I'm glad. Country sure looks bare and bleak about. This half-light's the time for them though and I seen big witches, big black dames about this time all over these states.

Trooper *sunken fearfully into himself.*

James   That be marvels! What they do to you, Blakely?

Blakely   Singing only.

James   They was singing? What would they be singing, Blakely?

Blakely   I don't know, Jim. They were singing though. Something like so . . . (*Tries a song.*) 'There were nine and ninety in the fold . . .'

Trooper   I never seen a witch singing maybe, but I never seen a witch singing a hymn, if you follow me.

Blakely   You not a witch-seeing man, Trooper. Some sees, some don't sees. You just a red-haired man and a red-haired man don't see much.

James   I heard as much right enough – down South.

Blakely   Fact, fact. Can't look a fact in the face and say it i'n't a fact. A fact stares right back. I wasn't intending to offend you, Trooper.

Trooper   No – I don't mind not seeing witches.

Blakely   So, some people would, see?

Trooper   Not me, Blakely.

Blakely (*rising*)   Any way I can take that glum out of you, Trooper? My, you getting to have an old man's manner of sitting. What's up with you?

Mo   Leave him be. He got the high dumps. It's a passing thing with us all. Less of the old man.

Blakely *standing nearer* **Trooper**.

Blakely   Maybe I can dance for you? Ever seen my dances?

Trooper (*looking up bleakly enough*)   Guess I have. None too pretty a sight.

Blakely   You thinking? (*Starts a waltz alone, hands high, leathers flapping, watching* **Trooper**.) Eh, eh? Footwork, footwork. Look and learn.

Trooper (*slight smile*)   Bear dances better, Blakely.

Nathaniel   Smells a damn sight better too.

Blakely   That's acause I han't got no partner.

Moves towards **Mo**.

Mo   Not on your black life, Blakely, you keep back from me.

James *and* **Nathaniel** *laughing, looking to* **Trooper**, **Trooper** *laughing now*.

Blakely   What about it, Missy Mo, maybe you care to shoot the leg?

Mo   Christ in his bed. I never saw the like. If I was a maiden, I'd surely cry. (**Blakely** *drags* **Mo** *up*.) God love you, leave an old man after a day of horses.

Blakely *stands before him formally, raises his hands to join* **Mo**'s, *then ducks his hands down to button the edge of his coat back, in a flap to the side*.

James   Ah, that disgusting, Blakely.

Blakely   See, that what we used to do, to get a spur on them fillies . . .

Mo   Jesus Christ, Blakely, am going to spew!

Trooper *laughing now,* **Nathaniel** *strikes up a waltzing tune loudly.*

Blakely　Ready, my dove? (*He takes* **Mo**'s *hands, starts to waltz him.*) Let's show the style now. (*They go a few steps.*) My, my, what a dainty little thing you are, Miss Mo. (**Nathaniel** *and* **James** *laughing hard,* **Trooper** *following.* **Blakely** *hits his crotch a couple of times against* **Mo**.) Ha! Ha!

Trooper *away in laughter. They dance a little further.* **Trooper** *in deep laughter. They part, awkward, laughing, the others laughing, clapping.*

Blakely　Now, Trooper. I got you smiling.

Laughing again.

Trooper　Right. You did, Blakely.

Blakely *throws himself down, panting.* **Mo** *sits down carefully.*

Mo　Going to ache after that. (*They sit staring into the fire a moment, the moon has begun to rise behind.*) One time me and Trooper come into a bar-room in Texas. East Texas. We been two weeks deep country. Now we see the frost of money over people's eyes. But there was this fella standing stiff against the bar . . .

Trooper　I remember . . .

Blakely　I don't remember. Weren't I with you then?

Mo　Stiff against the bar, holding up the world you'd say – and he was roaring around at the clients saying, You the worst bunch of two-cent hustling no-hopes a man ever did see in America. And when we come in, he put it on worse, shouting at Trooper because of those old army pants, and giving out about the king of England and how America got rid of England when it suited her by God, and such items of history, and Trooper just turns and says, 'Mr, you need to scream, go ahead, we like screaming,' says he, 'we connoisseurs of screaming.' Educated, you know. 'Connoisseurs,' said the man, 'what you mean, some kind of song-birds, you meaning?' Ignorant, you know. And Trooper

says, 'No – but you stopped screaming. Scream some more!'
The man comes over and puts an arm about Trooper sort of
like in a music-hall skit, all friendly and joking, and he says,
'Fella, you a tomato.' Trooper says, 'You meaning, a peach?'
Man thinks for a moment and says, 'No, a tomato,' and
Trooper laughs. Trooper got a pleasant laughter. And that
was Blakely and how we met him.

Blakely *up again, looking around, gobsmacked.* **Nathaniel** *and*
James *enjoying it.*

Mo   Tomato!

Blakely   No, boys, no. Never was. I didn't remember that.
That right? You got me, Mo, you got me.

James *takes out a long clay pipe and fills it, things settle again. The
moon well risen, a small spring moon. Smoke rises from* **James**'s *pipe.*

James   What be the picking there on that train. Trooper?

Trooper   That fine train of ours we going to abuse? (**James**
nods.) Easter pay. Easter pay for the fort at Chagrin and
Bolivar – forts I should have said. That train going through
few days after that good and holy time. This time we're in
now, I should have said.

James   Gold – I might be a true man with gold in Ashville.
Gold can turn a human creature any colour. Make me shine.
Black with a gold shine. Could set up a gent in Ashville, with
that same gold. If a fella could bear the company. You did
say gold, Trooper?

Trooper   Part gold. Sides of beef, chuck, cornmeal, onions,
linen, hats, beans green, beans black, barley, whisky,
gunpowder, saltpetre, traps for varmints, bullets, bandages,
ribbons and eggs.

Nathaniel   For the Easter?

Trooper   How's that, Nathaniel?

Nathaniel   Easter eggs?

Trooper   Nope – hen's eggs.

Nathaniel   You know what I meaning by Easter eggs?

Trooper   I know what you meaning. You think the army sends Easter eggs to grown men in a gold train?

Nathaniel   I seen men as old as Mo getting eggs at the Easter-time in Brooklyn. That a Russian habit, boys.

Blakely   Darn fool Russians.

Trooper   Don't know rightly if I ever saw an Easter egg. I saw a duck's egg often enough, that a soft blue one, and one rare time I saw a heron's egg – hard to find. Sligo i'n't no fancy-dandy place like your Brooklyn. Children lucky to get dried ling at Christmas, leave alone eggs at Easter. Aister, we used to say. In my own house maybe you might have expected an egg, but I don't recall one. May be forgetting such things . . .

Nathaniel   Little painted eggs, Mo. You'd a liked them. Wood, kind of paper with flour water, a wild bird's egg.

Blakely (*in the background, vaguely to* **James**)   Lucky to get dried ling – that old shit of Trooper's . . .

Mo *smiles at* **Nathaniel**.

Trooper (*quietly singing*)   Eggs and eggs and marrowbones
                                    Mix them all up well.
(*To himself.*) That's what we used to sing. Lucky to have eggs.

Blakely (*mockingly*)   Lucky to have bones, Trooper.

Nathaniel   You get the big noises in the churches at this time, in my Pa's town, out there in Russia. Prayers, blazing away. Old women singing like banditti and the gold everywhere. Big fellas with black beards doing the holy words. The name of that town, the name of that town . . . Snow would be gone then and the river eased out of its ice. There was this old white church across the watermeadows that old dead sailors built, you got big white-masted ships there in very old days, sails shrugging there among the fields and a deep river for the sea-going keels and that was two hundred miles inland. China merchants maybe, China bound. But the white church got lit with candles, three thousand and more, and you could stand on the meadows under the trees by the train station and look across at it, over the flooded meadows. That light burst out of it just the same as it was so much yellow water.

Blakely How come you know that, Nathaniel, that never was in Russia? I assume you speaking about Russia?

Nathaniel I seeing through my Pa's eyes now for you. See, I shut my own, and seeing through his.

Blakely You got your father's eyes in there under your lids?

Nathaniel I hope so.

Blakely I don't know if you a crazy Russian sometimes.

Nathaniel No, crazy come from my Ma – she were a Chinee. She used to say, herself in America, like a wingless bird in the Land of Fire.

James (*suddenly, mostly to himself*) We don't got molasses, salt beef, Mex beans or flat-bread flour – five prime vittals – and we don't got one of them!

Mo On the morrow, Jim, as much store-buying as you like. Maybe we could be for turning in now.

Trooper Someone got to go down to the brook and fill the nose-sack with fresh water for them horses there. Otherwise, they'll break their tethers towards dawn. Indians will get them for sure.

Blakely No Indians now, Trooper. You surely shot them all.

Trooper Never could shoot an Indian.

Blakely Well – that what the Yankee government were paying you for. Weren't you in all them Indian wars in the eighties? You said so.

Trooper I said I was in them since I was. Still wearing the duds, hah? Didn't say never that I was shooting Indians.

Nathaniel　Why didn't you shoot them, Trooper? You had
an employment there to shoot Indians. You the only one of
us ever held a proper employment, aside from breaking
stones. You should have shot a few for the look of things.

Trooper　Be like shooting you, Nathaniel. You ever see a
true Indian place? Don't mean the places they give them
now. Don't mean where the missionary men have them
cooped now and giving them new words and shirts, and
trying to get them to look dandy and plough and not be
drinking and stabbing. Ever see an Indian town – the tent
towns? (**Nathaniel** *uncomprehending*.) Put me in mind of
certain Sligo hills, and certain men in certain Sligo hills. The
English had done for us, I was thinking, and now we're
doing for the Indians. You asking Trooper why he never
killed? I *seen* plenty killed, I don't say I didn't. Girls hiding in
brushwood, taken for a soldier's violent pleasure. Brothel and
butcher shop. Well – didn't seem . . . Unless you been to war
you don't . . . These weren't fellas drinking all day and
churched at Sunday . . . These were (*smiling*) oh, characters.
We'd go in and have to . . . You couldn't leave nothing alive.
You know.

Mo　That years back, Trooper. Lord love you, that years
back.

Trooper　Yeh. Who'll fetch the water?

Blakely　Here (*taking the sack*), I do it. (*Looking down at*
Trooper.) Guess we weren't there, Trooper.

*He goes to fill water from the brook. The others settle into their
blankets, grunting and shifting. Scratching.* **Blakely** *crosses to the
horses with the water-sack. They make stamping noises, whinnies to
see him.* **Blakely** *chuckles.*

Blakely　Thirsty men, i'n't ye? You want some more
trickling water, Mr Thunder? Keep you fresh for speed
tomorrow, boy. Never shot an Indian! He think I believing
him? He were a full-pay Trooper then – a-course he shot
himself Indians. Probably shot whole towns of them. I bet all
that glistening gold in that train, I bet it all that what he

says there i'n't true. Hold up, Queenie, hold up, you'll get
your share. Because, his face look like he shot them . . . I
know how them Irish are where Trooper come from. Savage
they living. Han't got shoes. Han't got food most of them.
Eating nettles and prayers I'll be bound. Lucky to have
bones, Trooper! I seen Irish like that, holed up in the
crevices of America just as cockroaches do, or the very lice
on my body, and I never saw an Indian as bad as an Irish. I
didn't. Maybe just nearly as bad. Maybe the same. I'm
betting he shot his fair share. Why wouldn't an Irish shoot
an Indian? Trooper shot thousands. Shot more Redmen than
King Buffalo, I'm saying. What you think, Mr Thunder?
And they had buffalo too up there in those damned Sligo
hills, till the Irish ate them, raw from the hoof up. You want
to get wisdom, Trooper, talking to Blakely. Blakely knows.
(*The horses whinny.*) What frights you, boys, what frights you?

In the darkened camp, **Trooper** *wakes suddenly. He gives a cry.*

Mo   Easy, easy, child.

Trooper   I an't no fearful child, Mo.

The trees silver now in the moon, **Blakely** *silvered.*

Mo   Why don't you bring your blanket a shade nearer to
me, Trooper?

Trooper   You say I might, Mo?

Mo   A shade, a shade.

Trooper *a little closer.*

Trooper   What was I doing here in wide America?

Mo   Sleeping, sleeping. Not like me. (**Trooper** *asleep again
nearly.*) I'm wide awake in wide America.

Act Two

Clear morning, the men packing up their horses. The fire only a black mark on the clay. **Mo** *stamping it out firmly.* **Trooper** *by him and the other three nearly mounted and ready.*

Mo   One time I was in Kansas droving hogs for a syndicate. Long before I met you. Through the yellow gullies of Kansas. One morning I catch a change in the weather, by the way those hogs kept stopping and looking round for holes, caves, and such – well. Shortly up the country comes, comes walking, a fury of a dust cloud, tornado, ripping up plantings yonder, stirring through the great blue – in a fury. Saddest single thing I ever saw – the anger of that twisting wind. Disturbing where farmers had things set. The lack of use in it. Not a plougher or a planter, nor a drover. Empty-headed anger. Saddest thing. But, the hogs two steps ahead of it.

Trooper (*moving with* **Mo** *towards the horses*)   You want me (*putting his rifle in its holder*) to be more like them hogs, Mo?

Mo   Don't sit so raw up in the wind, maybe.

Blakely   Heading out, fellas. What time on your fob-watch, Trooper?

Trooper (*drawing it out, looking, shaking it, listening to it*)   The hands is stuck or stopped.

Blakely   You sat on it, Trooper, maybe.

Trooper   Wharf-watch. My father timed ships by it and tides and workings of men.

Mo   Who'll need a timepiece while the sun shines and the moon?

Trooper   All right. (*Mounting.*) Suits me just as fine.

Blakely (**Mo** *mounting nimbly*)   You i'n't so stiff, after dancing!

Mo Morning, noon, evening, night – those things are there if you have a timepiece or not.

Riding through green shadows. **Blakely** *more dressed in light, riding, excited.*

Blakely You i'n't so stiff, Mo Mason, you i'n't so stiff. You flush with life! Never will get tired of the motley bushes of America! Any wilderness suits Blakely. There were nine and ninety in the fold! And one was lost – shepherd got himself scratched by briars (*shading his eyes with one hand*) looking for his ransomed Blakely! Better and more life than my old faither. Faither, toilsome, hardy, a black rabbit, a dark stoat, a velvet-jacketed mole. And all about the white streets lay the dust of his mines, heaping, holding, hardening, till the clear granite of Lincolnshire turned to basalt and hellstone, and the trout-flying streams coiled bleakely about dead dogs and debris of love, and the crest of the King withered from the wall of the town hall, and my faither found his age, and we threw him down into the soil, and we felt the soil shake under our shoes, and his soul thundered into the disused tunnels, and someone cast after him a pleasant rose! (*Up in his stirrups now, streaming.*) More life, Mo, more life!

Mo's *great cry! They ride in fast unison, music. A flail of travelling. The attitudes of their faces, the style of their riding, painterly, eyes lost to the movement. Sunlight breaks over them in falls of gold. They dismount, looking down on White Woman Street.*

Mo That a fair-looking town.

Trooper White Woman Street. She grown a little right enough. Hard to make out the waterways now. Canal must be sneaking out there behind those red roofs. Town's mopping it up.

Mo Queer-named spot.

Trooper Yep, got its name from that famous girl used to see to business here. Only white woman for five hundred miles of wilderness.

Blakely You say so, Trooper?

Trooper Canal builders used to spend majorities of their wages on that woman. Every step west you forgot what beauty of women was, till you hit White Woman Street and that sweat-drenched withered girl was more perfect than first love. All Ireland's emigrants knew that furrow, and set their seeds against her, but I expecting nothing grew. If you was poor or lost your bills in cards, you shacked with an Indian. That time Indian weren't said to be even just a human person, but a kind of running hare or doe – fellas said they were going to rut a deer since money was fresh lost. One old sailor, who had lain with dolphins, as sailors sometimes do, said dolphins were more pleasing to him than any Indian girl. And what was they that spoke but local Irish eels lost and growing in that Sargasso sea? They was simpler times and it seemed the same to me and all I wished was to see that white woman and be her cash lover.

Nathaniel Ever rise to such dignity?

Trooper I nearly.

Blakely I knew you did.

Trooper How you say, Blakely?

Blakely I knew you did go in – any Christian man would have.

Trooper Well – went in to her by God one time when flush with cash. My troop brought in two hundred scalps and we were bonus. I had my token in my hand as good as gold, a little tin plate with a star on it, and she was there, Nathaniel, kind of saying nothing in the dark. Oh, I was, I was young, you know? But I catched my arm in her shabby curtains as I passed and what I did see shocked my poor soul.

Blakely Pox, was it, Trooper? Woman like that, lying down with mere Irish?

Trooper It weren't nothing of that kind, Blakely. It were a devious trick out of the wilderness. Weren't she like a saint to those men, a place for pilgrimage. Tober nAlt she was, a holy well, a shrine, St Bridget, some powerful class of folk that would bring you luck and ease your longing?

Blakely   God-damned street-woman sounds to me.

James   Shush, Blakely. Trooper remembering.

Trooper   I sounding like a fool, I know that, Blakely. I were seeing her in light, like no man before me, by grace of hooking part of me in a curtain. I'd a chose the darkness!

Nathaniel   Was it age, Trooper?

Trooper   Age? She had no age to mention. Less than you. Just a girl. With two circles of rouge on her cheeks and her wild green eyes lost as emeralds in a Texas stream. Never seed a child so frighted, holding out her arms to me, as if to shut my eyes, a dusty pilgrim that had walked some twenty miles to give her my best coin. No one could ever measure that need I feeling, a boy sullied up by wars, Indian wars. That need to view a sight of home, a goddess of my own countrymen. Men from my troop had swore she was from Listowel! You don't know that town – a little city of Ireland. But, boys, the dark of the room was her only whiteness, and in the light of day she was one so lovely Indian girl, a sparkling doe, a hare bright in the haggard, a hunter's reproach.

Mo   Guess that white woman were dead or old and they liked to keep that trade.

Blakely   I do hope you whupped her, Trooper.

James   Whupping don't answer, Blakely.

Trooper   Was all that pay and dreaming of my countrymen I thinking of, those farms they left when food got scarce, those long black nights aboard the famous ships, their arms pushing spades and hauling up axes in America, digging and cutting like pigs and dogs, men whose children had froze in ditches, brothers died with that green about their lips, the smear of nettles, whose religion was washed clear out of them by hunger – clear, tested, cursing men that no one could wager was worth two farts, filthy flotsam of Ireland, letterless, stumbling, crooked men that had nothing to believe on but that there were one white woman here, a woman of a hundred stories, a hundred boasts, a kind of fire-hot legend of those days, such as had power over their talk and in truth, boys, let me say it, was likely a goddess, and surely built that canal.

Blakely   Makes a man wonder though.

Trooper   What wondering?

Blakely   How's you coming back here.

Trooper   Why coming back? Because I know about that train, and gold of that train has me sitting on my black-assed horse there. (**Nathaniel** *laughs*.)

Nathaniel   Maybe we ride down now, where them poor Irish got duped?

Blakely   I got to say it, Trooper, but an English wouldn't hunt rabbit in the dark.

Trooper   Well. We know our duty, boys. Where we stop first in town we know.

Blakely   We know? (*Mounting*.)

Nathaniel   You saying whorehouse? Our duty in the whorehouse? (*To* **Mo**.) Yes, sir.

Trooper   Not there first, Nathaniel. What we do ever first in a sweet town?

Nathaniel   Forgetting.

Trooper   You follow after me. Then you remember your duty. We camp on that lower hill, you see that section, and walk down from there. Go down, Queenie, go down.

*The stage dark with glints of gold, specks of iconry here and there.
The men have exited. A dark cloth over the horses.*

Blakely (*off*)   What class of a chapel this be?

James (*off*)   Baptist, Blakely.

Blakely (*off*)   Whoah!

James (*off*)   What difference?

Blakely (*off*)   None, none . . .

*They come on respectfully in the half-light. They strike their breeches
to get the dust off.* **Nathaniel** *raises his hat and smoothes back his
hair. The other hats are removed in a chain reaction.* **Trooper** *kneels
on one knee, hat held there, other hand over his head, Irish fashion.
They pray vigorously.* **Nathaniel**, *and* **Mo** *in his Amish fashion, out
loud.*

Nathaniel   Nathaniel he wicked – can't see the good in
Nathaniel. Here because Trooper say we should – he right. I
was thinking only of – that wicked house a-down the
street . . .

Mo   More love!

Nathaniel   Maybe, maybe you should pour some of that
hellfire down on it, only – maybe spare the girls.

Blakely (*glancing at* **Trooper**)   That be prayers?

Trooper   Good as any else. Got some of your own, han't
you, Blakely?

Blakely   Acres of them – acres.

Trooper   Pray them so . . .

Nathaniel   Nathaniel Yeshov is a Brooklyn man and what
they pray in Russia he forget. What prayers of China he
never knew, though some day, in that land of fire . . .
Forgetting a deal of things. Wilderness do that, mister.
Scatter the thoughts of a simple man. Maybe you look out

for me. You know the truth of me I guess – see it all. Sad picture.

Mo   More love!

Nathaniel   Well, thanking you, mister.

He gets up, looks down at the others, taps his hat. **James** *unexpectedly begins.*

James   That was Jimmy's luck to meet these boys. The arms of these men have cradled me, given me a place to rest, a kind of home, though we moving our home day to day. For these boys I be willing to hang, to fester in prison, to take the fall. When I run first I run out to see the marvels of America, that was my wish. I had seen the dead part long enough. Ashville i'n't no paradise of ease and I was told by many that in the North you could walk careless, even so far after the bitter lies of that war. Richmond. So out I run to see them marvels of America and here I am to note it down and praise it. These four men have shown me the free silver of all daybreaks, the shrug of grass when it growing across a hundred acres, freely and finely, and shown me that a heart's friend don't cause too many aches, but heals the hurt of many old ones, with a bit of laughter, and easiness I wasn't used to knowing. And if that muddy slough bar my way, they shown me how to leap it. Careless! This world can throw what it might at me, but I am among the beauties of America with these friends, and we are mighty enough in it, and are pleased. It i'n't work for angels, what we doing, so we don't sing innocent, but say we done it all, we done all that, because we are robbermen that know our work and know the beauties of America.

Nathaniel *tries to see back into the gloom.*

Nathaniel   Thanking you too, padre!

James (*rising*)   That not the padre, Nathaniel. That just a statue.

Nathaniel   Dark in this holy place, Jim.

James   We go the store now, Trooper?

Trooper (*rising, confused*)   Sure, Jim. (*After a little.*) Seen an eatery corner of this street. (*Smiling.*) Some good Ohio food make new men of us.

Mo   Ohio grub, believe me, cattle grits and longshadow beef – lead on, Trooper.

Blakely *makes a face to* **Nathaniel**. *They go off upstage left. The white dusty sunlight of the street outside. PATS BEST EATS written over a door. The men come back out by it.* **James** *with a sack of provisions.*

Blakely (*reading the sign*)   Pat's God-damned Best Eats. Merciful Christ. Them beans was like chewing little river stones.

Nathaniel   I couldn't eat, what with paradise at hand.

Bar counter swings in.

Mo (*rubbing his stomach*)   Going to nurse that beef all night. Still moving, one way or another.

Blakely *standing nearer the bar counter, light of the whorehouse there growing, displacing the street.*

Blakely   El Dorado, boys – God's heaven!

They herd into the poorly lit room.

Mo   Quiet for a place of joy. This the same old place you spoke of, Trooper?

Trooper   Could be, could be. Everything looking very different. But, maybe so.

An old man comes out, an Indian, **Clarke**, *dressed much the same as themselves.*

Mo   You know that old man?

Trooper   I never seen that old man.

Clarke   You want women, boys – or what?

Mo   We want women. Well – these fellas want them. Me, I want a woman, but couldn't locate no bathhouse, and I reckon I smell too high. These other gents been soaping in innocent rivers betimes. I could never abide open-air washing.

Clarke   Women in there, dollar each. We don't want no biting and no fighting.

Mo   Right. Now, boys. No biting and no fighting. (**Nathaniel, James** *and* **Blakely** *file out upstage centre.*) Right. So, Trooper, you?

Trooper *staring after the others.*

Trooper   No – just later. Drop of whisky down here, mister, meantime.

Trooper *stands at lonelier end of the bar,* **Mo** *moves to* **Clarke,** *the bar between them.* **Mo** *sets his hat on the bar,* **Clarke** *puts whisky by* **Trooper**, *silently asks if* **Mo** *wants some.*

Mo   No, sir. Never did touch it. Only bit of religion ever stuck.

Trooper *drinks,* **Mo** *and* **Clarke** *quiet for the moment.*

(*After a bit.*) You mind me asking, mister, what that shiny thing be there? (*Pointing to a locket around* **Clarke**'s *neck.*)

Clarke   This here? What you think it is?

Mo   Is what I'm asking.

Clarke   My mother, you want to know.

Mo   Now you surprise me, mister.

Clarke   Can't buy it.

Mo   No, that understood, that understood.

Clarke   Ashes of her head only, sorry to report. Soldier's woman at Gettyburg. First bombardment, she serving the officers their chuck, big shell lobbed over, explosion, mother gone. They find her head, cremate it. (*Holds out locket.*) Death of a good woman. Only good woman in this town.

Mo   That a grievous violent death, mister.

Clarke I'n't nothing to these parts. Fellas knocking each other down in Ohio all day. Considered a pleasantry to stab someone. Like a compliment. See it here on pay days. I had two murders here on that very floor. And years ago, when there were no civilisation going at all, some fool killed a woman here.

Mo That was low work.

Clarke You're saying. Fella drew his knife across her throat, just like she was a pig to bleed. Happened in there, one of the rooms.

Mo Man caught?

Clarke Caught? Lawless days. Anyways, he never was caught. And she weren't no bad woman neither. Better call her a girl – sixteen, little Ohio river girl, not like me. I hail from the Smoky Mountains myself. Little Indian girl – came up from the river somewhere, like they used to then. She done her best to get by and some disgraceful man he do her in.

Mo You never see him again, that murdering man?

Clarke Never seen him in the first place. I weren't officially connected to this premises at that time. Scouting for army then, I was. Some other poor man standing here. Old negra man, I remember him, in those early days, and another Indian that still wore crow's feathers in his head, and carried his hair longer than the preacher would let you now. And spoke no English words – not like me doing here – easy as white man.

Mo You got damn good English, mister, damn best of that English I been hearing these seventy years of my life. I hear many men gabbling English and you the best at it. You riding the best pony of English I seen.

Blakely (*off*) Whoop!

Clarke Thank you, mister. That's kind. My name just Clarke, you want to know.

Mo   I meaning it, that complimenting I was doing to you.
Name's Mo Mason, I were born in Ohio and have wandered
extensive since them days . . . (*About to shake* **Clarke**'s *hand,
but* **Blakely** *reappears.*) Well, Blakely. Didn't expect you so
soon. (**Blakely** *strides over between* **Mo** *and* **Trooper**.) You
looking like the cat that got the milk. (**Blakely** *puts an arm on*
Mo's *back, leans towards* **Trooper**.)

Blakely   Whooooo, Trooper.

Trooper   Don't trouble me, Blakely.

Blakely   Trouble you? No, sir. (*Turning to* **Mo**.) I can
recommend that, Mo Mason. Any man could rise nimble
after that. (**Nathaniel** *and* **James** *coming out*.) Look at these
boys of paradise. Step over, boys, if you can still move your
legs, and take whisky with Blakely. (**Clarke** *serves them*.)
There's your three dollars, mister, and a dollar for what
whisky we can drink.

Clarke   Sure.

Blakely   Why don't you give us your song, Mo? The
Mighty Ohio. Ah, that a good song, Mo.

Mo   Singing regular, Mr Clarke?

Clarke   No biting and no fighting. But singing's regular.

Mo *shapes himself to sing*.

Blakely   That's it.

James   Shush, Blakely. Mo fixing to sing.

Mo   I singing 'bout the mighty Ohio
that flowing through this sweet land
Working men are seeing her and saying
she soft and white like a maiden's hand

The men listening.

Ohio she bring water to the harvest
making corn and tobacco plant grow

But that i'n't nothing to the drifter
he just like how her white waters flow

Nathaniel *quietly joins in.*

Mo *and* **Nathaniel**

Maybe he left his sweet home lately
where the honeysuckle twine by the door
He feeling the calling of the Ohio River
and whole wide America what's more

Blakely *gently takes the arm of* **James** *and brings him out from the bar and dances with him. The voices of* **Mo** *and* **Nathaniel** *flow freely now.* **Trooper** *alone buried into himself.*

Man he can pray to the mighty Ohio
to bring him to a sweet place at last
where he be finding a wife for to nurture
and throw his old grief to the past

Blakely *and* **James** *awkwardly stop. They're silent for a few moments.* **Blakely** *by the 'door'.*

Blakely   Night's fallen.

Clarke   That right singing, Mr Mo, and done me good to hear about that Ohio River. (*Lighting candle.*)

Nathaniel   You wouldn't find a singer finer on Coney Island itself.

Blakely   What you saying, Trooper? (**Trooper** *glances across at him, frightened.*) Eggs and eggs and marrowbones! Be drinking with your pals!

Mo   Blakely, Blakely, how long I know you?

Blakely   Me, Mo? How long you know Blakely? You know Blakely five year this Eastertime – no, sir, this first May coming.

Clarke   Easter a good time in the world. Preacher worn out by this time, telling the business in the chapel – I hear him myself, all last week.

Blakely   Now, what a whorehouse injun doing in the blessed chapel?

Mo   Blakely, in them long five years, I ever ask you to clam up a piece?

Blakely (*innocently*)   Not that I recollect, Mo. You want me to . . . Sure. A little more whisky. That be it. I be just minding to myself what happened in yonder, just recent. I understand you. I ain't a fool. Not this Blakely.

Nathaniel   Guess I missed Easter proper. The Sunday and all, and the hanging on the Friday. I'n't that the road for you? Missed the thing. Where we are I don't know half the time, summer, Easter. You think it was prison the way I be in the head betimes. But, here's to freedom, boys!

They drink.

All *but* **Trooper** *and* **Clarke**   To freedom.

Blakely   Blakely die if he ever see the gates opening again for him. If ever you see them leading Blakely to the cells, and you have a gun, you have a knife, shoot Blakely, stab him down – he don't want to live!

Blakely *collapses.*

Nathaniel   I shoot him now if he likes.

Clarke   Your friend shipshape?

Mo   Pay no heed. Two drinks always knocks down Blakely. That's how an English drinks, I guess. You best carry him, Nathaniel, since you slayed him. (**Nathaniel** *lifting him up and across one shoulder*.) Be thankful you a free man and don't be mentioning no prison out here where we happy to forget such places and do our work like respectable men.

Nathaniel *heads off with* **Blakely**.

James   Russia carrying England, Mo. What's bothering Trooper? He don't laugh, he don't sing.

Mo   Don't know, Jim.

James   You be bringing him along?

Mo   He i'n't pie-eyed, he just quiet. You go with Nathaniel, case he drops that varmint.

James   Oh, she were such a sweet woman.

Mo   Who, Jim?

James   In there, Mo.

He follows after **Nathaniel**, *and off.*

Clarke   You and your friend got a few minutes?

Mo   Sure. Don't we, Trooper?

Trooper   Sure.

Clarke   Can you do a man a favour, Mr Mo? (*Drawing out a newspaper from his coat.*) Don't mean to presume on our friendship so far.

Mo   I can. (*Takes newspaper.*) *White Woman Street Gazette and Advertiser.* You want me to . . .

Clarke   I like to get the news. Business slow tonight or I could get a regular to read it to me. I don't know what it is, but when I hear the happenings of the world I am contented.

Mo   Kind of starved for news myself. You just got the front part here, Clarke, or maybe there i'n't much news around here. Well . . .

Clarke   What is it?

Mo   Garters, 50c.

Clarke   Oh, good. Well, tell you the truth, Mr Mo, I don't wear stockings.

Mo   Me neither, Clarke. You desire me to read some item?

Clarke   Why don't you? Lord Jesus, I enjoy it.

Mo   Big fellas here, they say three men took for some robbery – they was hanged anyhow.

Clarke   That how they put it?

Mo   No. Allan gang hanged, would be what they have here.

Clarke Allan gang hanged. That really something. What they do, Mr Mo?

Mo Says, see page three. We ha'n't got page three, Clarke. Some devilment of poor outlaws, I expect. (*After a bit.*) That war there in Europe i'n't doing the boys of England much good – so this saying. Great tally of deaths . . .

Clarke (*expectant*) Yes?

Mo Says, see page seven. Well (*handing back paper*), that's the height of it, leaving aside corsets and such.

Clarke I sure like to get the news.

Mo All right, Trooper?

Trooper We shift if you want, Mo.

Mo (*to* **Clarke**) Well . . . (*Setting his hat on his head.*)

Trooper We got everything, Mo? Ah, hell. Did Jim have that fool sack of his?

Mo Good thinking. I don't think he did. You see our friend carry his sack?

Clarke The negra? Don't recall it. Must have left it where he was. (*To* **Trooper**.) You go in and fetch it, girls won't have touched it – they sitting out on the veranda now, with the slow business, drinking chicory – I hear them chattering. Take the candle in. It be dark in there. Take them moths and the squeeters with you . . .

Mo You want to go, Trooper?

Trooper I can't go, Mo. I can't go in there.

Clarke I'n't nobody there, mister.

Trooper I couldn't. I thinking I could and I couldn't. Mo, I thinking I could. But we'll leave that sack.

Mo I go. (*Holding the candle.*) Can't leave Jim's store-bought vittals. What would he think of us. Be angered with us.

Mo *goes upstage,* **Trooper** *watching hard.* **Mo** *disappears into the inner brothel, taking the light with him. There's the glimmer of it* *filling the doorway.* **Trooper** *and* **Clarke** *left in the dark more or less,* **Trooper**'s *eyes fixed on the changeable light.*

Clarke   What you afeard of, mister? Just a few rooms in there.

Trooper   Nothing. Just ghosts maybe. Just old ghosts.

Clarke   My grandpa he saying that moths and such be the spirits of the dead ones. If you quiet now you can hear them banging the window glass to get back out to the moon. You hear them? No. Maybe they follow Mr Mo. My grandpa saying that but I saying they just nuisances, catching in your face and burning theyselves. (**Trooper** *staring.*) Where you from, mister?

Trooper   Where from? Ireland.

Clarke   I knew. We get plenty Irish in here. Place there burning like Richmond, I hear. Some big mail depot or someplace. Fire and ruin in Dublin. Fellas put in jail and likely to be shot. Fighting the English.

Trooper (*not listening, fixed on the door*)   That right?

Clarke   So I hear. I sure like to get the news. Fighting the English. My grandpa fighting the English too. English won. You ever hear tell of them Indian wars? A-course you did.

Trooper   He gone a long time.

Clarke   He dead a long time right enough. Virginia.

Trooper   I meaning Mo is.

Clarke   It dark in there. (*Light growing again in the doorway.*) Here he is. (**Mo** *emerges. Brushes away a white moth.*)

Trooper   What you see?

Mo   I didn't see nothing but this sack, Trooper. (**Mo** *sets down the candle.*) Look, thanking you, Mr Clarke, for all your kindness.

Clarke   All right, Mr Mo.

Trooper *fixed.* **Mo** *takes his arm.*

Mo   Come on, Trooper. Whisky has you spooked.

Mo *and* **Trooper** *go out together into the starlight,* **Trooper**
remembering to lift his hand silently in farewell to **Clarke, Clarke**
likewise.

Clarke   Good journey, mister.

After a bit **Trooper** *stops in the shadowy street.*

Mo   We want to get along, seeing as the boys are waiting
for us.

Trooper   Where we going now anyhow?

Mo   Just up there that ways, outside of town. Boys are
waiting for us.

Trooper *nods.*

Trooper   A-course we are. A-course we are. I like the boys.
That was a sweet song you sang, Mo. Don't think I weren't
listening. I heard you and what you meaning. Sometimes,
don't we all wonder why we left home where we were known
and came out to see these plains and towns? We do.

Mo   This be the closest I been to home in forty years. But it
still too far to go.

Trooper   Mo, I come back to White Woman Street to see if
maybe Trooper O'Hara can wipe the slate clean and go back
to being what he was.

Mo   You don't need to say nothing to me about that.

Trooper   That because you a king of men, Mo. You saying
your brother Ezekiel more of a king than you? No, no.
Maybe Mo you hear dark things from that Indian Clarke
and you thinking about me?

Mo *looking at* **Trooper,** *thinking, going back over what Clarke*
said. He remembers, almost steps back from **Trooper.**

Mo   I know better than I know my own boots that you
never kill no woman like that . . .

Trooper See, Mo, and if you did think it, you would be saying nothing, and when I was waking up sudden in the night you wouldn't scorn to comfort me.

Mo Because I seeing you as my brother, Trooper, and a man don't care to think too dark about his brother.

Trooper I'm going to tell you now, Mo Mason, so you won't need to put this from your mind and just be Trooper's innocent brother. I didn't kill her like they said she was done, but I killed her just the same, no matter what mighty judge say different. She were an Indian girl pretty as the dawn with emerald eyes like a wolf's and I bedded her. And I looks down after and that woman is bleeding the way a first-time woman does, and she not crying in her face but I see the thing worse than tears, that dry and fearful look. A lost look. Then fast as a wolf she dips down to take my cold English blade from my breeches belt, and dragged it flashing like a kingfisher across her throat. She dragged it with force. Jesus of the world, I couldn't put her together again, Mo, she had a waterfall coming from her wound, and making a sound of water too. She just choked and died in front of me.

Mo Trooper, you didn't kill that poor lonesome girl.

Trooper I just run like a rabbit.

Mo Why ever you come back, Trooper?

Trooper Well, I don't know. I don't know why I left home and I don't know why I come back to White Woman Street. I thought, if I was in that room again, I could say something to her, I could do something kinder.

Mo But she dead thirty years, Trooper.

Trooper I know, I know she dead. I don't know what I was . . . Couldn't look at them girls tonight. Couldn't go into the room. Couldn't recall the look of the place hardly . . .

Mo Trooper, this world be darker than a mine for sin and hurt, but I saying to you, Trooper, without a lie, that you still lighting well enough, you still a man deserving life and a

measure of happiness, in spite of all. You carried that poor
girl a long way and time now you laid her down gentle and
let her be buried where maybe she don't belong, but any field
of the earth be good for such a sleep. What happen in
America is like a rover flood, everything lifted and dragged
away from its place. Not just Trooper hurt by this flood and
I'm telling you, Trooper, that rain of America i'n't your
doing.

Mo *pulls the dark cloth off the 'horses'. Early morning sunlight floods
the stage. The three other men just waking.* **Mo** *moves upstage.*
Blakely *shakily out of his blanket.*

Blakely Whoah. (*Seeing* **Trooper**.) Trooper?

Trooper Yes, Blakely?

Blakely Trooper, I offend you?

Trooper No, Blakely.

Blakely *goes to* **Trooper**, *puts an arm on his shoulder.*

Blakely I offend you in that whorehouse and not know
how I was dong it because I be a God's fool?

Trooper No.

Blakely Trooper, you a peach.

Trooper You meaning a tomato?

Blakely No, a peach.

James *rises quite nimbly from his blanket.* **Blakely** *heads back to
pack his gear up.*

(*Surprised.*) Morning, Mr Lazarus!

James *fixing the fire and the coffee.* **Mo** *trailing back past*
Trooper. **Mo** *looking at something in his hand.*

Trooper Sun up maybe these twenty minutes. Train
coming in below the sun. When we see the sun half-risen we
be near that freight of gold. (**Mo** *nods pleasantly.*)

James (*fixing the coffee*) If she's there.

Nathaniel (*still in his blanket*) She'll be there. And don't mind if she there or not. I feel just a lifetime of fine trains ahead of me. I'm going to pick the innards of every train from here to Argentina in this allotted span. (*Rising up.* **Mo** *by him.*)

Mo See this, Nathaniel.

Nathaniel (**Mo** *hands him something*) What's this, Mo?

Mo Found it under my hand in the grasses. In that deep dry grass. I can't say what colour you call that. Kind of speckled anyhow. (**Nathaniel** *peering at it.*)

Nathaniel That's kind of you, Mo. Why for giving it to me?

Mo Easter egg. Russian Easter egg.

The men gather for the coffee. **Blakely** *takes a slug from his cup.*

Blakely What man in creation but Jim Miranda could make Blakely feel better after whisky?

James You feel better?

Blakely Nope, but . . .

They laugh.

Nathaniel And who carried you home, Blakely?

Blakely Who carried me?

Nathaniel Why you think my back's broke?

Blakely All your sinning.

They laugh.

Trooper We're mounting up now. We're going. In fine fettle and with the best intentions.

The fling their dregs into the fire. A local music. They mount up. The freshening sun. Cantering now. Their faces eager and happy. Age falls away. The gold frost of the sun opens the sky, opens the woods and the hearts. The train is heard now in the distance, it blows its whistle as it passes through White Woman Street. They ride, the train's noise increases, it rushes upon them, the sky engoldens, and suddenly they are under the mass of the golden train, rushing and Leviathan.

Blakely   Trooper, Trooper, that be the golden train herself!

Trooper   Train of redemption, boys, ride for that train of redemption!

Nathaniel   Redemption for Brooklyn, boys, for Russia!

James   Redemption for the beauties of America!

In that moment fire opens up from the train, there's a mingling of smoke and steam and shouting. The gold fades into darkness. When things clear, the horses and the men are gone. Only **Blakely** *on his own in gold light.*

Blakely   Blakely be alone. One time Blakely was a Grimsby lad and talked good Grimsby talk but he lost all them words. That good shepherd, scratched though he be by briars, still can't find Blakely. Now he speaks like a mighty American, he got the lingo of the mighty Ohio, humming and hawing in that Yankee fashion. Let me tell you a tale. We had no food for eating which is why I was leaving Grimsby. Some years before me other Grimsby men left Grimsby. Wild, religious-minded men that called each other Father and the womenfolk Mother and such. What they do, they rose into America – leaving Grimsby and rose into America. Now Blakely don't recall his own first name. But he do recall where those long-dead travellers left from, same place he left from years after, and what was the name of the place. Blakely couldn't forget such a good name, such a fine name, and it still in his head, singing to Blakely, though Blakely don't ever know which way to go – Killinghome Creek, Killinghome Creek.

His light gone. In normal daylight, **Mo** *comes on helping* **Trooper**, *whose chest is stained with blood.*

Mo   You still hurting, Trooper?

Trooper   You see the others?

Mo   I seen Jim and Nathaniel going like hares for the wilderness.

Trooper   And Blakely?

Mo   Didn't see Blakely. He were more nearer the train.

Trooper   Safe if I rest up here a little while?

Mo   Safe enough here, Trooper.

Trooper   Just a share of sleep. (*Eyes closed.*) I seeing that shining hawthorn, Mo, you seeing it?

Mo   I seeing it. Go on, you sleep. I'll hunker here by you. You sleep, Trooper. May your eyes not see me, Trooper. May your eyes see the hawthorns of home. Look, Trooper. See the dances? Old rattling dances? (*Raising his arms slightly.*) More love, Trooper, more love. Look, Trooper – Ireland.

He looks off, raising his gun slowly in his fashion. A local music.

Dark-suited men coming up the hill to us, Trooper. Who they be? That you, Jimmy? That you, boys?

Blakely, *with* **Nathaniel** *and* **James**.

Blakely   A-course it is.

Nathaniel *and* **James** *look down at* **Trooper**. **Blakely** *kneels to him.*

Who else it be? Not those fool guards.

Mo (*after a bit*)   Jees Christ . . .

Blakely   No. Jees Christ don't walk in these woods.

Music. Dark. Curtain.

The Only True History of
Lizzie Finn

For Ali

Characters

Lizzie Finn, *mid to late thirties, a strong good-looking person*
Jelly Jane, *robust, handsome, late thirties*
Robert Gibson, *early forties, black hair, a little rough-looking*
Birdy Doyle, *a small pinched man in his forties*
Tilly, *a thin healthy-looking person in her twenties*
Colonel Cody, *a very striking American gentleman*
Bartholomew Grady, *seventies, a plume of white hair*
Lucinda Gibson, *Robert's mother, late sixties, dark like him*
Teresa, *same actor as Tilly but transformed*
Lord Castlemaine, *same actor as Colonel Cody but transformed*
Lady Castlemaine, *same actor as Jelly Jane but transformed*
Factotum, *same actor as Birdy Doyle*
Rector, *same actor as Factotum and Birdy Doyle*
A few **waltzers** *of any description*

The play is set in Weston-super-Mare, Avon, and Inch, Kerry, in the early 1900s.

The Only True History of Lizzie Finn was first performed in the Abbey Theatre, Dublin, on 4 October 1995, with the following cast:

Lizzie Finn	Alison Deegan
Jelly Jane/Lady Castlemaine	Marion O'Dwyer
Robert Gibson	Lorcan Cranitch
Birdy Doyle/Factotum/Rector	Birdy Sweeney
Tilly/Teresa	Fionnuala Murphy
Colonel Cody/Lord Castlemaine	Roy Hanlon
Bartholomew Grady	Eamon Kelly
Lucinda Gibson	Joan O'Hara

Director Patrick Mason
Set Designer Joe Vanek
Costume Designer Joan O'Clery
Lighting Designer Mick Hughes
Music Shaun Davey
Choreographer David Bolger

Act One

Weston-super-Mare, early 1900s. Stage left, two chairs, where light makes **Lizzie Finn** *and* **Jelly Jane***'s dressing room a nook of soft gaslight.* **Lizzie** *strides on, arriving for her work, starts to take off her day clothes.* **Jelly Jane** *arrives, carrying their stage dresses. They kiss. The low tinkering of the hall beyond.*

Jelly Jane That old washerwoman would want to watch her work. (*Feeling the dresses.*) They're still damp, Lizzie.

Lizzie It's the layers. They're hard to get dry. It's the best laundry in Weston-super-Mare. She's a demon with a ribbon iron.

Jelly Jane (*changing*) I'm that bilious today. I ate two pork pies and now I'm paying twice. I'm like Harry Giles that ate his wife Daisy and was hanged in London last year. They asked him what he wanted for his last breakfast. Stomach powders, he said.

Lizzie (*sitting on a chair in her underthings, gazing at a shoe hanging from its lace*) That came from King's and Co., the well-known boot and shoe retailer.

Jelly Jane A girl with a dicky stomach shouldn't high kick for a living.

Lizzie The salt air's got into it. (*Putting the shoe on.*) It'll look all right in the footlights. Everything does, thank God. (*Her other foot.*) Look at those corns, would you, Jelly Jane? They're worse than my mother's. And she had an excuse for them, wandering the roads of Corcaguiney.

Jelly Jane (*getting into her stage dress*) The apothecary by the African cenotaph has a yellow balm for them.

Lizzie An Irish road would kill you.

Jelly Jane Christ, Lizzie, that Ireland of yours is no good for a holiday anyhow. You're always thinking of your Ireland. I seldom think of my moors.

Lizzie   Since maybe it was you were happy there.

Jelly Jane   Oh, I was. My mother was cushions. (*They face each other, applying each other's white make-up and red lips and cheeks.*) She was too fond of my father though. Fifteen wee'uns, eight living. But she was cushions.

Lizzie   That's our music there now, Jelly Jane.

They pull on their starry knickers, solid garments with gold stars sewn into the crotches to catch the light in the cancan. **Jelly Jane** *half-trips into them.*

Jelly Jane   I'm tired to dance. Man-traps these knickers be, Lizzie.

Before they go onstage they give each other a quick look over.

Lizzie   Shipshape as ships, dear.

Jelly Jane   Yes, yes? Is this old girl presentable? Next year we'll open the shop. What do you say?

Lizzie   Next year. Let us show these provincial boys the style.

They turn smoothly and face out, an arc of limelight falls on them, they're underlit by harsh footlights. They dance the cancan bravely. At the close they throw up their skirts and show their starry knickers. Light only there, the glitter of the gold stars in the darkness. Music.

The yellow whorled light of the beach, a heavy bluster of wind, the spindly shadow of the pier in the distance. Windy music. After a little, **Lizzie** *comes on against the wind, in her good coat, pinning her hat with hatpins.*

Lizzie   All praise to the beggar that invented hatpins. (*Stopping.*) There'll be no little chaps out today, pushing their sailboats through the tide pools.

A man's black hat comes blowing along the sand. She traps it under her foot and lifts it up, and looks in the lining.

(*Reading.*) Robert Godfrey Gibson, Esquire. Now where are you, Robert Godfrey Gibson Esquire that puts your foolish head in here betimes?

Splashing feet. **Robert** *arrives panting, his handsome clothes spattered and speckled with sand and salt water. His hair is a bit wild and black without the hat.*

Robert   Success! When a hat gets the wind into it, good Lord. Running along like a blessed dog.

Lizzie (*laughing*)   I have it a bit dented after my shoe.

Robert (*taking the offered hat*)   It's a Kerry hat, it don't dent easy. Kerry hatters know about storms and dents. (*He gives the inside a determined puck.*) See now? I'll get it brushed and sure it won't know itself.

Lizzie *smiles but now* **Robert** *isn't sure how to proceed. He sets the hat on again and nods and is about to go. Another bluster of wind threatens the hat.* **Lizzie** *laughs and makes a leap at it.*

Lizzie   Oh, nearly.

They laugh. **Robert** *puts the hat softly under an arm.*

Robert   Best tuck it under my oxter like an army man.

Lizzie   Were you in the war that everyone goes to?

Robert   I was, with my three brothers. The Transvaal.

Lizzie   Everyone goes to the wars these times.

Robert   I suppose they do. Thank you for saving my hat, miss.

Lizzie   All right, Mr Gibson. (**Robert** *surprised.*) I read it on the lining – before I knew its owner was near.

Robert   Oh, that's fine. A hat's not a letter, is it? I thought you knew me. Because, may I ask, before I go, by your way of talking, you are a Kerry person also, are you not?

Lizzie   In other days. I don't know what I am now.

Robert   No more than myself. (*Makes to go.*)

Lizzie Here. (*Fetching out a hatpin from her own hat.*) Shove that in your hat. You can't go about barehead. You can take it out again when you reach the esplanade. (*Gives him the pin. He laughs loudly, sets his hat on his head and sticks in the pin.*)

Robert *wanders off, laughing still.* **Lizzie** *watches him go.*

Robert (*mostly to himself*) Thank you, thank you.

Lizzie *sings quietly, staring after him.*

Lizzie Billy and Maisie and I
Billy and Maisie and I
Try as we try as we try
We can't stop
Because Maisie keeps showing her mop her mop
Because Maisie keeps showing her mop

Robert *comes back as she knew he would.*

Robert Do you walk here a great deal, Miss?

Lizzie I walk here only rarely.

Robert Ah. Rarely. (*Nods and goes obediently.*)

The planky yellow of the music-hall. **Robert** *comes on with a chair and a beer and a playbill, sits himself down, rests the beer on his knee, tries to peruse the bill. Into the limelight steps a little man with a sharp face. He speaks very sadly.* **Robert** *lifts the beer halfway to his lips but the man's voice stills him. He doesn't move again till the end of the turn.*

Birdy Doyle Good evening to you. My name is Birdy Doyle. I will be doing for you now the Birds of Ohio. (*Pause.*) The Crested Jackhammer. (*Whistles it.*) The Yellow Miner Bird. (*Whistles it.*) The Ohion Sparrow. (*Whistles it.*) The Ohion Spotted Dove. (*Whistles it.*) The American Wood pigeon. (*Calls it.*) The Broken Man. (*Calls it.*) The Red-throated Thrush. (*Whistles it.*) The Lonesome Plover. (*Calls *it*.) That was, The Birds of Ohio. My name is Birdy Doyle. Thank you. (*Goes solemnly*.)

Robert, *the beer still halfway, looks about him, quite taken aback.*

Robert   Good Lord.

The music of the cancan. **Robert** *settles in to watch it.* **Lizzie** *and* **Jelly Jane** *come on, begin the dance, with a scattered hoot here and there. It's only after a while that* **Robert** *recognises* **Lizzie**. *He scans the playbill, touches the hatpin briefly that's still in his hat, gets up, puts down the beer messily, starts to peel off his greatcoat, and in a fever rushes the stage, and wraps, or tries to, his coat about* **Lizzie**.

Wait, wait!

Jelly Jane   A murderer!

Lizzie   What are you doing, mister?

Robert   Covering you with this coat.

Lizzie   And for why?

Robert   You're for better than showing yourself to these broken men.

Lizzie   It's my true work. Go away from me in my work!

Robert   You needn't show yourself again.

Lizzie   You're a stranger. Take your stranger's coat from me.

Jelly Jane   Take it from her! (*She strikes him down with great strength.* **Robert** *falls but keeps talking up to* **Lizzie**, *as if falling were nothing to him.*)

Robert   What work is it, for a woman that speaks like you?

Lizzie   How do I speak? Are you a madman from the asylum up the hill?

Robert   No, no, but a man, with a coat.

Jelly Jane *draws* **Lizzie** *away.* **Robert** *stumbles from the stage, coat dragging behind him.*

Lizzie (*shouting after him*)   You shame me, before this hall.
You shame me, you blackguard!

Poor light of the dressing room, **Lizzie** *agitated,* **Jelly Jane** *trying
to get her to sit.*

Jelly Jane   Was yon man known to you, Lizzie?

Lizzie   I gave him the time of day, one of my best times of
day, and a hatpin.

Jelly Jane   You gave that man a hatpin?

Lizzie   Yes.

Jelly Jane   But why, my Lizzie?

Lizzie   One of my sixpenny hatpins from the Orient
Bazaar!

Jelly Jane (*shocked*)   In Rhodes Street? (*To herself mostly.*)
She's met him. He'll be one of those false types. To break a
woman's heart – a dancing woman's heart.

Lizzie   Top bill, we are. Names over the sentimental
singers, and the humorous turns. Contract!

Jelly Jane   We are!

Lizzie   I have it all written down, in writing.

Jelly Jane   In bloody writing.

Lizzie   You'll find nowhere just as respectable as theatre
life!

Jelly Jane (*almost jumping at the force of* **Lizzie**)   So I find!

Lizzie (*differently, sitting finally*)   Kerry. Kerry. He's bringing
Kerry in on me.

Jelly Jane   Is that where he's from? The poor man. Maybe
he couldn't help himself so.

Lizzie Don't be sensible now, Jelly Jane. I don't want to be sensible now. I want to rage and speak nonsense.

Jelly Jane (*sitting close*) Well now, it's just all you've ever told me about Kerry . . . Will I get something soothing from the corner, pet? Something to still tha hurt? Foreign wine or porter, or Ladies' Gin?

Lizzie (*quietly*) I want to rage and speak nonsense.

Jelly Jane (*softly*) Please, please, rage, dear.

Lizzie I don't like a person to put shame to me. (*After a little.*) My mother went barefoot all her life, but the roads were green all over Corcaguiney then, if there were roads. There used to be a saying about the roads of Corcaguiney, as being things that did not exist. They might say a particular person's virtue was like the roads of Corcaguiney – you know?

Jelly Jane (*listening hard*) Ah ha.

Lizzie But in our time there were roads enough, to carry my father and his singing voice about the place. He knew songs from the islands that he didn't sing much, unless we were rowed over to the Blasket on a sweet summer day. He knew tradesmen's songs and tinkers' songs and he knew little parts out of operettas that he could sing for the rich people if he were asked. He liked to sing for the rich because he had a great love of fine chairs and carpets and plates – he liked to look at them in the rooms. But then he'd be as happy to go out on the frosty road again, and be gone, the three of us, be a memory, a memory of singing. And he knew that the people all over Corcaguiney would be humming his tunes about the hills if they wandered there, or about the strands, or in their houses. He was the very singing soul of Corcaguiney. He never let shame be put to us. Singing or dancing to him were the highest things a person could put himself to. And he always said the very heart of a person was revealed in their singing. You could take a dairymaid out of a byre, and set her in the shitty yard, and if she could sing, all paradise and Beulah would appear about her and the

listeners would be transported there and then. He took fever
from a hungry ditch and my mother followed after him. I
will never forget him or dishonour his memory, that singing
man. For a man with a singing voice like that is God, or the
shadow of God on this earth. And I am the daughter forever
of that singing man.

Jelly Jane   You are, Lizzie.

Lizzie   I am.

*Bundles of mist unbundling themselves at the edge of the beach, a sense
of wetness on the holiday boards, the beach obscured. A neat young
woman,* **Tilly** *comes on with a folding billboard and sets it in its
morning position.* **Robert** *wanders on, trying to see down on to the
beach for* **Lizzie**.

Tilly (*nervously*)   Good morning to you, sir.

Robert   Good morning. (*A mite gruffly.*) Misty.

Tilly (*relieved*)   There won't be many on the strand today,
sir. Except the regular worm diggers and the gentlemen with
the shell nets.

Robert   No – thank God! (*Peering into the mist.*) Is the tide
out?

Tilly   Oh, yes, sir. The tide's been like that a long time,
since they built the great sea wall at Bristol. Thirty years
ago, sir.

Robert   Is that a fact? So what's your name then?

Tilly   Tilly Johns, sir.

Robert   Did you see by any chance, Tilly Johns, a
handsome woman, with a green hat maybe, go out upon the
strand, walking?

Tilly   No, sir. But she may be there for all that. I know the lady you mean.

Robert   Oh, you do?

Tilly   Lizzie Finn, do you mean, sir, the famous dancer? She's as neat and lovely as a florin, sir. I see her most days.

Robert   Oh, do you now?

Tilly   She loves the strand. I never had the nerve to speak to her. In the high summer you'll have bands of lads lining the esplanade, watching her go, and I expect longing they knew her.

Robert   Is that so now? Bands of them.

Tilly   Oh, she's very admired in Weston-super-Mare.

Robert   Well. (*He has a good read of the playbill.*) 'Colonel Cody's Wild West Show.' Is that on at the minute?

Tilly   It's coming Thursday. It'll be great. They have Indians and everything, and fighting. They'll hold it in the pleasure gardens. Oh, you should go, sir.

Robert   I will, I will go. I have a great interest in America. More so than Africa, let me tell you.

Tilly   It's tailormade for you then, sir. Buffalo Bill Cody is as much a legend as Lizzie Finn, nearly.

Robert   That much? Bless me.

Tilly   Well, I've things to do, sir, things to do. It was a great pleasure talking to you, sir. You're kindly.

Robert   Oh, thank you. Well. (*She starts to go.*) Goodbye now. (*Looking again at the poster.*) Well, now. Well, now.

Tilly (*stopping up short*)   But I forgot, sir!

Robert (*startled*)   What?

Tilly   I doubt if she'll be here today.

Robert   Why so?

Tilly   She was attacked last night in the music-hall. It's all over the town. It was in the *Gazette*. An Irishman, sir, with a great head of black hair and a wild face, and eyes that would burn your heart out of your chest. He sounds like the very devil himself, doesn't he, sir? She'd hardly come down for her walk today.

Robert   But she wasn't injured.

Tilly   I don't know, sir. I hope not. They're looking for the man, to lock the demon up. But I expect he ran for it. He'll be in Dublin now. You've heard of Dublin? It's the big town over there in Ireland.

Robert   I've heard of Dublin.

Tilly (*going*)   There you are now. How did I forget such a thing? It's the mist, must be. (*She goes.* **Robert** *looks about nervously.*)

Low lights of evening, the mist still enduring, coiling about, drifting across a sign at the back of the music-hall, that reads STAGE. **Robert** *comes on with a fist of red roses that are melting in the mist, the petals dropping, much to his concern.*

Robert   I'm bringing stalks to her, stalks. That won't help me.

Lizzie *comes to the sign, looks out, examining the weather, pulling on yellow gloves, and sees* **Robert**. *She stills.*

Lizzie Finn, Lizzie Finn, is that you?

Lizzie   Who wants to know? I have fine big strong men inside to call to if I need.

Robert   It's myself, and I am most dreadfully sorry to have assaulted you last night with my coat. It wasn't till I heard that the authorities were looking for me that I understood the full horror of what I had done. Now I'm in fear of them taking me away before I can apologise to you.

Lizzie So you should be. (*Quietly.*) You blackguard.

Robert Indeed and I am, and I've brought you these . . . (*Looking at the ruined flowers.*) These sorry, sorry blooms . . . The mist has dissolved them and loosened these red sparks on to the lane . . .

Lizzie You'd better take that out of your hat.

Robert Take what?

Lizzie That, what I gave you.

Robert (*touching it*) The hatpin? I'd forgotten all about it.

Lizzie Well, I told them you might be wearing one. They gave each other very queer looks about it, I can tell you.

Robert (*taking it out*) I've never been sought by the police before . . .

Lizzie Oh, it's not only the police.

Robert Who else?

Lizzie The asylum men. They want you up there on the hill to teach you your manners. They've a nice white jacket for you in place of your coat.

Robert If you could understand why I did it . . .

Lizzie I don't need to, do I? Jelly Jane is the chief witness but you were considerate enough to attack me in front of a hundred of my most devoted followers, the Monday night crowd itself.

Robert No, you don't need to. I should submit to them really. You've no idea how tired I am. I haven't slept for months.

Lizzie Well, you'll get a good sleep maybe up the hill, if they catch you.

Robert I suppose so. (*Breaks down.*)

After a little, **Lizzie** *comes down to him bravely.*

Lizzie What is it then, Mr Gibson, that has you so trigger-happy with your coat in music-halls?

Robert Bless me, I don't think I can say now, after breaking down so. Oh, it's a foolish world. Full of foolishness and foolish actions. Don't you think?

Lizzie You better tell me, or I'll call to my cohorts within.

Robert It was Africa, Lizzie Finn. Africa. I'm half a year coming home like a lame dog cut up in the hunt. I've no heart for staying and no heart for going. I'd rather be a spirit, you know, a little puff of a what-do-they-call-it, a ghost. It was Africa. I buried my three brothers there.

Lizzie (*after a little*) Here, I'll take your nice roses, Mr Gibson. (*She does.*)

Robert Thank you.

Lizzie Will you meet me again, in the daylight?

Robert Oh, yes. Oh, yes, Miss Finn.

Lizzie Off you go. You'll sleep tonight. Go on. (*He does.*) Is all the wars in the world worth these broken gentlemen?

A simple nest of linen bolstered by feathers. A dim light is thrown up from the foot of the bed, by a meagre summer fire. **Lizzie** *and* **Jelly Jane** *lit snug in the mass of white linen,* **Jelly Jane** *with a fierce nightcap,* **Lizzie**'s *famous hair spread down a pillow. They have their arms out, still and straight before them on their stomachs. All the rest of the stage in pleasant darkness.*

Lizzie He's a very strange man, Jelly Jane.

Jelly Jane Do you think you should meet a man like that? Maybe, do you know, he has a little silver knife he likes to stick into ladies, like the Manchester Prowler. Or maybe, do

you know, a taste for you, boiled in a big pot, like poor
Harry Giles that was.

Lizzie   No, he's just a big sad sort of a fella.

Jelly Jane   I suppose he's just a wanderer coming through
Weston-super-Mare like many another. (**Lizzie** *acknowledges
this*.) I suppose he's as much flotsam and jetsam as a
thousand others you'd see in the halls of England? (**Lizzie**
acknowledges this.) I suppose as women we go for the ones that
we go for and no explanations. (**Lizzie** *acknowledges this*.) I
suppose that's how it happens.

Lizzie   I suppose, Jelly Jane.

Jelly Jane   Well, it's very mysterious and a girl would do as
well to be philosophic about it, as aught else.

Lizzie   Oh, yes.

*Across the stage from them slowly a crescent moon appears small and
high, and then the intermittent thrown light of a lighthouse.* **Robert**
*stands in the dark alone, it's somewhere high above the town, and
solitary, with a fall to the sounding sea below, and a stirring cliff
breeze against him. He's gazing down.*

Jelly Jane (*holding one of* **Lizzie**'*s hands across the linen*)   I'll
say the one thing, dear, and then hold my whist, as you'd
say. (**Lizzie** *looks at her peacefully*.) I do hope he's not like the
roads of Corcaguiney. (**Lizzie** *lays her head in against* **Jelly
Jane**'*s*.)

Lizzie   What can you do, dear?

Jelly Jane (*staring forward into the firelight*)   Not much, is the
answer to that, Lizzie. Not much.

Robert (*makes to jump but doesn't*)   If I were Isambard
Kingdom Brunel I'd throw a bridge from here to Wales.

*He raises his arms up. The light from the lighthouse washes across
him. He laughs in his privacy.*

I would, I would!

The many-coloured bunting of the pleasure gardens a week later, the colours flying, a rail upstage to protect the spectators, beyond which Colonel Cody and his Show will take place off. **Robert** *in highly polished shoes and* **Lizzie** *in her summer finery stroll on, accompanied by* **Jelly Jane**, *looking a little awkward.*

Jelly Jane It's a wonder, I'm told, by ones who were here last week. The American Waggoners get put upon by Savage Redmen and the Colonel saves them with his Horsemen. Well, you wouldn't think grown people would pay four shillings for that, on a lovely summer's afternoon, when they could be away at the bathing huts for naught and be putting sand in their knickers. And I never did like shepherding folk.

Lizzie Chaperoning, is what you're doing, girl, not shepherding, and I am very grateful to you for it, as you know.

Jelly Jane (*mostly to herself*) Shepherding's more like it, with that big black sheep beside you. There's it starting up now. They're fierce-looking chaps, them Redmen, all the same. It's all miles off, I can't see a thing. (*She ducks under the rail and disappears off.*)

A clatter of gunfire and whoops of the Indians and an explosion of spectacle off.

Lizzie (*grabbing* **Robert***'s arm*) They're blasting them, they're blasting them!

Robert (*laughing*) But they'll be fine just after!

Lizzie But see that blood, that drenching of blood! And the terrible fire from the guns of the outlaws!

Robert Settlers, Lizzie. Don't you want the Settlers to win America?

Lizzie I do not, I do not! Hurrah the Redmen, hurrah the Redmen!

A pause as they watch something.

Robert Is that our chaperone?

Lizzie (*hands up to her cheeks*)   Oh my good Lord! Oh, my Lord! Oh, Jelly Jane!

Robert   Christ, he rode right across her. Stay here, Lizzie, I'll go out there and fetch her! (*He ducks under the rail and rushes off.*)

Lizzie   Oh, oh, oh, oh, oh.

Robert *struggles back carrying an indignant* **Jelly Jane**.

Is she all right, Robert?

Jelly Jane   Would you . . . I'm not hurt, you fool. Put me down.

Robert (*laying her on the ground gently*)   She's hurt her leg, Lizzie, don't mind her.

Jelly Jane   Look, he's after me now.

Robert (*raising her skirt*)   You're all right, Miss Jane, you're all right. I was a soldier. I know a wound like this. Let me assist you, won't you.

Jelly Jane   Are you so sure you know tha way about my legs?

Robert   I do. (*He rips part of her drawers.* **Jelly Jane** *screams.*)

Jelly Jane   What sort of doctoring is that? I paid seven shillings for those Belgian drawers.

Lizzie   Hush a moment, he has to bind you, I think.

Colonel Cody *in all his moustached splendour comes out to them. He's quite elderly but very striking in his working outfit. There's a few moments of silence as* **Jelly Jane** *takes him in.* **Robert** *instinctively rises from* **Jelly Jane**, **Colonel Cody** *takes his place.*

Cody   A thousand abject apologies, my dear. I do believe you caught a blow of a hoof on your lovely leg. (*He examines it.*)

Jelly Jane   You don't have to mind if you touch my leg a little.

Cody   Why, think of me as a medical man, for the moment, my dear.

Jelly Jane   Oh, yes.

Just the spectacle of them for a while, **Robert** *and* **Lizzie** *looking down at* **Jelly Jane**, **Jelly Jane** *looking into* **Colonel Cody's** *face.*

Oh, Lizzie. Oh. (*Dizzy.*) Now I feel it. Oh. (*Blacks out.*)

Towards evening, on the spot where **Robert** *stood in the darkness.* **Lizzie** *and* **Robert** *face each other, their hands held forward and joined.*

Robert   Look at that trawler below, so far, so clear, like an almond on the sea. I was up here just a week ago, the night I brought you the roses, there was just a bit of a moon and the lighthouse on the point washing its light on me now and then.

Lizzie   That's a lonely life. I hope he gets into the hall betimes, so he can see what fun is.

Robert   Who, Lizzie?

Lizzie   The lighthouse keeper.

Robert   Of course, yes. (*After a moment.*) Can I tell you a very strange thing? William Rowan Hamilton, the mathematician, was walking along the Royal Canal near Finglas, puzzling the secret of quoternian multiplication, when suddenly a kingfisher came firing out of the green bank, like a blue bullet, a blue revelation. And in that moment of strange blue fire, jolted by it, it came to him: $i^2 = j^2 = k^2 = ijk = -1$. And he scratched it hurriedly on the stone of the bridge nearby. Blue fire, Lizzie Finn, blue fire. (*After a moment.*) Lizzie, I would like to take you home with me, if you'll come. I don't think I'd care very much to go now without you.

Lizzie   Won't you stay and be my Robert here and watch me dance in England? It's not so easy to dance in Ireland.

Robert   Lizzie, if you give me your kiss, it may be easy enough.

Lizzie   You can take my kiss. Here, take it.

They kiss.

Robert (*close to her*)   I took your kiss.

Lizzie   You took it. And when they blame me for it I'll tell them to the last you took it. But I think they won't believe me.

A convivial gathering backstage, in farewell to **Lizzie** *and* **Robert**. **Jelly Jane** *in a chair with her wounded leg up,* **Colonel Cody** *attending her assiduously.* **Birdy Doyle** *rather alone on a chair.* **Lizzie** *standing, aglow, and* **Robert** *pouring out a fine red liquid into* **Jelly Jane**'s *glass.*

Birdy Doyle   We must drink a fond farewell.

Robert   I hope your lovely leg heals quickly, Jelly Jane, and you'll be back dancing for the autumn season.

Jelly Jane   Oh, mercy, Robert Gibson, I'll dance no more if my present luck holds out, and the Colonel will give me a job as a Western Waggoner, he says.

Cody   And so I shall!

Jelly Jane   I'm to be overwhelmed by Redmen every day of the week, Lizzie. Come here to me, girl, so we can whisper. (**Lizzie** *kneels in to her.*) That we lived so long, Lizzie, to witness these miracles that stun our hearts.

Birdy Doyle   We must drink a fond farewell!

Jelly Jane   And so we must. A farewell to music-halls and maidenhood, perhaps, if I prove a decent Western Waggoner in the upshot. Here's to Lizzie and her Robert and their Ireland, and may they prosper there as they deserve. Seven

years Lizzie and I did show our legs to the English lads, and
they have been the dearest and the fondest days of my life!

Lizzie   Oh, Jelly Jane.

They all drink.

Jelly Jane   We're going to have to have singing now, or
we're not worth our salt. For if you can't sing when you're
sad you can't sing when you're happy.

Birdy Doyle   We must drink a fond farewell!

Jelly Jane   We've done that now, Birdy. Now Robert
Gibson, a soldier always has songs, come on now, as bawdy
as you like.

Robert   I think I only have hymns. I don't think hymns is
what we want just now.

Lizzie   Oh, Robert, only hymns? I'll have to be teaching
you good wicked songs.

Jelly Jane   All right then, Lizzie, girl, a wicked song. Let
his education begin tonight!

Lizzie *fits herself to sing. She does the full act on it, striding and
smiling, putting it over. It's true that her voice is poor enough, but it
doesn't hinder her.*

Lizzie   I never knew a man that didn't like lemon
              that didn't like a lemon in his tea
              I never knew a man that didn't like singing
              if he's singing to my doh-ray-me

         Spoken chorus: What's she on about?

         I never knew a man that didn't like kisses
         that didn't like some kisses now and then
         I never knew a man that didn't go a-hunting
         a-hunting for my sweet little wren

             Chorus.

         I never knew a man that didn't care for dancing
         dancing with the ladies of the town

> Oh but I never knew a man that didn't like sitting
> Sitting on my sweet Fanny Brown
>
> *Chorus.*

General laughter and raising of glasses.

Well, Colonel, I hope you'll favour us with a song. It's always a privilege to hear a foreign song.

Cody   Well, ladies and gentlemen, I'm not noted for the beauty of my voice, it's true. But if you'll bear with me, I'll sing you a song that a man in Wyoming wrote for me especial, in the old gone days of my youth.

> I went out to shoot the buffalo
> with my gun so bright
> I saw them moving like the sea
> in the dying light
>
> *Chorus:*
> I saw them moving like the sea
> as I let my pony rest
> I was thinking to myself right then
> I love this West the best
>
> The hills were high and ranged about
> the river was like gold
> a man could live here all his life
> and never would grow old
>
> *Chorus.*
>
> But days they come and days they go
> and changes are our lot
> and I travel now no more, my friends,
> in the Land that Time Forgot
>
> *Chorus.*

A bit of a silence. **Jelly Jane** *touches* **Colonel Cody**'s *arm.*

Birdy Doyle   We must bid a fond farewell.

The stage of the music-hall in the late night. **Lizzie** *alone in the dimness, looking out over the empty hall. She gives a half-swish to the front of her day dress, as if her dance was running through her head. Out of the shadows comes* **Jelly Jane**, *hobbling along on her stick.*

Jelly Jane   Look at me, Lizzie. A far cry.

Lizzie *smiles at her.*

Lizzie   Well, girl, to give it all up, it isn't easy after all.

Jelly Jane   Ah, girl, it's high time. We're getting so long in the tooth we'd have to start putting more comedy into the dancing, because they like to see young legs when they look at legs.

Lizzie   I suppose so. But you are the one dearest to me besides Robert. You must come and see us in Ireland.

Jelly Jane (*not believing it*) Oh, yes.

Lizzie   I know I'm supposed to be brave Lizzie Finn, but, I tell you, girl, I'm half-afraid to go.

Jelly Jane   Think of the grandeur of it, Lizzie. The train will take you away through the Welsh farms, there'll be lamps across the fields in the dark towns, and you'll sit knee to knee with him. Don't be afraid ever to go back to your own people.

Lizzie   Oh, Jelly Jane, Jelly Jane. I'll miss all this. I was warm in our bed.

Jelly Jane   Ah, girl. Here, I wanted to give you this. (*Handing her a little stone figure.*)

Lizzie   What is it, Jelly Jane?

Jelly Jane   It's a little stone angel, you see. My father dug it up one time in his field. Some say it was in there from the time of the giants, I don't know. He gave it to me when I was going south and I'm giving it to you now.

Lizzie   I can't take your father's gift.

Jelly Jane   Something to watch over you, Lizzie. (*Closing her hands around hers with the figure in them.*) Something of Yorkshire, where you've never been. Something of Jelly Jane.

Lizzie   She's beautiful.

Jelly Jane   You can give it to any child of yours if you wish. Let it protect you and yours and bring you safely through whatever troubles there must be.

Lizzie   These have been very strange and unexpected days.

Jelly Jane   Love always comes mysteriously, girl. Didn't we know that? I'll leave you in peace and bid you goodnight.

Lizzie   I'm very honoured by your gift, and by your friendship.

Jelly Jane (*winking*)   Likewise, likewise, Lizzie Finn. (*Going, then stopping, looking back.*) You're the dandiest girl a girl could know, Lizzie Finn.

Above Inch Strand in Kerry. Right, a structure suggesting the old house tower, a sort of lumber room, where rest bits of lawn sports, trophies from wars and old items, old dolls, a basin to catch a quiet drip, the newest thing being three army uniforms on a rough rack, all in a dusty solitude, with a few wooden steps leading up to it. Left, the comfortable sitting area of a drawing room, appropriate to a small gentleman's house, good chairs and a richly embroidered sofa, and a little elegant table for a lamp and a vase. There's a little pair of reading glasses on this table. Downstage, the garden leading off from the drawing room, a roll of trim lawn, with a deal of rhododendron, fuschia and peony, and roses. A simple well and a bucket. An open enough feeling, but also the sense of shelter from the high wilderness beyond the house. The garden thick with birds, the fresh pounding of the sea in Dingle Bay below, running in on to Inch Strand. A fresh, hot high summer's day towards late afternoon. Now through the pulse of sun comes **Bartholomew Grady**, *the gardener, a stocky man of about seventy with a fire of white hair still. He carries a basket lined with wet dock leaves which he will put cut roses into for moistness. He*

*waves his old cutting knife, a contraption tied about with ancient
string, at the retinue of black flies above his head.*

Bartholomew Can not a Christian gardener cross his lawn
without assassins? All winter, wrapped by my fire, I think of
you sleeping in the icy stones, waiting for these sprightly
summer days. (*He manages, however, to select a few blooms,
expertly snipping them into his basket.*)

Lucinda Gibson, *Robert's mother, tall, dark, with a plain silver
cross on the breast of her brocaded black mourning dress, comes through
the drawing room with a rectangle of paper, looking for good light to
read it by. She steps out into the garden, closely scanning the paper.*

Lady, now, don't come out here without your netted hat –
these black men will divide in the air, like demons, and
ambush you too.

Lucinda A little rough boy has just come running along
the sea road from Castlemaine with a telegraph message. I'm
sure his father sent him, with all the haste that is due to a
telegraph message. And, look, I can't read it at all,
Bartholomew. It is smudged of course.

Bartholomew I've the responsibility of these blooms, lady.
You know how the heat runs in under the dock leaves. I
can't be scanning over messages at the same time. You'd best
be burning a thing like that, lady – that's my counsel.

Lucinda Of your charity, Bartholomew Grady. (*She gives
him the telegram.*)

Bartholomew Fortunate for you I've still immaculate
sight. Here, hold it for me again, please, lady. (*He hands her
the telegram back and she holds it unfolded for him. He steps back a
few paces.*) By Napoleon's ghost, I can read anything, at four
paces. There now. All nicely read now. (*Heading off.*)

Lucinda But what does it say, Bartholomew? Is it good or
bad?

Bartholomew I don't know if it's good or bad. It will be as
well for me to say nothing, lady. (*He heads off, stooping at the
bucket briefly to skite a handful of moisture on to his selections.*)

Lucinda I'll fetch on my reading glasses. (*She goes to the little table where her glasses are, examines the paper.*) That old man doesn't get any saner. (*Reads.*) What could this be? Bartholomew?

Bartholomew (*just about to escape*) Yes, lady?

Lucinda (*coming back out*) Was there anything in your newspaper about Robert?

Bartholomew No, lady.

Lucinda Nothing at all?

Bartholomew The *Castlemaine Herald* confines itself mostly to the state of the country and the frequent occurrence of murder in Irish life.

Lucinda You spotted nothing throughout the newspaper that would cast light on this telegraph message?

Bartholomew Believe me, lady, I combed it through as is my custom when I am ingesting my sausages at noon and, *mirabile dictu*, as Virgil often said, there wasn't a blessed thing about your son.

Lucinda (*ignoring his sarcasm*) Then it's a mistake. (*Stuffing the message away.*) It has been taken down wrongly at the post office. Honoria Fanning is half-deaf as we all know and her husband is half-blind. The perfect people to run a post office. (*She goes back into the house.*)

Bartholomew Half-blind, says she. (*Goes off.*)

The ringing of a telephone somewhere deeper in the house. Light on **Robert** *upstage at a wall telephone, his back turned. The telephone rings for a while. Then, offstage,* **Lucinda**'s *voice.*

Lucinda (*off*) Yes, yes, Red House.

Robert Hello, Robert – this is Mother.

Lucinda No, you are Robert, I am Mother. Robert, dear, how lovely to hear your voice. How lovely. It's three years, isn't it, dear? Do you know they sent me the uniforms back, all the way from Africa? I was astonished.

Robert   Did you receive my telegraph?

Lucinda   Yes, I received it, dear.

A pause.

Robert   I'm here at the station in Castlemaine. Do you think Honoria Fanning is still on the line? We're married, abruptly I'll grant, but married all the same. I know it seems strange and ill-mannered, but it seemed the best course to take.

Lucinda   Are you telling me that you and Honoria Fanning are married?

Robert   Mother, don't be satirical.

Lucinda   It's just the way you put it. I knew she already had a husband, of sorts. Robert, I really must attend to Teresa in the kitchens. She's been trying her hand at a strawberry fool and it may need rescuing. Goodbye, Robert.

Robert   Mother, Mother. I'm coming out on the trap . . . Mother . . . Oh, dear. (*Light away from him.*)

Bartholomew *wanders on again with his pipe, directing the smoke purposefully at the flies.*

The sky above is reddening into long streaks, with lines of gold. The birds are hushed. He stops at the well.

A well is a kind of unturned bell, that will ring neither matins nor evensong. Ah, yes. (*Goes.*)

*The sky deepens to the slate and crimson of late sunset, the dark filling slowly. Upstage, on a high trap, with the strike of the pony's trotting hooves, **Robert** and **Lizzie**, with a chequered rug across their legs against the night.*

Robert (*exhilarated*)   Glorious, oh, glorious, my lovely Kerry. Three years, Lizzie.

Lizzie   Those are woods, aren't they, on the headland? I don't ever recall woods in Kerry. Isn't that strange?

Robert   They're my woods, Lizzie. Your woods. Our woods. See the lovely swagger of Inch Strand, Lizzie. That's your strand now.

Lizzie   It's white as a snow bear that I saw once in a menagerie.

Robert   It's famous all over for its beauty. I was happy there often with my brothers. That was our Africa once. And now we'll fill it again with brothers and sisters!

Lizzie   It's handsome, Robert.

Robert   There's the house peeking through the trees – Bartholomew's windbreakers, they are, to protect his garden. I've missed his bitter tongue. Oh, I'm so proud to be bringing you here, Lizzie.

Lizzie   I don't see the house you mean. That little place there by the strand?

Robert   Lizzie, that's the village, as we call it. There was an old body there that gathered the periwinkles.

Lizzie   Not those big roofs and the dark tower?

Robert   That's your home.

Lizzie   But, Robert, that's a landlord's house, isn't it?

Robert   Well, and if it is? What did you think you were coming to?

Lizzie   Not a great place like that, dark against the incoming night.

Robert   It's not so great, believe me. Just a little place, Lizzie. Just a little place for the Gibsons to lay their heads. Are you so shy of it? Will we rest up another night in the hotel in Castlemaine?

Lizzie   I might have been happier approaching in daylight. Twilight is so full of things past. But since we're this far, let's drive on. I can imagine the three of us, my father and mother and me, on this road.

Robert   Remember, Lizzie, you're my wife. You're strong and right and legal here.

Lizzie   Oh, I'm not afraid.

Robert   There's nothing to fear.

Lizzie   Go on away up so.

A deep light in the drawing room, brown shadows shoaling between the chairs. **Teresa**, *the general servant, a birdlike young woman of twenty, comes in, with Bartholomew's roses carefully in her arms. She sets them down gently and digs in her pocket for a Lucifer, strikes it, removes the glass of the lamp, lights it. The room shrugs in the blowing light till she replaces the glass. She arranges the roses in the vase intently, casting shadows everywhere. At the other side of the house, the iron clanging of the bell. She hurries excitedly from the room. Echoing phrases, bang of things, silence for a little, then* **Teresa** *reappears showing* **Lizzie** *into the drawing room.*

Teresa (*breathless*)   You go in there, do, miss, there's a heap of nice places for sitting. (*Watching* **Lizzie** *all the while.*) Would you like your coat off, missy? (*She takes* **Lizzie**'*s coat, lays it on her arm, stroking the material. She takes* **Lizzie**'*s hat in further wonder.*) I never seen an English lady before, missy. You do look lovely if I may say. Are everyone in England so trim? I imagine so, missy.

Lizzie   England has its style, that's true, girl. But that's a nice frock you're wearing yourself.

Teresa (*overcome*)   This old thing, missy? It's only a yard of dross material the mistress bought for me in Tralee.

Lizzie   Well, it's not the dress but the girl in the dress, we used to say.

Teresa Oh, missy. You've no notion of the excitement you've caused me. Barty has been sputtering by the stoves with all sorts of black words, poking at the ashes with his pruning knife and doing it no good, but I couldn't get my rest last night for thinking of you. Oh, don't mind my give-out, missy. I'm worse than a goose. (*Going, then worriedly.*) You know what a goose is?

Lizzie I do.

Teresa Ah, geese are all over. I knew that! (*Goes.*)

Lizzie *left alone. She looks about for a mirror or something to see herself in, attends to her hair.*

Lizzie I didn't know he was a king, I didn't know. (*She sits ill at ease on a chair, looks at the fireplace.*) He'd be set there on a hearth like that, singing. My father. Lovely Neapolitan songs to break your heart. He'd be given a pair of hard shoes to stand in, so as not to cause offence. Then they'd take them off him at the door. And off into the night with us with our sixpence. Oh, Lord.

A while later, **Robert** *sitting beside* **Lizzie**, *and* **Lucinda** *facing them. There's a certain strain in the room.* **Teresa** *arrives with tea-things on a tray.*

Lucinda Well done, Teresa, well done. Set it down there. Good girl. (*Smiling out to* **Robert** *and* **Lizzie**.) Yes. Will you do the salmon for the travellers' supper?

Teresa Oh, it's well on now, lady, well on.

Lucinda Poached, I trust, Teresa? I can't abide salmon, really, unless someone poaches it.

Lizzie You mean stolen?

Teresa No, no, missy – broiled. It is, lady – just as you told me.

Lucinda Thank God. (*She pours the tea with* **Teresa**'s *help.* **Teresa** *hands out the cups.*) That's the girl. She has trained up beautifully, hasn't she?

Teresa   Will I bring in candles, lady? Now that there's more folk than one?

Lucinda   Do we need candles?

Robert   There's light enough.

Lucinda   The light of candles draws us in from outdoors, I always think. Draws our hearts within the house. The countryside lies about us, but the candles draw us away from it. Usher in our souls, as it were. A lamp doesn't have the same effect somehow.

Lizzie   You like the garden and the countryside?

Lucinda   I could stand all evening in the garden listening to the bay running in on Inch, I could. Do you like the tea?

Lizzie   Yes, I do, Mrs Gibson.

Lucinda   Oh, Lady Gibson, it is. My husband was knighted for his jurisprudence hereabout, but, Lord knows, they flattered him.

Lizzie   Excuse me – I didn't know.

Lucinda   At any rate, you're Mrs Gibson now, so there won't be too much confusion between us. (*Seeing that* **Teresa** *hasn't moved for a while*.) What's amiss, Teresa, are you all right?

Teresa   I have a scream coming on, lady, you must forgive me. I got a terrible cold feeling in my bones when you spoke of souls and suchlike.

Lucinda   Well, don't scream in here, please. You go and scream in peace in the kitchens. When you get a chance, you may unpack their suitcases and portmanteaus.

Teresa   Yes, lady.

Lucinda   We'll manage here.

Teresa   Yes, lady. Thank you, lady. (*She goes.*)

Robert   Still mad as a March hare.

Lucinda   But very malleable, very. I'm quite pleased with her. (*To* **Lizzie**.) Of course, she'll be yours now to perfect.

Lizzie   I don't understand you, Lady Gibson.

Lucinda   This is Robert's house, you know. You've married him, and you must be mistress. Of course, if you wish, I can go to my people in Yorkshire.

Lizzie   Oh, Yorkshire.

Robert   Your people in Yorkshire are underground these many years. There's no question of you being ousted in any way.

Lucinda   Oh, dear me, ousted, no. Thank you, Robert. The plain fact is, dear, since the government transferred the bulk of our farms, it has proved quite difficult to keep things going. Since our whole economy was based on rents.

Robert   I mean to look into all that. I'm sure we can manage for the three of us.

Lucinda   So many in recent years have had to leave their efforts here and go. It's quite sad, really.

Robert   We have a touch of new capital now.

Lucinda (*looking at* **Lizzie**)   Oh, have we? How nice. Where are your people from, Mrs Gibson?

Lizzie   My mother was from Ventry and my father I believe from somewhere near Caherconree, but they moved about Corcaguiney.

Lucinda   They moved about?

Lizzie   He travelled from place to place with us.

Lucinda   And did he have property here?

Lizzie   He had a wife and a child and a splendid singing voice.

Lucinda   You mean your father moved about, singing?

Lizzie   Yes.

Lucinda How unusual, Robert. And they are both deceased, sadly, your parents?

Lizzie Yes, Lady Gibson. They died of fever.

Lucinda So much death. Robert, after giving me an account of his brothers, tells me you were married in the Presbyterian church in Rutland Square. Does he mean you are a Presbyterian rather than of the Established Church?

Lizzie Yes, of course.

Lucinda I don't want you to think me bigoted, you see. I just wished to know. It's the kind of thing one likes to know about one's daughter-in-law. If you have a little fortune, dear, how did it come to be?

Lizzie I gathered it for myself over the years.

Lucinda How very extraordinary. How did you do that remarkable thing?

Lizzie You don't follow the halls, I think.

Lucinda The halls?

Lizzie The music-halls.

Lucinda Oh, no, dear. Do you?

Robert Lizzie is a very independent woman, Mamma, and has lived an independent life, for which she is to be admired. She suffered here in Corcaguiney as a young girl, and I think it is wrong of you to question her like this, if I may say so.

Lucinda Well, Robert, you know I have the highest regard for you, and I understand how dreadful it has been for you out there in Africa, and indeed I feel the force of our tragedy just as horribly as I know you do, but this is the plain world out here in Kerry, and the people hereabouts will want to know about your wife before they bring her into their houses. That's just how things are. I know these are modern times, and we are surely heading into darker times yet, but people are very simple and they like to know who they are talking to. That's all.

Robert   I should think they must be proud to know Lizzie.

Lucinda   My dear, these are very ordinary people out here. They expect a marriage in Christ Church like all your family before you. They want to read about her trousseau in the *Irish Times* and they want to feel that their world is going on at least as it always has gone on. You can't expect any better of them, especially in these hard times. I hope you won't disregard that. Because I myself feel quite put out, even to a degree, put upon, by this, I'm sorry to say.

Robert   I don't know why you would be, Mamma.

Lucinda   Well, I've tried to explain to you as gently as I can. I can see you have fine qualities, Mrs Gibson, but you mustn't expect to thrive here immediately. Go about with some care for people's foolish expectations. If you wish to gain your ground eventually. You are very different to the run of girls we get around here.

Lizzie   I expect so.

Lucinda (*rising*)   Now, if you wish me to, I'll see to dinner. I'm sure you're both famished. In a private sense, I bid you welcome to Red House. In other senses, I don't know how I will enjoy describing you to people, but be that as it may.

Robert   You needn't try, Mamma, believe me.

Lucinda   We shall see, my dear.

A few minutes later. **Robert** *kneels before* **Lizzie**, *holding her because she's upset.*

Robert   It's only history chooses a person's circumstance.

Lizzie   Partly I love you because you don't care about all that.

Robert   That's it. I admire you, Lizzie. You didn't lie down and die in Corcaguiney. We are all very much equal under the clothes that history lends us. If you can sing or dance or go soldiering, so much the better for you. No one knows exactly the through-going of their days. You made yourself secure in England. You don't require telling whether it was well or ill done.

Lizzie It was better than many of the doings of Corcaguiney, let me tell you, Robert. How it comes back to me, sitting under these dark skies.

Robert You are the finest person I've ever met, and I've met my share of fine people, in the army and generally.

Lizzie Shall I go up and help little Teresa to unpack our things? She's a nice little creature, I think.

Robert We'll both go up. We'll put on our finery and have a lovely supper of Corcaguiney salmon and the devil take the lingerer.

Lizzie You haven't let me down, sweet.

Robert Nor will I ever, Lizzie.

They go.

The house as if empty, the little ruckus of moonlight through it and the fresh falling of the sea below. A rising and falling music. After a little, **Teresa** *emerges, staggering under the weight of some empty cases. She climbs the steps to the house tower, and lets the cases drop.* **Lizzie***'s stage knickers fall out of one of them.*

Teresa My, what dust! I'll ignore it. For I can't bide long near these poor uniforms. Three such lovely boys, and naught left of them but this tired cloth, by God. (*Sensing a scream coming on.*) Ah, I won't scream, because they are poor killed lads now. (*To the uniforms.*) I might offend ye. (*Attending the cases.*) That new missis is full of style. She has dresses! (*She spots the knickers, takes them up, examines them in some wonder.*) Ho, there's style for you. Will you take a gander at them stars. Would you deck them? (*Holds the knickers against herself. They seem enormous.*) Ha, ha. Oh. They must be winter knickers.

The heaviness of them. Now I've seen the heaven of knickers. She must have been a empress before Robert Gibson found her. Oh, the Holy Christ, that'll keep me going till Christmas. I needs see nothing else till then. (*Holding them aloft.*) Oh, what knickers!

Curtain.

Act Two

The reverse side of the house, represented by, left, broad granite steps up to the open hall. A sense of pillars. It's late September, and there's a big fire in the marble hearth, a bracket of unlit candles on a wall. Twilight infects the piece of gravel before the steps. But mostly, right and downstage, there's a broad bare area, for the strand, and a tufted dune upstage right, and a sense of an old shell midden there. A cold-looking moon has arisen. There's a heap of tangled greenery piled left, Bartholomew's, with a pitchfork stuck into it. A strong sense of the slightly agitated night tide, and of frost. Teresa comes across the hall bearing logs, drops them with a clatter on to the hearth, and carefully places some on to the fire. She takes a long taper from her waistband and lights it in the fire, takes it to the candles, sets a chair under them, and lights them with some effort. The pleasing light grows in the hall. Now Bartholomew drags on further debris on a big cloth, bringing it to the heap, groaning as he straightens again. Teresa comes to the top of the steps.

Teresa Do you not feel that chill on you, Barty? Of course, my poor mother will say this is winter. Her summer is the first week of June, when she gets her journey home to us, for the few holy days given her by Lady Castlemaine. The rest of the year is winter. By her calendar. Isn't that strange? But September is maybe winter, is it, Barty?

Bartholomew It is for various growing things, I don't know about your mother.

Teresa Ah, she was hired to a farmer up beyond Mary's Mountain when she was but five years old. She was a little slave to work. Which is the why she takes such a bleak view of the seasons, I'm sure. And the poor girl fifty-five now. Barty?

Bartholomew (*hoisting some of the garden refuse on to the heap with the pitchfork*) Yes, doty?

Teresa Barty, dear, what do you say about the new missis, now we've had a while to know her?

Bartholomew (*resting*)   Well, doty – fact is – she will never do.

Teresa   Oh, but you see her clothes, Barty. The solidest style of clothes I ever saw. It does my soul good to watch them.

Bartholomew   Clothes are very well.

Teresa   I depend on you for wisdom, Barty. I'm disappointed at you. (*Going in again.*) Her clothes speak well for her. (*Coming back a moment, indignant.*) If I ever had such attire, I'd expect you to think well of me.

Bartholomew (*surprised*)   And I would, surely.

Teresa *goes in having made her point.* **Bartholomew**, *shaking his head, starts to fix an old pipe for himself, in the growing dark. At length* **Robert** *comes on wearing an old working coat and a battered hat. He has a sack of tools.* **Bartholomew** *spies the figure, extracts the pitchfork, and with force brandishes the pitchfork at him, not seeing who it is.*

What do you do there? Clear off. I'm not afraid, mind.

Robert   Is that how you talk to beggars?

Bartholomew   It's how I talk to thieves! I'll put this in your ragged coat for you! Go back away!

Robert (*holding up the bag to protect himself*)   I heard you were a fierce old warrior.

Bartholomew   I'll give you old, I'll give you old, you blackguard! (*Starts to rush at him with the pitchfork.*)

Robert (*shoving the bag into the way of the fork*)   Heavens, I'm only playing a game with you, don't kill me. (*Raising his hat.*)

Bartholomew (*halted*) Oh, Mr Robert. Forgive me, do. Why couldn't you say your name in the dark?

Robert   You hardly gave me a chance, Bartholomew.

Bartholomew   You weren't on the public road dressed like that?

Robert   I was mending fences down at the river. The flood tore some posts out. I was expecting two fellows to help me but they didn't come. So I saw to it myself.

Bartholomew   They wouldn't come to you? Would you credit that? That's for because they think they're all kings now, with the new laws – kings of thistles and rushes.

Robert   Well, kings can linger by their fires, if they wish. Isn't it for the better, Bartholomew?

Bartholomew   No, is the short answer.

Robert (*going up the steps*) This is a lovely night now. Look at the strand. I feel better for the labour. I thought you were going to kill me for certain, Bartholomew, with your nice pitchfork. (*Goes in across the hall.*)

Movement and clatter in the hall now as **Robert**, *come back again, draws chairs up to the hall fire for the evening.* **Lizzie** *comes on carrying a folded cloth on her arm, with* **Teresa** *worriedly beside her.*

Teresa   But that's old Ventry linen, missy, you wouldn't want to go cutting that up – would you? It's fine stuff off the beds.

Lizzie   Well, girl, if it makes a fine sheet won't it make a fine dress? You'll have a fine dress made of old Ventry linen, and you can say it to who you like, can't she, Robert?

Robert (*into the fire, with a book*)   I should think so.

Lizzie   It will be honoured more as a dress than a sheet, girl.

Teresa   Well, if you say.

Lizzie   I have pieces of silk we can sew on to it in plaquettes. And I have gold ribbon too. You'll have a lovely dress for your November dances. Now, stand, while I measure you.

Lizzie *takes out a long tape and a piece of paper, and begins to take measurements of* **Teresa***, noting them down as she goes.*

Teresa *(after a little)*   Mercy . . .

Lizzie   What, child?

Teresa   It's like a holy day.

Lizzie   And that's a good thing when it comes.

Teresa   But I can't grow idle and lose my good character. (**Robert** *scoffing.*)

Lizzie *(seriously)*   And you won't. (*Measuring,* **Robert** *watching, smiling.*) What a perfect little person you are, Teresa. Everything matching up like a goddess.

Teresa   Oh, jackanapes, missy.

A little later and darker, the fire enclosing **Lizzie** *and* **Robert***. He reads, she makes measurements on a piece of transparent paper.*

Lizzie *(licking the pencil lead to encourage it)*   There's terrific burning in the wood, isn't there?

Robert *(half-attentive)*   Driftwood. (*Silence for a little, then, looking up.*) You know, they used to tie a lamp between the horns of a cow, and put it out to wander on Inch Strand, so that ships, trying to go up to Castlemaine Harbour, would take a course by it on a dark night, thinking it was a beacon, and run themselves on to the strand. There's many beds and tables in the houses around here that came out of such old ships. That was a savage thing to do, wasn't it? (*Back to his book.*)

Lizzie   The Gibsons did that?

Robert   No, no, the people, the people.

Lizzie   Oh, them. (*Marking the paper.*) I intend to make a good dress for Teresa. Why shouldn't she have a fine dress? She has a great interest in clothes. With her stature she could

make her fortune as a child act. Singing, I mean. She could
be a child till she was sixty, with the proper painting of her
face. (*After a little.*) What are you reading?

Robert   Horace.

Lizzie   Oh, Horace. And what does he say, Horace?

Robert   What does he say? He recommends a life of narrow
poverty. *Angustam pauperiam.*

Lizzie   Oh, that old thing.

Robert   Which is just as well, Lizzie, because that's how
we'll end up, the way things are going.

Lizzie   Po – he recommends poverty? He doesn't know
much about it, I think.

Robert   Maybe so – his father was an auctioneer, right
enough.

They laugh together.

Lizzie   An auctioneer – good God! (*Goes on working for a
little.*) I knew another man once that liked Horace. A big
Scottish fellow, in the Presbyterian orphanage. He told us
one time we were the future of Ireland. I can hear his lovely
accent now. 'The roses of the Presbyterian Mission in the
West.' A roomful of bony girls, gawping up at him. When I
think of it. (*Holding up the paper.*) Would you look at poor
Teresa, there's nothing to her.

Robert   The future. So you are, Lizzie, I'm sure.

Lizzie   Ho! Future. In those days it was my dream to go to
America and marry a Redman and live in a wigwam in the
wilderness. That didn't come to pass, did it?

Robert   No, sadly.

Lucinda *appears rather suddenly upstage, looking a little lonesome
and dishevelled.*

Lucinda Oh, here you are, of course. I got rather muddled. We're not in the drawing-room at this time of year. I will forget that.

Robert Mamma, dear, good evening.

Lucinda (*coming to the fire tentatively*) It's quite nice, isn't it, in here, with the fire lit. You always used to sit in here, the four of you, making a lot of noise talking and singing.

Lizzie Singing? (*To* **Robert**, *teasing*.) Hymns, was it?

Robert Mamma, come nearer to the fire here, it's blessed cold over by the door.

She approaches tentatively.

I like to listen to the sea as long as I can, and this is the best room for that, certainly.

Lucinda Do you remember playing croquet in here, with old Mrs Thomson's wool?

Robert No, I don't, Mamma.

Lucinda (*standing near the fire but awkwardly*) Your father wanted to remodel this room to look like a little side chapel in Christ Church Cathedral. I wouldn't have it. He said it looked like someone's tomb already and why not go the whole hog? Well, it was always very difficult to tell whether your father was being humorous or not.

Robert I hope he was being humorous on that occasion.

Lucinda The truth is, you know, my dear, I only miss your father at this – butt-end of the year. In the summer, well, somehow I blow along quite nicely. But just here, where the year turns so insidiously . . .

Robert He was always up the hillside this time of year, blasting the life out of little birds. I'm sure you never saw him.

Lucinda (*laughing*) Little birds. (*Laughing*.) The only other man who could ever make Lucinda Gibson chuckle was your great-uncle John Godfrey. He was an interesting man, Mrs Gibson. He helped to lay the telegraph cable across the

Atlantic, it goes out there somewhere into the sea, by Ventry,
is it, I forget? They wanted to knight him too, but he was
much too immersed in his books. He used to sit in here in
those old fled days, talking to your father and me. We
thought him very romantic, with huge moustaches as was the
fashion of the time. Yes, he put that heavy cable, cased in
lead, he used to say, like a long thin grandee in his coffin,
from here to New York, unwinding it off a big wheel on a
neat little ship they had. And as soon as they had it laid
down, why, the Irish deaths began to meet the American
births running along the cable the other direction. You
know? It was a triumph for him. How odd to think men like
him can actually die. 'Isn't one bay enough, if it's your bay?'
he used to say, when your father would be bemoaning the
size of these lands, 'Isn't one bay enough,' as if, heaven
knows, we owned the whole of Corcaguiney and the waters
by it.

Robert　Well, he was certainly a favourite of yours,
Mamma.

Lucinda　Oh, yes. Most definitely. If your father had had
an ounce of his gusto, his learning, or his strength. Not that
your father was a complete waste of time.

Lizzie　He gave you a nice enough son, Lady Gibson.

Lucinda　Jingo, he gave me four sons, the rogue. Well, I'll
go up to my bed. I'm sorry to pester you with memories that
are undoubtedly of no interest to you. You know how a
human creature likes to talk of what it knows and knew.
Goodnight, dear. Goodnight, Mrs Gibson.

Robert　Oh, I like to hear about the old fellows you had a
bit of a *grá* for, Mamma.

Lucinda　I see. Goodnight. (*She goes.*)

Lizzie　Goodnight, Lady Gibson.

Robert *and* **Lizzie** *share a look.*

She detests me, would you say?

Robert　Not at all.

Lizzie Why does the woman always call me Mrs Gibson? I never know who she's talking to. I look around for this Mrs Gibson.

Robert She's very old-fashioned. That was the way of it in her generation. She used to call my father Mr Gibson.

Lizzie She didn't!

Robert Oh, yes. Publicly, at any rate. If she felt really intimate, or was telling a story about him — because he went all over Corcaguiney as a magistrate, and was always courting disasters — if she was really being affectionate and warm towards him, she called him Magistrate.

Lizzie My God, Robert.

Robert Oh, yes. Just that touch formal, my Mamma. It was the fashion of manners in her young days. I don't think she notices how peculiar it sounds to our ears.

Lizzie Imagine me calling you Mr Gibson. May we go up to our doss now, Mr Gibson? Can we go up and have a good roll in the hay above, Mr Gibson?

Robert But of course, Mrs Gibson. My pleasure, I'm sure.

He leads her off as if to a dance.

Frosty daylight, **Bartholomew** *alone in the yard, raking the patch of gravel.* **Teresa** *comes on from the avenue. She's wearing a pair of old boots, which makes it hard for her to hurry. There's mud on her spindly legs.*

Bartholomew No coat, Teresa?

Teresa No, no, Barty. There's no fashion in my coat.

Bartholomew (*looking at her*) Fashion, is it? You were looked for earlier and not found. You were adjudged to be deep in your sculleries at your work, teeming potatoes and the like.

Teresa Oh, don't accuse me, Barty. I'll tell you where I was, if you can keep a priesteen's counsel.

Bartholomew   That's not as secure as you may think, doty. Where were you so?

Teresa   I was visiting my beau for five minutes.

Bartholomew   In my old boots? Which one of your beaux, Teresa, girl?

Teresa   The lovely pigman down at Kaiser Field. Oh. You won't say?

Bartholomew   You'll need a tin bath and a strong nose if that's a marriage, doty. However did you keep those boots up on you?

Teresa   I stuffed the blooming *Castlemaine Herald* into them!

She hurries up the steps and crosses the hall. **Lizzie** *and* **Robert**, *dressed for a walk, meet her halfway.*

Oh, Lord.

Robert   Someone's looking for you, Teresa. Someone with a cross face.

Teresa   Oh, Lord. (*Goes in.*)

They go down the steps to **Bartholomew**.

Bartholomew   Good morning to you. I hope it's all going well for you. (**Lizzie** *smiles.* **Bartholomew** *gets quite jaunty.*) There's a touch of rain about, you may find. This hat hates rain.

Lizzie   Does it?

Bartholomew   You see that house-field lying fallow there?

Lizzie   Yes.

Bartholomew   There'd be a great frolic on that same field every August in the old days.

Lizzie   Is that right?

Bartholomew   Oh, yes. There's no market for hay now and if there was there'd be few enough men to work willingly for so little and so long.

Robert   That's the truth, Bartholomew.

Bartholomew (*encouraged*)   A field like that with no market for it would kill a small man beyond Ventry if it was his one and only field!

Lizzie   Of course, it would, yes.

Bartholomew (*almost sweating*)   In former times, missy, the mistress of this house would come out from the house to the hay lying dry as dresses in that field, and take up the pitchfork like a very man and turn the first line to the sun for luck. For luck in the harvest and in the going-on of things.

Lizzie   Well, couldn't I come out next year, if you gave me the signal?

Bartholomew   Could you? Lucinda Gibson never did come out, and that was a pity.

Lizzie   If you give me the signal next year, I'm your girl.

Bartholomew   Every district has its custom by which a district endures. You must revere the custom of a place, or die away. You must turn the warm sheaves to the sun obediently, or die away.

A bit of a silence at this announcement.

Lizzie (*very seriously*)   Begod, Mr Grady. Thank you for sharing that with us.

Bartholomew (*subdued a little*)   My father used to say that to me. He got it out of Virgil, I believe.

Lizzie   Well, he was right, your father, he was right.

Bartholomew (*pleased*)   He was. Or was it Virgil was right?

Now, the falling September light on the strand. **Robert** *and* **Lizzie** *come down by the marram grass and the midden and walk a little downstage. The fresh sound of the waves running in broadly from Dingle Bay, the piping of birds.*

Robert   Did you notice that old midden there, Lizzie?

Lizzie   Where, sweet? That old heap of shells and such?

Robert   I met an Englishman on the strand years ago, who told me that midden was begun in the time of Christ. To think of people here all that while, living simply from the sea. Right down to the old picker of winkles who used to infest that little house by the strand.

Lizzie   A harsh cruel life, I'd say, out in the rain and the wind.

Robert   Of course, it would have been, yes. You're right, Lizzie.

Lizzie   People just like me in other days gone by, just like me, probably. Little hectic people that never heard of music-halls.

Robert   You think so? Maybe it was your crowd put the lamp on the cow so, and killed the poor mariners?

Lizzie   It does sound like something I'd do, you know. I didn't like to say last night, and spoil your story.

They wander away upstage and off. Just the emptiness and privacy of the strand for a little, with the subtle changes of light provided by the stirring sky. Gradually, the waltzing music of a little orchestra, distantly, the strand getting some hints of gold, and after a while, two splendid chandeliers lower and illumine the space, and now some couples appear, dressed richly and beautifully. The people themselves aren't as lovely as their clothes. **Lord Castlemaine**, *a tall powerful-looking man, dances with his wife,* **Lady Castlemaine**, *who is plump but energetic. Great glitter and appearance of happiness. A little* **Factotum**, *dressed blackly, is taking cards. Now* **Lizzie** *and* **Robert**, *looking splendid,* **Lizzie** *in her very best red dress, approach the* **Factotum**, *who takes their card balefully.*

Factotum   Mr and Mrs Robert Godfrey Gibson!

The dance continues, **Lady Castlemaine** *watching* **Lizzie** *as she looks on eagerly.* **Lizzie** *smiles up at* **Robert**. *Even* **Robert** *seems stirred. The dance ends,* **Lady Castlemaine** *whispers something to her husband and goes upstage to speak to one of the other women.* **Lord Castlemaine** *crosses to* **Robert**.

Lord Castlemaine Gibson, how nice to see you. We heard you were about again. How splendid you could come tonight. (*Shakes his hand.*)

Robert You haven't met my wife, Lizzie.

Lord Castlemaine No, I haven't. And it's a great pleasure. We heard that Robert had found himself a great – a great actress.

Robert Lord Castlemaine – Lizzie Gibson.

Lizzie How do you do, Lord Castlemaine? I was never a great actress, I'm sad to say.

Lord Castlemaine (*taking her hand*) You must never think we are so provincial here as not to honour the stage. We hear a great deal about the stage that is unsavoury, and we know it is bunkum. After all, my dear, Shakespeare himself was an actor.

Lizzie I'm proud enough to have known the stage life, I must admit.

Lord Castlemaine Excellent, excellent. I want you two to enjoy yourselves. My wife, Lady Castlemaine, took a good look at you, Mrs Gibson, while she danced, and whispered in my ear that you would do very well. I want you to know that. She can tell whether a person will wash or not from two hundred yards, if needs be.

Lizzie That's a talent, Lord Castlemaine.

Lord Castlemaine There now, Gibson. I haven't offended, I hope?

Robert No, no.

Lord Castlemaine *heads back to his wife.*

(*To* **Lizzie**.) The bloody fool.

Lord Castlemaine *turns again, a notion striking him.*

Lord Castlemaine   I would so like to talk to you, Gibson –
about Africa.

Robert   Oh, yes. Not a lot to say, really.

Lord Castlemaine   Oh, I think there is a little to say. In a
while, in a while.

He heads over to his wife again. The music begins.

(*Over his shoulder.*) And I'll have a dance with you, Mrs
Gibson, if you don't mind your feet crushed!

Lizzie (*to* **Robert**) Well?

Robert   You'd like to . . .

Lizzie   I'll kill myself if you don't. A dance to me is like raw
meat to a lion.

Robert   I'd never disappoint a hungry lion, Lizzie.

They join in the dance. It's true that **Lizzie** *never looked happier than
when she dances now, unless it was doing the cancan with* **Jelly
Jane**. **Robert** *and she are swept into a feeling of great union by the
music, as good as a marriage. Now the* **Factotum** *pulls onstage a
long table piled with food, covered in an immaculate white tablecloth,
trimmed with the colours of the Castlemaines. The inhabitants of the
countryside seem to have found their way on to the plates, along with
much beef and puddings and wines. The people gather in to eat, helped
to food by the* **Factotum**.

Lizzie (*whispering to* **Robert**)   If my father had ever seen a
spread-out like that, he'd of sang like a linnet all night in
hopes of a go at it.

Robert (*laughing*)   You can eat for him so. In his memory.

Lizzie   I will, Robert, I will. That's a fine compliment to
him. Thank you. (*She goes with her plate to the* **Factotum**.)

Factotum   Is it most things you're after?

Lizzie   Oh, yes. Most things will do nicely. Everything will
do better.

Factotum   Sure I'll give you everything so. Quail?

Lizzie   Oh, yes.

Factotum   You know the noise that fella makes?

Lizzie   No. (**Factotum** *does it.*) Remarkable.

Factotum   Partridge?

Lizzie   Oh, yes, lovely.

Factotum (*serving it*)   You know . . . (**Lizzie** *shakes her head nay. The* **Factotum** *does the sound of the partridge.*) Pheasant?

Lizzie   Yes. (*He does the pheasant.*) You know, you remind me of a man I knew once in the music-hall. You're the very spit of him. You don't know the birds of Ohio, by any chance, do you?

Factotum   No, ma'am, only the birds of Corcaguiney.

Lady Castlemaine *approaches* **Lizzie**.

Lady Castlemaine   Hello, my dear. My husband tells me you are perfectly delightful, and so I see you are. Isn't Peadar a wonder with his bird calls?

Lizzie   He is – just wonderful.

Lady Castlemaine   I told him when you arrived at Red House it wasn't the first time there was wild blood into Corcaguiney. People forget it now, because it suits them to forget, but my grandmother was a very beautiful woman who came from the very darkest thickets of Portugal. And, my dear, would you believe it, was one of those fanatical Catholics who were brought up never to talk to a Protestant if they could help it. She was reared by the Princess of Brazil in Lisbon, and really was the most wonderful, bigoted woman I ever knew. Even at ninety-three.

Lizzie *doesn't know how to take this*.

Am I being a fool? Am I bungling everything? I do bungle things so.

Lizzie   I know you mean it kindly, it's just – I'm not bigoted and I'm not Portuguese.

Lady Castlemaine I know, I know. Come with me, Mrs Gibson, and I'll show you her picture in the hall. Then we can get back to dancing, when our supper has settled.

Lizzie (*going off with her*) It'll take a good while enough for these poor birds to settle.

Lady Castlemaine (*disappearing*) The main thing is, my dear, for people to remain in their houses, to hold to Corcaguiney, make their stand here, if they can . . .

Robert *and* **Lord Castlemaine** *together now.*

Lord Castlemaine I just wanted to say, Gibson, I was very put out to hear about your brothers. Very much so. I was very fond of them all. As you know my own father fought in the Crimea. I feel a great kinship with your mother and you in your sorrow.

Robert It's not as simple as that, of course.

Lord Castlemaine No, indeed not, and this is no place to discuss war. But it's been on my mind to write to you. I wrote to your mother at the time.

Robert I'm sure that was very thoughtful of you.

Lord Castlemaine Let me say, and God knows you've the right to shut me up if you wish, but though they died, they died well, they died for these three kingdoms and in service of their great Queen. And you survive now, noble and good, having done your utmost and given your all for the same immortal lady.

Robert (*quietly*) You shouldn't assume, Lord Castlemaine.

Lord Castlemaine Excuse me?

Robert I simply say, you shouldn't presume.

Lord Castlemaine How so, Gibson?

Robert It's true Frank and Harry died as nobly as people can die, when your general is a fool, and your cause is unjust.

Lord Castlemaine Unjust!

Robert   I resigned my commission two years ago after they were so wastefully killed. Wastefully.

Lord Castlemaine   What?

Robert   They never even saw the Boer guns that killed them. They were found in the morning with their companions all dusty and dead in the brushwood, half-eaten by the wild dogs of Africa.

Lord Castlemaine   War's not pretty, Gibson. You know that. And Charles? Did Charles also resign his commission? He died, didn't he, wearing his uniform?

Robert   Charlie died of drink in Cape Town. That's how he took the news. He died in my arms screaming blue murder and seeing demons. Not a pretty death, really. But, in his uniform.

Lord Castlemaine (*after a moment*)   I did assume, didn't I? So dreadfully assume. (*Touches* **Robert**'s *arm*.)

Robert   I resigned my commission and shortly afterwards accepted a captaincy in the Boer army. I crossed to Kruger, as it were. His Irish Brigade, to be exact.

Lord Castlemaine (*after a moment, taking back his hand*)   That rabble?

Lizzie *and* **Lady Castlemaine** *join them.*

Lady Castlemaine   I showed her that wild grandmother of mine, Henry. She said she looked a bit peaky, didn't you, my dear? (*Catching the atmosphere.*)

Lord Castlemaine   These ruffians going about with guns, shooting landlords, and burning haycocks, they're all pro-Boer.

Robert   I think I can make a distinction between Africa and Ireland.

Lord Castlemaine   I hope you can. You must go now from my house. After we made an effort for this, this woman you've married.

Lady Castlemaine   What do you mean, dear? What's the matter?

Lord Castlemaine   We've been duped. Gibson has changed camps, you might say, haven't you, Gibson? He fought for the Boers!

Lady Castlemaine   I should think that's his business.

Lord Castlemaine   Well, really, my dear Lady Castlemaine, you are unshockable. But I am not. A man who is pro-Boer can eat his supper somewhere else. And take his dancing woman with him.

Lady Castlemaine   I don't think you want to say that, dear.

Robert   It's all right, Lady Castlemaine.

Lizzie   It isn't all right so much as you think, Robert.

Robert   It's all right, in the sense that we are going now.

Lizzie   There's many in England itself that were against that war without being against the soldiers.

Lord Castlemaine   Against the war without being against the soldiers? What sort of way is that to lead your life? They're all mad in England, I've always said so!

Robert   Come along with me, Lizzie Finn, and don't be fighting with him. He's not up to your mettle.

They head off undaunted. **Lizzie** *turns briefly to* **Lord Castlemaine**.

Lizzie   I won't have that dance with you now – if you don't mind.

Deep November, **Robert** *tucked in by the fire reading.* **Teresa** *stands on a chair in the middle of the hall, wearing the new dress, while* **Lizzie** *pins gold and silk trim on to it intently.*

Robert (*to himself, reading*)   What ought I say of autumn's storms and stars?

Teresa (*seeing a fallen heap of books beside* **Lizzie**'s *chair, and one open on the seat itself*)   You like to deck the books, missy, that's for certain.

Lizzie   I never had much time for them in olden days. I've taken a run at them now and I'll be hard to stop. I've read even manuals of grainstores and books about the care of forests in India.

Teresa   And what's that little fellow there you're looking at?

Lizzie   It's not one of the house, but one that Robert fetched home for me. It's called *The Only True History of Frank James, by Himself.* It's a mighty book about an outlaw in America, penned mightily by the man himself. He robbed great gobs of gold off trains and rode hard through the days with his brother Jesse. He's a man to like. Robert, who is a scholar, says Frank James never did write any book and it only says he did to make you believe it's the plain truth. I believe Robert, and I believe the book. It's wild and exciting, with guns and good times and running from the laws.

Teresa   Now, that would be a tale for Teresa.

Lizzie   You could steal it to your room after me.

Teresa   I would but, no shame to me, I've no letters. Lady wrote my name into my shifts and knickers when I came first. I hadn't the wit to tell her it was no advantage to me. I was young then, missy. I half-know my own letters. I'm staring at them often enough when the linen comes back from the laundry girls. Barty swore one time he'd teach me, but his pots and blooms have first call on Barty. Missy?

Lizzie   Yes, dear?

Teresa   Was it wild good at the Castlemaines' ball, tell us.

Lizzie   It was wild good, wasn't it, Robert?

Robert   Wild good.

Teresa   I heard so. My mother's always at me, at me, to get employment at Lady Castlemaine's. She does the dairy for them there. The maiding, you know.

Lizzie   Well, girl – maybe you will.

A longish pause. **Teresa** *not moving. Suddenly she's crying.*

Teresa   You don't think the pigman will have me so!

Lizzie   Oh, I do, I do!

Teresa   What would be the point of the dress otherwise? I might as well wear flour-sacks.

Robert   Shush now, Teresa, in the house.

Lizzie   Shush now.

Teresa   Oh, it's a lovely dress, and what you put on there. Gold ribbon! I never even laid eyes on gold ribbon before. And the square of satin there on my poor flat bosom. Who'd a credited Teresa with such an immensity of a dress? Of course, it won't impress Barty.

Lizzie   It does suit you, girl. I'm glad you like it. You can sew in the bits yourself.

Teresa   Amn't I delightful in this? (*Dancing a bit on the chair.*) Someday I'll get shoes for this in Tralee, and then God help the pigman. (*An inspiration.*) I know the perfect complement for this missy, I do! (*She leaps from the chair, heads off into the house.*)

Lizzie   Mind the pins, girl, mind the pins! (*To* **Robert**, *laughing.*) She's a lovely wild girl.

Robert   She's like two buckets banging together!

Lucinda *comes in slowly. She carries her prayerbook and gloves and was obviously out at chapel. She seems dazed.*

Are you all right, Mamma?

Lucinda (*stuck at the door*)   Curious, curious. I only wished to attend evensong. I drove myself in the trap, quite independently, quite happily. Frosty and pleasant the countryside looked. I thought of myself sitting among the other worshippers, clean and starched and pleasant, our girls singing in the gallery. The clockwork, the rightness of it all. The truth of it. All simplified before God by the singing. The balm that has been given to me.

Robert   What happened, Mamma?

Lucinda   The face of the rector surprised me. He was standing inside the doors, looking at me in horror. I thought it was a trick of the light, of the November light. Like a stone face in the shadows. Suddenly I thought some tragedy had befallen him, some terrible event, his wife was dead, his daughters had been taken . . . I hurried to him. I hurried to my doom!

Robert   Mamma, Mamma.

Lucinda   He's such a pale-faced creature, with that sing-songing voice. He said things to me that seemed terrible and stark from his lips. Things that seemed shocking to me suddenly, that seemed to freeze my heart, as if bags of summer ice were stacked about it. Things I knew, or I thought I knew, that seemed suddenly more terrible to me than death, more shocking than death. Because he was describing to me the death of truth and rightness in my own house.

Robert   No, Mamma.

Lucinda   Described those things to me, and seemed to bar me from entering, from joining the worshippers all dark within, my refuge, Robert. I drove back along the sea road like a ghost. Coldness is an illness like to cholera, it kills and infects. I am so cold.

Teresa *bursts back into the room triumphantly, hardly seeing* **Lucinda**. *She rushes centrestage, alive with her inspiration.*

Teresa See, missy, see, the perfect complement!

She hoists her new dress violently, to show **Lizzie** *the starry knickers.*

Later, **Robert** *and* **Lizzie** *alone by the fire.*

Robert It was a wicked thing to do, wicked. To keep her from the chapel.

Lizzie But she knew about me, and she knew about Africa, didn't she?

Robert Knowing it, and being told about it, may be different things. It's your money paid down the debts of this house, and the real scandal is the level of debts allowed to us after the farms were sold. I hate to put capital to debts rather than income, but there it is. She's secure for the first time in many a long year, and if I can correctly revolutionise the farms remaining and start us back to health, she'll be securer still. Maybe it's time she stopped imagining herself the Queen of Corcaguiney. Though I wouldn't chose such a method to sear off her wings.

Lizzie Her face was ashen. I never saw the like before.

Robert She's terrified. If you don't have visits and visiting in a district like this, you may go mad, I suppose.

Lizzie It was all her world to be Queen of Corcaguiney, I see that.

Robert Why are they so ruled by imaginary distinctions? In this wild place? Well, I suppose it's because I crossed to the Boers.

Lizzie God knows, doty, a man that has lost three brothers can do what he likes.

Robert The fact of it is, crossing to Kruger healed nothing. If your heart is almost broken, a change of uniform is a poor bandage. I don't know what bearing it has on my mother. Why did they go for her?

Lizzie   So they all may feel at home. I'll go up to her.

Robert   Do, Lizzie, do. That's kind.

Upstage, **Lucinda** *standing in front of* **Lizzie**. **Lucinda** *holds a dress across her arms.*

Lizzie   I've brought great grief to you. I'm sorry for it.

Lucinda   There's nothing to be done, and you are just what you are, and clear about it, and I have been foolish after my own fashion.

Lizzie   Not foolish at all.

Lucinda   Look, I was to give this to you at Christmastide, but I prefer to give it now, if I may.

Lizzie (*taking the dress*)   Thank you. It is so sombre and elegant. Thank you for a beautiful dress.

Lucinda   Why wouldn't I buy my own daughter a dress, Mrs Gibson?

Lizzie   It seems to me Spanish somehow. Like in the picture-book about the Moors in the library – the deep current of blue in the dark cloth.

Lucinda   Of course, it may be.

Lizzie   Well, well, thank you again.

Lucinda (*turning away*)   Do not think you are not loved in this house.

The light of the fire washing in on **Robert**, *his face lit. Faintly, fractured, the voice of a man singing from an operetta, to which* **Robert** *pays no heed.*

The next day, a cold blank November day. **Bartholomew** *works at inserting kindling under his bonfire, it's arduous for him to stoop, but he's absorbed in the work. He's looking forward to the flames.*

Bartholomew   The fire will wake flies nearby in the stones, but it will be a false awakening.

Lucinda *comes down the steps. She doesn't look at* **Bartholomew**, *which surprises him.*

Good morning, lady.

Lucinda (*vaguely*)   Yes, Bartholomew.

She goes on right and exits downstage. **Bartholomew** *returns to his task. He strikes a Lucifer and tries the kindling, watches the nest of flames grow. But something bothers him. He keeps looking after* **Lucinda**. *He goes a little right and looks down over the strand.*

Bartholomew   There she goes. (*Watches another while, now and then glancing back at the growing bonfire. Suddenly, in some alarm.*) Lady! Lady! She can't hear me! Mr Robert! (*No response.*) Lady! Don't! She's walked straight in! Oh, lady! (*He follows after, off.*)

The bonfire brightly.

Some days later. The telephone ringing in the hall. **Robert**, *looking famished, comes out to it at length. Then* **Lizzie**, *then* **Teresa**.

Robert   Yes, yes, Red House? Hello, Captain. (*To* **Lizzie** *and* **Teresa**, *who hold each other's hands.*) It's the captain of the lighthouse at Dunquin. Yes, Captain, I'm here. I see. Yes, I understand. In the sea-coves beyond Dingle. Yes, I'm sure, I'm sure. A black dress. Thank you, Captain. Difficult news, yes. I should think the tides could well do that, yes, I agree. No, no, the sea quite calm all that day. Freak wave? I don't know, I don't know. Is there any sign of Bartholomew Grady? No? Yes, we believe he went in after her. He was seen by the old woman by the strand, walking in. Indeed, very courageous, very. Who will bring her up to the house? I see. Very good. We'll be expecting them. Some hours, yes. Thank you again, Captain. Please don't worry. Goodbye. Thank you.

He looks at the receiver, trembling. **Teresa** *holds on to* **Lizzie**.

Teresa (*very quietly*)   It was me, wasn't it, missy? With the knickers?

Lizzie (*equally quietly*)   Never and no, sweet, never and no.

Later, **Lizzie** *on her knees trying to light the hall fire, there's a knack to it that eludes her.* **Robert** *comes up the steps with a few letters. He sees her at the fire, doesn't speak for a moment.*

Robert   Well. Is Teresa not about?

Lizzie   She's quite destitute. Everything here reminds her of one or other of them. I sent her down to Kaiser Field where she has a friend. (*Seeing the letters.*) What are they?

Robert   Condolences. There's a quite charming one from Johnson the fuel merchant in Castlemaine. In his very best schoolroom writing. (*Shows a letter.*) This one with the crest, is from Lord Castlemaine.

Lizzie   What does he want?

Robert   Oh, it's as formal as a hedge. I suppose he thinks he was Mamma's great friend.

Lizzie   I bet he does. (*Rising.*) I don't understand this fire. I don't.

Robert   Nobody does except Teresa.

The next day, a little reception in the hall after **Lucinda**'s *funeral. It's subdued enough.* **Lord** *and* **Lady Castlemaine** *with the* **Rector**, **Lizzie** *in the dress* **Lucinda** *gave her,* **Robert** *in black* *clothes.* **Teresa** *looking terrified and useless by the door.* **Robert** *takes the tray from her, and pours a dark sherry into the little glasses the guests are clutching, like straws.*

Lizzie (*the* **Rector** *bears a great resemblance to the* **Factotum**) *You* don't know the birds of Ohio, do you?

The **Rector** *looks at her.*

Rector (*quickly*)   I don't think I do, Mrs Gibson.

Lizzie (*to herself*)   Some day, somewhere, someone's going to call me Lizzie again.

Lord Castlemaine   Our man tells us there's a storm brewing down there in the bay. We don't want to be blown about the sea-road. We won't stay long. A lovely sherry, I must say.

Lizzie   Portuguese.

Lady Castlemaine   Really?

Lord Castlemaine   I must say, we expected a bit of a gathering. It's not like the old days, is it? You'd find a hundred mourners and more at a funeral, a hundred and more.

Robert   Oh, we might have had a few others, I suppose. My agent couldn't come down from Tralee, as it happens. But we thought the three of you would like to pay your respects properly, in the house itself.

Lord Castlemaine   Oh, indeed. I relish the opportunity. Very well put, Gibson. Indeed. Wasn't it, Lady Castlemaine?

Lady Castlemaine   It was, my dear.

Robert   She had few enough close friends in these later years. She was content to stay at home since Papa died. But loved to visit when she was able. When she was asked.

Lord Castlemaine   Of course.

Robert   I am just glad you let her lie inside the walls of the yard, rector. We must be grateful to the captain of the Dunquin Light and his theory of waves.

Rector   A freak wave is not as uncommon as people believe, I think.

Lord Castlemaine   Not at all as uncommon. They're an everyday occurrence, in fact. They really shouldn't be called freak at all.

Robert   Just waves, in fact.

Lord Castlemaine   Indeed. Waves. Waves.

At the door **Teresa** *hangs her head quietly and beings to cry. The* **Rector** *and the* **Castlemaines** *look at her.* **Lizzie** *goes and puts an arm about her.*

Lizzie (*softly*)   There, doty, don't cry. You go to your pigman and don't mind this here. (**Teresa** *looks up at her.*) Go on.

Teresa *escapes.* **Lizzie** *walks back towards the guests.*

Lady Castlemaine (*to* **Lizzie**)   They're so devoted, the people.

Lizzie *gives her an odd smile and goes on across the hall and down the step.*

She has a little bit of blue in her dress. I didn't like to say. It bothered me.

Robert *looks at her long and hard.*

A little later, **Lizzie** *at the left of the strand.*

Lizzie   Just sometimes, wouldn't you like to shoot people?

Robert *comes up behind her and puts a coat about her shoulders. She turns, remembers the coat in the music hall, laughs.*

That's the second time, my love.

Robert   What did you say, Lizzie?

Lizzie   Nothing – only blathering.

Robert   I'm sorry about that trio of lunatics. I shouldn't have asked them.

Lizzie   Oh, it doesn't matter, Robert. I wanted to get down to the strand before nightfall anyway. Did I ever show you this yoke?

She takes the stone angel from a pocket, and kneels to bury it in the sand.

Robert   What is it?

Lizzie   It's an old angel that Jelly Jane gave me, that her father dug up somewhere. It was to give to our child, should he show his nose, or she. (**Robert** *laughs*.) I hope she won't mind me putting it in here.

Robert   Why are you putting it there, Lizzie?

Lizzie   For your mother. It's a Yorkshire angel, and she was from Yorkshire, wasn't she?

Robert   Yes, she was.

Lizzie *rises, knocking the sand off her hands.*

Lizzie   There. It's not a very big monument, I suppose, not like you see on some of those tomb-houses in the yard at Castlemaine. Big, black-looking angels with wings the size of yachts.

Robert   It's a splendid monument. Mamma never had a *grá* for tombs. That's why we had her put under the yews, with a decent view down the bay to Inch.

Lizzie   For heaven's sake, sure you'd want that. At the very least. She was most of her life gawping down at it from the house there.

Robert   Exactly. Here. (*Fetching out something of his own from a little container, a vade-mecum.*) Put that in for Bartholomew.

Lizzie   What is it so?

Robert Did you never wonder what happened to it? I even chose a little box for it, a vade-mecum, Lizzie, to protect me from my own foolishness. The hatpin. The sacred hatpin.

Lizzie All right. (*Putting it in the sand. After a little.*) Well, Mr Gibson, what are we going to do for friends here?

Robert. I do not know.

Lizzie A girl likes to have great pals, you know. I suppose we could grow old and curmudgeonly and see no one and fill the house with scalded-looking brats and love them hugely, a little tribe of rasher-faced Gibsons.

Robert We mightn't have a choice. I don't see us dancing with the Castlemaines too often.

Lizzie God forbid! I would rather kill myself than dance with them, Robert Gibson!

Robert Ah. Lizzie, Lizzie, I've lead you astray to this useless place.

Lizzie No, heart. All the places of the world, where things are expected of a person, are the same. I'll call it home where Robert is, if you'll do the same. What's our history, Robert, but something like that poor Frank James had, a true history of lies, and written by nobody, as you told me yourself? There'll be nobody in the wide world to remember us, child, and all that will remain of us is an echo, a strain of dancing music, and the memory of a man that loved his brothers and his people, who was given a heart as restless as a frightened dog by wars and accidents. So what odds where we are?

Robert Perhaps we could make a better life for ourselves somewhere else?

Lizzie I've sometimes wondered why you needed to come back here at all. Apart from Lucinda.

Robert Love of the place. And it was mine, of course.

Lizzie That's good enough reason. I'm willing to stay on and be rude to as many toffs as I need to be. I am.

Robert I know. But you wouldn't really like it. I feel different about things now, with you. I'm not so keen to be at home. I'd rather be a foreigner some place. Like Cork, for instance.

Lizzie Cork? (*Laughs.*) Well, they have a new music-hall there in Cork, I was reading.

Robert I was reading too.

Lizzie It's the scandal of the *Castlemaine Herald*. We could try our luck there. And I'd be a fierce respectable act, married to you. They'll think I'm proper royalty. I could ask for some shocking rates, I could. And if I am a bit long in the tooth for showing my legs, couldn't I take up with the singing?

Robert Oh, I should stick with the dancing . . . (**Lizzie** *gives him a puck.*) I don't mind the sound of that. I can't be a farmer if there's no farms. I don't fancy falling into the sea with poor Red House. Better go off now while the going's good.

Lizzie Mr Gibson, you're a man to gladden my heart.

Robert We'll just spend the one last night up in the linen bed, and get that train in the evening tomorrow. The agent in Tralee can try and sell the place for us. We'll just walk out the blessed door and turn the old key in the lock. Why not?

The pull of the wind about them, drawing them closer.

Lizzie (*slowly*) Is it very far to Cork from here, Mr Gibson?

Robert I believe it's a terrible distance, Mrs Gibson.

Lizzie And are they very wild there? I've heard it said.

Robert Oh, they are, I'm sure.

Lizzie It will suit us so.

Echo of a song from an operetta. The wind about them. She includes him in her coat. Curtain.

The Steward of Christendom

For Donal

Characters

Thomas Dunne, *early to mid seventies at the time of the play, 1932*
Smith, *fiftyish*
Mrs O'Dea, *likewise or older*
Recruit, *eighteen*
Willie Dunne, *Thomas's son, born late 1890s, died in the First World War, thirteen or so as he appears in the play to Thomas, his voice not yet broken*
Annie Dunne, *Thomas's middle daughter, bowed back, about twenty in 1922, thirtyish 1932*
Maud Dunne, *Thomas's eldest daughter, early twenties in 1922*
Dolly Dunne, *Thomas's youngest daughter, about seventeen in 1922*
Matt Kirwin, *Maud's suitor and husband, mid to late twenties in 1922, mid to late thirties in 1932*

The play is set in the county home in Baltinglass, County Wicklow, in about 1932.

The Steward of Christendom was first performed in the Royal Court Theatre Upstairs, London, on 30 March 1995, with the following cast:

Thomas	Donal McCann
Smith	Kieran Ahern
Mrs O'Dea	Maggie McCarthy
Recruit	Rory Murray
Willie	Jonathan Newman
Annie	Tina Kellegher
Maud	Cara Kelly
Dolly	Aislín McGuckin
Matt	Rory Murray

Director Max Stafford-Clark
Designer Julian McGowan
Lighting Designer Johanna Town
Music Shaun Davey
Sound Designer Paul Arditti
Stage Management Rob Young, Sally McKenna, Caroline Boocock
Costume Supervisor Jennifer Cook
Production Electrician Matthew O'Connor

Act One

Circa 1932. **Thomas**'s *bare room in the county home in Baltinglass.*
A toiling music-hall music distantly. A poor table, an iron bed with a
thin mattress and yellowing sheets. A grey blanket, a three-legged
stool. A poor patch of morning light across **Thomas**, *a solitary man*
of seventy-five, in the bed. His accent is south-west Wicklow, with his
words clear.

Thomas   Da Da, Ma Ma, Ba Ba, Ba Ba. Clover, clover in
my mouth, clover honey-smelling, clover smelling of Ma
Ma's neck, and Ma Ma's soft breast when she opens her
floating blouse, and Da Da's bright boots in the grasses,
amid the wild clover, and the clover again, and me the Ba Ba
set in the waving grasses, and the smell of honey, and the
farmhands going away like an army of redcoats but without
the coats, up away up the headland with their scythes, and
every bit of the sun likes to run along the scythes and laugh
along the blades, now there are a score of shining scythes,
dipping and signalling from the backs of the men.

A sharp banging on the door.

Smith   Wakey, wakey!

Thomas   Who is there?

Smith   Black Jim. Black Jim in the morning.

Thomas   Oh, don't come in, Black Jim, with your
blackthorn stick raised high.

Smith   It's Black Jim.

Thomas   But don't you come in. There's no need. Is it Da
Da?

Smith   It's Black Jim, and he must come in.

Thomas   There's no need. Thomas sleepy sleepy, beddy
bye. Is it Da Da? (*No answer. More distantly on other doors there's*
a banging and the same 'Wakey, wakey' receding.) Da Da comes in,

Da Da comes in, Tom no sleepy, Tom no sleepy. Tom you sleep, says Da Da, or you get big stick. And when little Tom no sleepy sleep, big stick comes in and hitting Tom Tommy, but now the polished boots are gone, and the dark has closed over the fields, and the smell of the clover is damped down now by summer cold, and the dress of Ma Ma hangs on the chair, and her face is pressed into the goosey pillow, and all is silence in the wooden world of the house, except the tread of the Da Da, a-worrying, a-worrying, except the fall of the big stick, cut from the blackthorn tree in the hushed deeps of winter. Da Da is golden, golden, golden, nothing that Da Da do takes away the sheen and the swoon of gold.

He bestirs himself, wipes his big hands on his face vigorously, gets out of bed with good strength. He is big-framed but diminished by age, in a not-too-clean set of long johns.

You bloody mad old man. Gabbling and affrighting yourself in the dark. Baltinglass, Baltinglass, that's where you are. For your own good, safe from harm. Like the milking cow taken down from the sloping field when the frost begins to sit on her tail. When her shit is frosty. Snug in the byre. (*He sits on the stool and leans in to the table as if pressing his face against the cow.*) Come to it, Daisy now, give your milk. Go on. (*Slaps a leg.*) Ah, Daisy, Daisy, sweet, give it up, for Thomas. Oh. (*As if getting a jet into the bucket.*) Oh, oh. (*Happily.*) Aye. (*Catching himself, stopping.*) The county home in Baltinglass, that's where you're situated. Seventy-five summers on your head and mad as a stone mason. Safe, safe, safety, safe, safe, safety, mad as a barking stone mason. Because you were not civil to your daughter, no, you were not. You were ranting, you were raving, and so they put you where you were safe. Like a dog that won't work without using his teeth, like a dog under sentence. But please do not you talk to Black Jim, Thomas, please do not, there's the manny. Because he is not there. (*Singing.*) There was an old woman that lived in the wood, willa, willa, wallya.

His own silence.

Da Da?

Mrs O'Dea, *the seamstress, a small plump woman in an ill-made dress and a white apron with big pockets full of tape and needles and oddments of black cloth, opens the door with her key and comes in.*

Mrs O'Dea (*a local accent*)   Will you let me measure you today, Mr Dunne?

Thomas   What for indeed?

Mrs O'Dea   You can't wear those drawers forever.

Thomas   I won't need to, Mrs O'Dea, I won't live forever.

Mrs O'Dea   And what will you do when summer's gone? How can you bear to wear rags?

Thomas   I rarely go out, you see.

Mrs O'Dea   Look at the state of yourself. You're like something in a music-hall. Mrs Forbes, the Boneless Wonder, or some such.

Thomas   This is a madhouse, it suits me to look like a madman while I'm here.

Mrs O'Dea   If you allow me measure you, I'll make up a fine suit for you, as good as my own attire.

Thomas   With that black cloth you use for all the poor men?

Mrs O'Dea   Yes and indeed, it must be black, by regulation of the board.

Thomas   If you had a bit of gold or suchlike for the thread, something to perk the suit up, why then, Mrs O'Dea, I would let you measure me.

Mrs O'Dea   Gold thread? I have none of that, Mr Dunne.

Thomas   That's my bargain. Take it or leave it.

Mrs O'Dea   Would a yellow do?

Thomas   Yes, yes.

Mrs O'Dea   You're not afraid of looking like a big goose?

Thomas I go out but rarely. If I look like a goose, few will see me. (*As an inspiration.*) I won't venture out at Christmas!

Mrs O'Dea (*taking out her measuring tape*) Have you fleas?

Thomas No, madam.

Mrs O'Dea (*calling out the door*) Mr Smith! (*To* **Thomas**.) You won't mind Mr Smith washing you, just a little.

Thomas (*anxiously*) Don't let Black Jim in here. Don't let him, for I've no sugar lumps. It's only sugar lumps appeases him.

Mrs O'Dea He must wash you, Mr Dunne. It's just Mr Smith. You smell like a piece of pork left out of the dripping press, man dear.

Smith, *about fifty, balding, with the cheerfulness about him of the powerful orderly, comes in with a basin.*

Smith Raise 'em.

Thomas (*backing away*) The blackthorn stick hurts Tommy Tom. Sugar lumps, sugar lumps!

Mrs O'Dea Take off your old long johns, and be easy in yourself. It's only a sponging.

Thomas (*trying to hold his clothes fast*) Tum tum tum, bum bum bum.

Smith *roughly unbuttons the long johns and pulls them off,* **Thomas** *miserably covering himself.*

Smith I'd a mind once to join my brother on the Hudson river. He has a whale flensing business there, flourishing. Would that I had joined Jack, I say, when I have to wash down an old bugger like you. I would rather flense whales, and that's a stinking task, I'm told.

Thomas (*smiling red-faced at* **Mrs O'Dea**) Da Da.

Mrs O'Dea (**Smith** *beginning to sponge*) Good man yourself, Mr Dunne.

Thomas (*weeping*) Da Da, Ma Ma, Ba Ba.

Mrs O'Dea   My, my, that's a fine chest you have on you, Mr Dunne. What was your work formerly? I know you've told me often enough.

Thomas (*proudly enough*)   I was a policeman.

Mrs O'Dea   You had the chest for it.

Thomas   I had, madam.

Smith (*sponging*)   Dublin Metropolitan Police, weren't you, boyo? In your braid. The DMP, that are no more. Oh, la-di-da. Look at you.

Thomas (*smiling oddly*)   La-di-da.

Smith (*sponging*)   Castle Catholic bugger that you were. But you're just an old bastard in here with no one to sponge you but Smith.

Thomas   Black Jim no like Tommy Tom. No like Tommy Tom.

Smith   Chief superintendent, this big gobshite was, Mrs O'Dea, that killed four good men and true in O'Connell Street in the days of the lock-out. Larkin. Hah? His men it was struck down the strikers. (*A gentle hit with the drying cloth.*) Baton-charging. A big loyal Catholic gobshite killing poor hungry Irishmen. If you weren't an old madman we'd flay you.

Mrs O'Dea   That's fine, Mr Smith, leave him be. Can't you see you terrorise him? That's him scrubbed.

Smith (*going off with the basin*)   Excusing my language.

Mrs O'Dea   Can you put on your own clothes, Mr Dunne?

Thomas   I can, madam.

Mrs O'Dea   Is it true you gave your previous suit to a man in the walking meadow?

Thomas   It is. (*Dressing.*)

Mrs O'Dea   Why would you do a thing like that, and go in those rags yourself? Was the man you gave it to cold?

Thomas   No. He was hungry.

Mrs O'Dea   There's no eating in a suit, man dear.

Thomas   I was out a-walking in the lunatics' meadow, and Patrick O'Brien asked me for the suit. He was in former times the finest thrower of the bullet in Kiltegan. Do you know what a bullet is? It is a ball of granite whittled down in an evening by a boy. I could tell you tales of Patrick O'Brien and the bullet, on the roads there round about. All the men of the village milling there, raging to win fame at the bulleting if God shone the light of luck on them, the thrower slowly slowly raising the bullet, slowly dipping it, then away, with a great fling of the arm, down the road with it, and well beyond the next corner if he could. And if the bullet touched the grassy marge, a terrible groan would issue from the man and his supporters. And the young boys red in the face from ambition and desire. Patrick O'Brien, a tall yellow streak of a man now, that thinks he is a dog. A dog, Mrs O'Dea. When he asked for the suit, I couldn't refuse him, for memory of his great skill. They were evenings any human person would remember.

Mrs O'Dea (*measuring him now with the tape, putting up his arms and so on as necessary*)   What did he want with your suit?

Thomas   To eat, he said. To bury it and eat it, piecemeal, as the spirit took him.

Mrs O'Dea   You gave your good suit to a poor madman to be eaten?

Thomas   I was glad to give it to him. Though indeed truly, it was one of Harrison's suits, and the last of my finery from the old days. A nice civilian suit, made by Harrison, in North Great George's Street, years ago.

Mrs O'Dea   I can't believe that you gave away a suit like that. A lovely bespoke suit.

Thomas   Why not? Amn't I a lunatic myself?

Mrs O'Dea (*sensibly*)   Well, there must be a year's eating in a man's suit. You won't need to give him the new one.

Thomas   No, but it won't be much to me all the same, if it has no gold in it. The boy that sings to me betimes wears gold, and I have a hankering now for a suit with a touch of gold. There was never enough gold in that uniform. If I had made commissioner I might have had gold, but that wasn't a task for a Catholic, you understand, in the way of things, in those days.

Mrs O'Dea   You must have been a fine policeman, if they made you all of a chief superintendent.

Thomas   Maybe so. But, to tell you the truth, I was forty-five years in the DMP when they did so, and promotion was really a matter of service. Not that they would put a fool to such a task, when you think of the terrible responsibility of it. I had three hundred men in B Division, and kept all the great streets and squares of Dublin orderly and safe, and was proud, proud to do it well.

Mrs O'Dea   I am sure you did, Mr Dunne, because you carry yourself well yet. You mustn't mind Mr Smith. He's younger than yourself and one of his brothers was shot in the twenties, so he tells me.

Thomas   The DMP was never armed, not like the Royal Irish Constabulary. The RIC could go to war. That's why we were taken off the streets during that rebellion at Easter time, that they make so much of now. We were mostly country men, and Catholics to boot, and we loved our King and we loved our country. They never put those Black and Tans among us, because we were a force that belonged to Dublin and her streets. We did our best and followed our orders. Go out to Mount Jerome some day, in the city of Dublin, and see the old monument to the DMP men killed in the line of duty. Just ordinary country men keen to do well. And when the new government came in, they treated us badly. Our pensions were in disarray. Some said we had been traitors to Ireland. Though we sat in Dublin Castle all through twenty-two and tried to protect the city while the

whole world was at each other's throats. While the most
dreadful and heinous murders took place in the fields of
Ireland. With nothing but our batons and our pride. Maybe
we weren't much. You're thinking, of course he would speak
well for his crowd. Yes, I'll speak well for them. We were
part of a vanished world, and I don't know what's been put
in our place. I'd like to see them clear Sackville Street of an
illegal gathering without breaking a few heads. There was a
proclamation posted the week before that meeting. It was my
proper duty to clear the thoroughfare. There was no one
killed that day that I know of, there were scores of my men
in Jervis Street and the like, with head wounds. I'm sorry
Smith's brother was killed. I'm sorry for all the poor souls
killed these last years. Let them come and kill me if they
wish. But I know my own story of what happened, and I am
content with it.

Mrs O'Dea   Mercy, Mr Dunne, I didn't mean to prompt a
declaration. You're all in a sweat, man. The sooner you have
a new suit, the better.

Thomas   But I tell you, there's other things I regret, and I
regret them sorely, things of my own doing, and damn
history.

Mrs O'Dea   We all have our regrets, man dear. Do calm
yourself.

Thomas   I regret that day with my daughter Annie and the
sword, when we were home and snug in Kiltegan at last.

Mrs O'Dea   There, there, man dear. We'll see if we can't
keep the next suit on you, when you go a-walking in the
lunatics' meadow, as you call it. It's just the exercise field,
you know, the walking meadow. It will have plenty of yellow
in it.

Thomas (*differently, head down*)   I suppose it is very sad
about Patrick O'Brien. I suppose.

Mrs O'Dea   I have all your measurements now, Mr Dunne.
And a fine big-boned gentleman you are. (*Looking at his bare
feet.*) What became of your shoes, but?

Mrs O'Dea *and* **Thomas** (*after a moment, as one*)   Patrick O'Brien!

Mrs O'Dea   Maybe there's a pair of decent shoes about in the cupboards, that someone has left.

Thomas   Coffin shoes, you mean, I expect. Oh, I don't mind a dead man's shoes. And a nice suit, yes, that I can wear in my own coffin, to match, with yellow thread.

Mrs O'Dea   Not yet, Mr Dunne, not by a long chalk. (*Going out.*) I'll do my best for you. (*Locking the door.*)

Thomas (*alone, in an old summer light*) When the rain of autumn started that year, my mother and me went down into the valley by the green road. Myself trotting beside her in my boyish joy. We passed the witch's farm, where the witch crossed the fields in her dirty dress to milk her bloodied cow, that gave her bloodied milk, a thing to fear because she used the same well as ourselves, and washed her bucket there before drawing water. My father was the steward of Humewood and she should have feared to hurt our well, but you cannot withstand the mad. Well, we passed the nodding bell-flowers that I delighted to burst, and ventured out on to the Baltinglass road, to beg a perch for our bums on a cart. (*Sitting up on the bedstead.*) For my father would not let my mother take the pony and trap, because he said the high lamps made too great a show of pride, and we were proud people enough without having to show it. Not that he didn't drive the trap himself when he needed. But we were soon in the old metropolis of Baltinglass, a place of size and wonder to a boy. (*Pulling out his ragged socks from under the mattress.*) There we purchased a pair of lace-up boots. A pair of lace-up boots which banished bare feet, which I was soon able to lace and tighten for myself of a morning, when the air in the bedroom was chill as a well, and the icy cock crowed in the frosty yard, and Thomas Dunne was young and mightily shod. (*Looking down at his feet.*) And Dolly my daughter later polished my policeman's boots, and Annie and Maud brought me my clothes brushed and starched in the mornings, as the castle of soldiers and constables woke.

When my poor wife was dead those many years, and Little
Ship Street stirred with the milkman's cart. And the sun
herself brought gold to the river's back. (*He looks at the locked
door.*) If they lock that door how can my daughters come to
rescue me? (*He holds out a hand and takes it with his other hand,
and shakes.*) How do you do? How do you do? (*Very pleased.*)
How do you do? (*Holds out his arms, embraces someone.*) How do
you do? (*Gently.*) How do you do? Oh, how do you do?

Music. After a little, **Smith** *enters with a cracked bowl with a steam
of stew off it. He hands* **Thomas** *a big spoon which* **Thomas** *holds
obediently.*

Smith   You look just like an old saint there, Mr Dunne, an
old saint there, with your spoon. You may think me a rough
sort of man but I know my saints. I seen a picture of St
Jerome with a spoon like that and a bowl like that. (**Thomas**
sits to eat.) Eat away, man. You should see the cauldron of
that stuff the cooks have made. The kitchens are in a fog.
Seven lambs went into it, they say. Isn't it good stuff?
(*Friendly.*) What's it your name is again, your first name? I've
so many to remember.

Thomas   Thomas. They named me Thomas long ago for
my great-great-grandfather the first steward of Humewood,
the big place in Kiltegan, the main concern. Though all his
own days they called him White Meg on account of his fierce
white beard. He'd stride up the old street from his house to
the great gates and say nothing to no one. White Meg. But
Thomas it was, was his name.

Smith   With your spoon. St Thomas! When I brought Mrs
O'Dea her cocoa in at five, she had you all cut out and hung
up on a hook with the other inhabitants, and the breeze was
blowing you softly from the crack in the pane. She's a keen
seamstress. St Thomas. Do you like the stew?

Thomas (*expansively*)   Of all the dishes in the world I may
say I relish mostly a stew.

Smith   You, St Thomas, that knew kings and broke Larkin.
Stew.

Thomas (*alerted*)   Put a piece of lamb in it at the bottom, for the men that are working, and let the child eat off the top of it. The child's spoon is a shallow spoon. Parsnips. The secret of stew on our hillside was just a scrape of crab apple in it – just a scrape. But then we'd fierce crab apples. And not to curse while it was cooking. And not to spit while it was cooling.

Smith   What was the name of the patriot was killed years past in Thomas Street outside the church of St Thomas, in the city of Dublin?

Thomas (*thinking, innocently*)   Thomas Street wasn't in my division. But Emmet, was it, you mean? Robert Emmet?

Smith   That's the one. They hung him there and the people cried out against the soldiers and the peelers, and after they dragged his body over the parade ground till it was bleeding and broken in its bones, and then they got a loyal butcher to cut him into four pieces. He was dead then.

Thomas   I should think.

Smith   That's what they did to him, those official men, and a fine Protestant gentleman at that.

Thomas (*pleasantly*)   It's as well to throw a bit of rosemary across it too, if you have rosemary. Rosemary smells good when the land gets hot. Across the stew. Rosemary. Thyme would do either, if you've none. When you put in the spuds. Or lavender maybe. Did you ever try clover? A child will eat clover when he is set down on the meadow to sit. The bee's favourite. A cow makes fine milk from a field of clover. So put in rosemary, if you have it. Ah, fresh spuds, turned out of the blessed earth like – for all the world like newborn pups. (*Laughing.*)

Smith   I suppose you held the day of Emmet's death as a festive day. A victory day. I suppose you did. I suppose you were all very queer indeed up there in the Castle. I'm thinking too of the days when they used to put the pitch caps on the priests when they catched them, like they were only dogs, and behind the thick walls of the city hall all the English fellas would be laughing at the screams of the priests, while their brains boiled. I'm thinking of all that. I suppose you never put a pitch cap on anyone. They weren't in fashion in your time. A pity. It must have been a great sight, all the same.

Thomas (*eating rapidly*)   Good stew, good stew. Wicklow lambs.

Smith (*looking at him*)   St Thomas, isn't it?

Thomas (*smiling*)   St Thomas.

Smith *goes off with the empty bowl.*

I loved her for as long as she lived, I loved her as much as I loved Cissy my wife, and maybe more, or differently. When she died it was difficult to go from her to the men that came after her, Edward and George, they were good men but it was not the same. When I was a young recruit it used to frighten me how much I loved her. Because she had built everything up and made it strong, and made it shipshape. The great world that she owned was shipshape as a ship. All the harbours of the earth were trim with their granite piers, the ships were shining and strong. The trains went sleekly through the fields, and her mark was everywhere, Ireland, Africa, the Canadas, every blessed place. And men like me were there to make everything peaceable, to keep order in her kingdoms. She was our pride. Among her emblems was the gold harp, the same harp we wore on our helmets. We were secure, as if for eternity the orderly milk-drays would come up the streets in the morning, and her influence would reach everywhere, like the salt sea pouring up into the fresh waters of the Liffey. Ireland was hers for eternity, order was everywhere, if we could but honour her example. She loved her Prince. I loved my wife. The world was a wedding of loyalty, of steward to Queen, she was the very flower and perfecter of Christendom. Even as the simple man I was I could love her fiercely. Victoria.

The **Recruit**, *a young man of eighteen or so comes on. He has obviously made a great effort to smarten himself for this meeting. He is tall and broad, and stoops a little as he takes off his hat.*

Good morning, son. How are you?

Recruit   Oh, most pleasant, sir, most pleasant.

Thomas   You had a good journey up from your home place?

Recruit   It didn't take a feather out of me, sir.

Thomas   Good man. What age are you?

Recruit   Eighteen, sir, this November past.

Thomas   Height?

Recruit   Six foot three, sir, in my winter socks.

Thomas   Well, you look a very fine man indeed. You were never in trouble yourself, son?

Recruit   Oh, no, sir.

Thomas   And did you serve in the Great War? I don't suppose you could have.

Recruit   No, sir. I was too young.

Thomas   Of course. A soldier doesn't always make a good policeman. There's too much – sorrow – in a soldier. You're a drinking man?

Recruit   I'll drink a glass of porter, with my father.

Thomas   Very good. I've read your father's letter. And I want to tell you, we are going to give you a go at it. I have a big book in my office within, bound in gold, that has the name of every DMP man that has ever served the crown. Do you wish for your own name to be added in due course?

Recruit   Oh – indeed and I do, sir. Most fervently.

Thomas   I hope you will do well, son. These are troubled times, and men like yourself are sorely needed. I will be watching your progress – watching, you understand, in a fatherly way. Do your best.

Recruit   I will, sir. Thank you, sir!

Thomas (*taking his hand*)   I was a young recruit myself once. I know what this means to you.

Recruit   The world, sir, it means the world.

Thomas   Good man. I'll write to your father in Longford. Take this now as a token of our good faith. (*Handing him the spoon.*)

Recruit   Thank you, sir, thank you.

The **Recruit** *shadows away.* **Thomas** *kneels at the end of his bed and grips the metal tightly.*

Thomas   I must not speak to shadows. When you see the shadows, Thomas, you must not speak. Sleep in the afternoon, that's the ticket. How did I get myself into this pickle, is it age just? I know I did what Annie said I did, but was it really me, and not some old disreputable creature that isn't me? When it was over, I knew suddenly in the car coming here what had happened, but at the time, at the time, I knew nothing, or I knew something else. And it was the gap between the two things that caused me to cry out in the car, the pain of it, the pain of it, the fright of it, and no one in the world to look at me again in a manner that would suggest that Thomas Dunne is still human, still himself. Everything is as clear as a glass. I can remember how lovely Cissy was the day we married, and that smile she gave me when the priest was finished, how she looked up at me in front of all our people, her face shining, astonishing me. You don't expect to see love like that. And that's a long time ago. And I can remember, now, the last day with Annie, and how I was feeling that day, and I can see myself there in the kitchen, and I know how mad I was. And I am ashamed. I am ashamed. I am ashamed. (*After a while of breathing like a runner.*) Hail Mary, full of Grace, the Lord is with thee, blessed art Thou amongst women, and blessed is the fruit of thy womb. (*He gets stuck, bangs his head with his right palm.*) – Jesus. Holy Mary, mother of. Holy Mary, mother of. I remember, I do remember. Hail Mary full of grace the Lord is with me blessed art Thou amongst women and blessed is the fruit of Thy womb Jesus holy Mary Mother of . . . of . . . of God! Of God! (*Climbs into bed.*) Robert Emmet. (*Pulls the sheet over his face.*) Robert Emmet. (*Spits the t's so the sheet blows up from his lips.*) Rober*t* Emme*t*. (*After a moment.*) Sleep, sleep, that's the ticket.

His son, **Willie**, *neat and round, comes in and sits on the end of his bed and sings to him Schubert's* Ave Maria. *At the end,* **Thomas** *looks over the sheet.* **Willie** *wears his army uniform.*

Hello, child. Are you warm?

Willie   It's cold in the mud, Father.

Thomas   I know child. I'm so sorry.

Sunlight grows slowly over the scene, banishing **Willie**. *The imagined stir and calling of the Castle below.* **Thomas** *is at ease suddenly. His middle daughter,* **Annie**, *in a light cotton dress of the early twenties, a bow in her spine, carries on a white shirt, which illumines like a lantern when she crosses the windowlight. There's an old music.*

Annie   Now, Papa – there's the best-ironed shirt in Christendom.

Thomas   Thank you, dear.

Annie   It took the best part of an hour to heat the hearth, to heat the iron. There's enough starch in the breast to bolster Jericho.

Thomas   Thank you, dear.

Annie   If Dolly had ironed it, you'd look at it more intently.

Thomas   I am looking at it, Annie. Or I would, if it weren't so blinding white.

Annie   And it isn't that white, Papa. And you've things on your mind today, I know. A black day.

Thomas   I expect it is.

Annie Why Collins of all people to give the Castle to? Couldn't they find a gentleman?

Thomas He is the head of the new government, Annie.

Annie Government! We know what sort of men they are. Coming in here to the likes of you. Whose son gave his life for Ireland.

Thomas (*coming over to her, kindly*) Will gave his life to save Europe, Annie, which isn't the same thing.

Annie I miss Willie, Papa. I miss him. We need him today.

Thomas I blame myself. There was no need for him to go off, except, he hadn't the height to be a policeman. The army were glad to take him. I blame myself.

Annie Will was proud, Papa, proud to be in the Rifles. It was his life.

Thomas It was the death of him. You cannot lose a son without blaming yourself. But that's all history now. Annie.

Maud, *his eldest, a very plain woman with black hair, dressed heavily for the bright day, carries on his dress uniform, struggling to balance the ceremonial sword.*

Let me help you.

Maud It's all right, Papa, I'll plonk it on the bed.

Thomas Where's Dolly?

Maud Polishing the boots. I hate to see a woman spit. Lord, Lord, she's a spitter, when it's Papa's old shoes. And she was away out this morning, I know not why, all secretive.

Annie Away out this morning? She didn't touch her bed all night. Up at that dance at the Rotunda. She should be whipped.

Maud And did you say she could go to that dance?

Annie I didn't say she could take all night to walk home.

Thomas   Thoughtful daughters you are, to be helping me so. How did you get the creases so firm?

Maud   I slept on them. In as much as I slept. I cannot sleep these times.

Thomas   I could meet the emperor of the world with those creases.

Annie   You'll have to make do with Michael Collins.

Maud   Oh, don't start that old story, Annie. We've had enough of it now, God knows.

Annie   I was only saying.

Maud   Well, don't be only saying. Go and stir the teapot, can't you, and give over the politics.

Annie   I was only saying.

Maud   You're only always only saying, and you have me stark wide-eyed in the bed all night, worrying and turning and fretting, and a great headache pounding away, because you can leave nothing alone, Annie, till you have us all miserable and mad with concern.

Thomas   Now, girls, think of your mother. Would she want you to be talking like this?

Maud   No, Papa, of course not. She would not.

Annie   Mam? What do you know about Mam, if I may ask?

Maud   Don't I see her often when I sleep? Don't I see her blue polka-dot dress, yes, and her bending down to me and making me laugh?

Annie   That's only ould stuff Willie told us.

Maud   Oh, Annie, Annie, I was four years old, you were only two!

Thomas   Daughters, daughters – what a terrible thing to be arguing about!

Annie   Oh, a thing indeed.

Maud (*after a little*)   I'm sorry, Annie.

Annie   That's all right, girl. It's not your fault Collins is a criminal.

Maud   I'll be dead, that's it! I'll be dead by day's end. I can't take everything in! My head's bursting with Papa and Michael Collins and I don't know what . . .

Dolly, *holding out the polished boots carefully from her dress, starts across to* **Thomas**, *smiling.* **Thomas***'s face lights like a lamp.*

Thomas   Oh, Dolly, Dolly, Dolly!

Before she reaches him, an intrusion of darkness, the scattering of his daughters. **Thomas** *roars, with pain and confusion. He lifts his arms and roars. He beats the bed. He hits the table. He roars.* **Smith** *unlocks the door and hurries in, brandishing a pacifier. It looks like a baton.*

Smith   What the hell is all the shouting? You have the pauper lunatics in a swelter! Crying and banging their heads, and laughing like fairground mechanicals, and spitting, and cutting themselves with items. (*Looking back out.*) Mrs O'Dea, Mrs O'Dea – try and sort those screamers!

Mrs O'Dea (*off*)   I will, I will!

Smith   Even the long ward of old dames with their dead brains, have some of them opened their eyes and are weeping to be woken, with your bloody shouting. Do you want to go in with them, old man? After I beat you!

Thomas (*hurrying back into his bed*)   I only shouted the one time. It must have been the moon woke them. (*Drawing the sheet high.*) My daughter Annie gives you the shillings for the room, Black Jim.

Smith   She can give all the shillings she likes. She won't know where we throw you.

Thomas Don't put Thomas with the poor dribblers. I've seen them. I've seen that terrible long ward of women, belonging to no one at all, no one to pay shillings for them. Don't put me there.

Smith Then show me silence. (*Striking the end of the bed.*)

Thomas Don't strike there. My son sits there.

Smith You are a violent, stupid man, Mr Dunne, and I want silence out of you!

Thomas (*a finger to his lips*) Silence.

Smith *goes, banging the door, locking it harshly.*

(*Pulling up the sheet.*) Robert Emmet.

Annie *has slipped over to his bed.*

Annie Papa.

Thomas (*looking out again*) I must be silent, child.

Annie Papa, please will you tell me.

Thomas What, child?

Annie Why is my back bowed, Papa?

Thomas Why, child, because of your polio.

Annie Why, Papa?

Thomas I don't know, Annie. Because it afflicts some and leaves others clear. I don't know.

Annie Will I ever have a husband, Papa?

Thomas I do hope so.

Annie I think a woman with such a back will not find a husband.

Thomas She might.

Annie I see the prams going by in Stephen's Green, glistening big prams, and I look in when the nannies are polite, and I look in, and I see the babies, with their round

faces, and their smells of milk and clean linen, and their
heat, and Papa –

Thomas   Yes, child?

Annie   They all look like my babies.

Annie *goes,* **Thomas** *looks after her, then covers his face again. A
country music. He sleeps, he sleeps. The moon, the emblem of lunacy,
appears overhead, pauses there faintly, fades again. It is a very
delicate, strange sleep. The calling of a cock distantly, birdsong, the
cock louder. An arm of sunlight creeps into the room and across*
Thomas*'s covered face. His hand creeps out and his fingers wave in
the light. He pulls down the sheet and the noises cease. He listens.
Imitates the cock softly.*

Thomas   The cock crows in the morning yard, banishing all
night fears. No person, that has not woken to the crowing of
a familiar cock, can know how tender that cry is evermore,
stirring the child out into the fresh fingers of sunlight, into
the ever-widening armfuls of sunlight. How stray the child
looks in the yard, bare feet on the old pack-stones in the clay,
all his people have come out in their own vanished times, as
small as him, surrounded by the quiet byres just wakening
now, the noses of the calves wet in the closed dark, the sitting
hens in the coop anxious to be released, out away from the
night fear of foxes, so they may lay their eggs beyond finding
in the hayshed and the hawthorn bushes. Only the boy
knows their terrible tricks. He inserts an arm into the known
places and feels the warm eggs, smells them happily in his
brown palms, and searches out the newest places of the hens
in the deepest bowers of the straw. He carries them back in
to his Ma Ma, folded in his gansey, with the glow of pride
about him as big as the sun. Then he goes back out into the
yard while the eggs are boiling, or put aside carefully for the
cake, and tries to read the story of the day in the huge pages
of the clouds. And he sees the milking cow driven up on to
the top field where the summer grass is rich and moist, and
how well he knows the wild garden there of meadowsweet,
where the dragonfly is hard as pencil. And the boy's Ma Ma

is calling him, and he goes, and there is no greater morning, no morning in his life of greater importance.

Smith *enters with a newspaper. He fetches out* **Thomas**'*s po. It's empty.*

Smith I hope you're not blocking up like some of the old fellows.

Thomas A deserted house needs no gutter. Is that my newspaper?

Smith It is. (*Throws it to him.* **Thomas** *opens it.*) Can you not order a decent newspaper?

Thomas *Irish Times* suits me.

Smith It's all fools on horseback.

Thomas Not so much. I'm trying to keep up on the activities, if I may call them that, of a certain Hinky Dink Kenna, who runs the first ward in Chicago. I tell you, you'd have to call him a criminal here. Himself and Bath-house John Coughlan. Villains. If they had never left Ireland, I'd have had to lock them up in Mountjoy. But you can do what you like in America, or so it seems.

Smith Is that right? And what do they get up to, those two?

Thomas Oh, they're in the liquor trade, you might say. It makes powerful reading.

Mrs O'Dea *comes in with big flaps of black cloth –* **Thomas**'*s suit in its unsewn parts.*

Smith He hasn't washed himself.

Mrs O'Dea Didn't you wash him yesterday? Do you want to rub him out? Come on up, Mr Dunne, and let me pin these to you for a look at it.

Smith Can't you see he's reading.

Thomas (*getting out of bed*) Oh, I've time for reading. In my retirement.

He stands for the fitting. **Mrs O'Dea** *begins to pin the sections of the suit to his long johns.*

Mrs O'Dea   You're the cleanest man in Baltinglass.

Thomas *seems agitated, looking down at the sections.*

What's the matter, Mr Dunne?

Thomas   That's just the old black stuff.

Mrs O'Dea   And what if it is?

Thomas (*so* **Smith** *won't hear*)   Didn't we discuss yellow?

Mrs O'Dea   Yellow thread, Mr Dunne. I can only stitch the sections together with yellow. The trustees buy us in the black cloth from Antrim.

Thomas   But it's fierce, foul stuff, isn't it?

Smith   I'll leave you to it, Mrs O'Dea. I'll be over in the Monkey Ward, sluicing them out, if you need me. Be good, Mr Dunne. (*Goes.*)

Mrs O'Dea (*taking a bobbin from her apron*)   Look it, isn't that the bee's knees? That's from my own sewing box, that Mr O'Dea gave me in the old days. I can't do fairer than that.

Thomas   Oh, it's very sunny.

Mrs O'Dea   Now. (*Pinning again.*) It'll do beautifully. Can't your daughter bring you in clothes, if you don't like mine?

Thomas   I wouldn't go bothering her. All my daughters are good, considerate women. We looked after each other, in that fled time, when their mother was dead.

Mrs O'Dea   I'm sorry, Mr Dunne. And how did she die?

Thomas   They never failed their father, their Papa, in that fled time. You should have seen them when they were little. Three little terrors going round with the knicks to their knees.

Mrs O'Dea (*pricking him by mistake*)   Oh, sorry. And where are your other daughters, Mr Dunne, these days?

Thomas We stood under the hawthorn, while the bees broke their hearts at the bell-flowers, because the fringes of darkness had closed them.

Mrs O'Dea Who did, Mr Dunne?

Thomas My wife Cissy and myself. Cecilia. In courting days. Old courting days.

Mrs O'Dea And what did she die of, did you say? (*Pricking.*)

Thomas Nothing at all. Her farm was Lathaleer, her father's farm. The most beautiful piece of land. He was woodsman and keeper at Humewood, but he was a most dexterous farmer. The Cullens of Lathaleer. What a match she was for me! A strong, straight-backed, sensible person that loved old steps and tunes. She'd rather learn a new step than boil turnips, old Cullen said to me – but it wasn't so. What does a father know? King Edward himself praised her hair, when we were presented in nineteen-three. A thorough mole-black devious hair she had.

Mrs O'Dea I'm sure. And didn't you do well by her, rising so high, and everything?

Thomas Our happiest days were when I was only an inspector in Dalkey village. We lived there in a house called Polly Villa. There was precious little villainy in Dalkey. Three girls she bore there, three girls. And the boy already, before we came.

Mrs O'Dea You have a son too? You have a lot.

Thomas No. No, he didn't come back from France that time. He wrote me a lovely letter.

Mrs O'Dea (*after a little*) And King Edward praised your wife's hair. Fancy.

Thomas Aye – All the ladies loved him. Of course, he was old in that time. But a true king.

Mrs O'Dea (*finished with the fitting, unpinning him again*)   What would you say about King De Valera?

Thomas   I would say very little about him, in that I wouldn't know much to say. Of course, I see a bit about him in the papers.

Mrs O'Dea   As much a foreigner as the King of England ever was, Mr O'Dea used to say, when he was overground. Mr O'Dea was a pundit, I'm afraid.

Thomas   He wants to buy the Irish ports back from Mr Churchill. I think that's a great pity. A man that loves his King might still have gone to live in Crosshaven or Cobh, and called himself loyal and true. But soon there'll be nowhere in Ireland where such hearts may rest.

Mrs O'Dea   You're as well to keep up with the news, Mr Dunne.

Thomas   I had an admiration for the other man though, the general that was shot, I forget his name.

Mrs O'Dea (*ready to go*)   Who was that?

Thomas   I forget. I remember the shock of sorrow when he was killed. I remember Annie and me crying in the old parlour of our quarters in the Castle. A curiosity. I met him, you see, the one time. He was very courteous and praised Wicklow and said a few things to me that rather eased my heart, at the time. But they shot him.

Mrs O'Dea (*going*)   They shot a lot of people. Was it Collins?

Thomas   I don't know, I forget. I remember the sorrow but not the name. Maybe that was the name.

Mrs O'Dea   I may have left a few pins in you, Mr Dunne, so don't go dancing about unduly.

Thomas   Dancing? I never danced in my life. I was a tree at a dance.

Mrs O'Dea *goes off.* **Thomas** *discovers a pin and holds it up.*

Where are your other daughters, Mr Dunne, these days? (*After a little, moving the pin about like a tiny sword.*) The barracks of Ireland filled with new faces. And all the proud regiments gone, the Dublin Rifles and the Dublin Fusiliers. All the lovely uniforms. All the long traditions, broken up and flung out, like so many morning eggs on to the dung heap. Where are your other daughters, Mr Dunne, these days? Dolly of the hats. Annie told me the name of the place. Somewhere in America. What was the name?

The light of their parlour in the Castle. **Annie** *comes on with a big bundle of socks to sort. She sits on the three-legged stool. The socks are all the same. She looks in the socks for holes by thrusting her right hand into each of them, sorts the good from the bad.*

Annie   There's a terrible queer sort of a quietness settled over this Castle. How Papa expects to hang on here now till September. The city will be rubble, rubble by September.

Maud *follows on looking pale and alarmed.*

Maud   Have you seen that Dolly?

Annie   No.

Maud   I can't keep a hoult on her at all these days.

Annie   She'll be down the town, as usual.

Maud   How can she go shopping in times like these?

Annie   What's civil unrest to Dolly and her shopping?

Maud (*feeling the back of her head*)   Oh, dear.

Annie   What is it, Maud?

Maud   Nothing, nothing at all.

Annie   Maud, what is it now?

Maud   I have an ache here, Annie, at the base of the skull, do you think it might be something deadly?

Annie   I never knew a one to worry like you do, girl.

Maud   Do you want to feel it? Is there a lump?

Annie   Don't come near me with your head! It's nothing.
It's called a headache. Any normal person would accept that
it's a headache. Girl, sometimes I don't wonder if you
mightn't be seriously astray in your wits, girl.

Maud   Oh, don't say that, Annie.

Annie   Am I not allowed sort the darning in peace?

Dolly *comes in to them, wearing a neat outfit. She looks subdued.*

What's happened you, Dolly?

Maud   I was all over the yards looking for you, Dolly,
where on earth do you get to, these days?

Dolly   I was down at the North Wall with the Galligan
sisters.

Maud   At the North Wall?

Annie   What were you doing there, Dolly?

Dolly   Mary Galligan was going out with one of the
Tommies, and he and his troop were heading off home
today, so we went down to see them off.

Annie (*sorting away*)   Well, well, I don't know, Dolly, if you
aren't the biggest fool in Christendom.

Dolly   No, I'm no fool. They were nice lads. There was a
good crowd down there, and the Tommies were in high
spirits, singing and so on. It was very joyful.

Maud   You've to keep your skirts long these times, Dolly.
You're not to be seen waving to soldiers.

Dolly   They're going from Ireland and they'll never be
back, why shouldn't we say goodbye? Do you know every
barracks in Ireland has lost its officers and men? Regiments
that protected us in the war, who went out and left
thousands behind in France. Willie's own regiment is to be
disbanded, and that's almost entirely Dublin lads.

Annie   Dolly, why are you so surprised? Haven't we known
for the last six months that Ireland is to be destroyed? I

don't know why it's such news to you. Haven't you listened?
Haven't you seen your father's face? Haven't you felt for him,
Dolly?

Dolly It's different when you see it.

Annie You're a fool, Dolly.

Dolly I'm no fool.

Annie *picks up in one hand the good socks and in the other the ones
needing mending – they look like two woolly hands themselves.*

And I'll tell you. Coming home in the tram, up the docks
road, Mary Galligan was crying, and we were talking kindly
to her, and trying to comfort her, and I don't know what we
said exactly, but this woman, a middle-aged woman, quite
well-to-do, she rises up and stands beside us like a long
streak of misery, staring at us. And she struck Mary Galligan
on the cheek, so as she left the marks of her hand there. And
she would have attacked me too, but that the conductor
came down and spoke to the woman. And she said we were
Jezebels and should have our heads shaved and be whipped,
for following the Tommies. And the conductor looked at her,
and hadn't he served in France himself, as one of the
Volunteers, oh, it was painful, the way she looked back at
him, as if he were a viper, or a traitor. The depth of
foolishness in her. A man that had risked himself, like Willie,
but that had reached home at last.

Dolly *crying.* **Annie** *gets up and puts her arms around her, still
holding the socks.*

Annie Things will sort themselves out, Dolly dear.

Dolly If she had shot us it wouldn't have been so bad.

Annie Things will sort themselves out.

Maud *feeling the back of her head again, confused.*

We'll put on our aprons and get the tea. We'll go on
ourselves as if we were living in paradise. (*The three go out.*)

Thomas Their father's face. Their father's face.

He puts his hands over his face. **Matt**, *a youngish man in a hat, his shirt sleeves held by metal circlets, sets up his easel centrestage. Sunlight gathers about him, clearing the sense of* **Thomas**'s *room. Rooks. A suggestion of meadow grass.* **Matt** *holds a square of cut-out cardboard to the view, deciding on a composition. He wipes at his face.*

Matt   Midges! The artist's bane!

Thomas *approaches him, a little wildly.*

Thomas   Patrick O'Brien, Patrick O'Brien, wherever did you bury my suit, man dear? They are tormenting me with dark cloth, and I hope you will give it back to me, despite your great prowess and fame, as a bulleter.

Matt   It isn't who you think, Thomas. It is Matt Kirwin that married your daughter Maud.

Thomas (*astonished*)   Oh – is it? (*After a moment.*) You have a strong look of Patrick about you. Except I see now, you are not on all fours, as I would expect. Are you a hero too?

Matt (*kindly*)   How are you getting on, Thomas?

Thomas   How does it come that you are here in the walking meadow? I only ask, as I am used to seeing people hither and thither and yon. (*Feeling his arms for solidity.*) Have you lost your wits also?

Matt   Maybe so, but I have brought Annie over in the Ford. We're over there in Kiltegan for a week or two with the little boys. I thought I might capture a water-colour while I waited.

Thomas   You might, like a man might capture a butterfly. You haven't started your capturing.

Matt   In a minute, when I decide the view I want. The painting itself will only take a moment.

Thomas   They're all choice views. Where's Maud then?

Matt   She stayed in Dublin this time.

Thomas   It isn't the melancholy?

Matt I don't know what it is. She has certainly kept to her bed of recent months. Has she been right since the second boy came? I don't know.

Thomas Her mother was always very jolly. I don't know where she gets it from.

Matt The sea air of Howth will cure all that, in time, the sea air, the quieter nature of life there in Howth, and the boys. She does love to see the boys, and they are most dignified and splendid boys.

Thomas You say? (*Warmly.*) Well, Matt (*taking* **Matt**'s *hand*), how are you? (*Oddly.*) How do you do?

Matt We're going along fine. I'm teaching in the technical school in Irishtown – for my sins. And painting for myself when I can. I have done a great deal of work on the Great South Wall, in my lunchtimes. The Poolbeg Lighthouse? But we couldn't get by at all without Annie. She keeps everything going.

Thomas Yes, yes, she told me you had one of your drawings printed up in a book, didn't you, yes, of the Bailey Lighthouse I think she said. You will be a great expert soon on lighthouses.

Matt (*pleased*) It was little enough.

Thomas Ah, Matthew, it is good to see you. You're looking so well. I forget, you know, I forget how much I like you. And the boys, the two grand boys, will I see them today? Are they in the Ford?

Matt No, Thomas. They're so little still, and this is such a strange spot, for children, and, you know, they were a bit upset the last time. The elder boy has read his *Oliver Twist* and you were all mixed up in his mind with Fagan. Do you remember, at the end of the book, when the child is brought in to see Fagan before Fagan is hanged?

Thomas Hanged? No.

Matt Maud was worried that . . .

Thomas   Certainly, certainly. You must excuse my long johns. I lost my suit only recently. As a matter of fact, it must be buried around here somewhere. Well, no matter, they'll make me another, and then maybe you will bring my grandsons again to see me? Or you could fetch me over to Kiltegan in the Ford if they were afraid of this place. I'd be very quiet for you in the Ford.

Matt   Of course, Thomas.

Thomas   I know I look a sight. And that won't do for such fine boys. I only saw them those few times, but, I think it is the smell of children that gets in upon you. You long for it then. And the roundness of them, and the love they show you. It could be anywhere about here, my suit. But I'm having a touch of gold put into the new one – well, yellow, anyhow.

Matt   You'll find Annie in your room if you go up, I'll be bound. She thought you were inside, you know.

Thomas   Yellow thread, you know?

Matt   All right.

Thomas   Matt, I don't like to ask Annie, to bother her, but do you think there's any great likelihood of my getting away from here at all in the coming times?

Matt   I don't know rightly, Thomas.

Thomas   Of course, of course. It is quite a pleasant station. You see all the country air we have. Not like the city. The city would ruin a man's health. Though it has its beauties. Do you know, I used at one time to be a policeman? Do you know I used at one time be Chief Superintendent of B Division? With responsibility for the Castle herself? It was I cleared all the vermin out of Yorke Street, that time, the fancy men from the Curragh and all their girls – it *was* me, wasn't it, Matt? I held that post? You must bring the boys to Kiltegan as often as you can.

Matt Well, we do, Thomas. You have a fine vista here,
look. (*Having him look into the cardboard framer.*) You do, what
with those oaks, and the field of wheat beyond.

Thomas (*peering, after a moment*)   It's only grass just.

Matt Oh, is it grass?

Thomas Paint away, Matthew.

Matt Thank you.

The light of **Thomas**'s *room again finds* **Annie**, *more spinsterish
now, strong, bony, simply dressed, with her handbag and a brown
paper bag. She looks anxious.* **Thomas** *goes to her with a great
smile, raising his arms.*

Thomas (*searching in his mind for her name*)   Dolly – Maud –
Annie!

Annie Papa.

Thomas (*his arms collapsing slowly*)   What has happened to
you, Annie? You look very different to how you were just this
morning.

Annie What happened to your clothes, Papa?

Thomas I don't know, Dolly.

Annie Annie, it is.

Thomas Annie. I don't know. I think I heard there was a
bit of thievery going on, but I don't think there's any truth in
it. Nothing for the magistrate. I'll deal with it. You know Mr
Collins is to take over the Castle in January. I'll need all my
clothes done over like new.

Annie No, Papa. That was all years ago. In bygone times.
You are in Baltinglass County Home, Papa.

Thomas I know. And I tell myself, so I won't forget. I had
it written down somewhere, but I lost the bit of paper. What
is it about the old head? Give me the name of any street in
Dublin and I'll name every lane, alleyway, road, terrace and

street around it. I could knit you the whole thing with
names, and if you forgot a few places, and found a hole there
in your memory, I could darn it for you. I am in effect a sort
of Dublin Street Directory. But when it comes to the brass
tacks of things, everyday matters, as, for instance, where in
the name of God I am, well, daughter dear, I'm not so quick
then. But look, girl, what Annie gave me. (*Going to his mattress
and fetching a book out.*) A wonderful strange story about a boy
on the Mississippi. And his friend. They are lost in a cave
together, the two boys, and the poor bit of a greasy candle
they have is burning lower and lower, and the demons of the
dark are surely approaching . . . I feel I know that cave. Do
you see, Dolly? I can see it when I put my hands over my
face. Like this. Yes, there she is, the mighty Mississippi,
going along like Godly pewter. And those poor boys,
Huckleberry and Tom, and the yellow walls of the cave, and
the big drips of water. Oh, Dolly, and the old granite bathing
place at Vico Rock. And there's the terrible suck-up of water
when Davy Barnes the newspaper vendor takes his dive, the
fattest man in Ireland, and there's Annie, all decked out in
her first communion regalia like a princess, oh, mercy, and
there's the moon over a bay that reputable people have
compared to Naples – Sorrento, Vico, beautiful Italian
names living the life of Reilly in old Killiney and Dalkey. On
a summer's night, you were born, Dolly, deep in the fresh
dark, just when the need for candles failed. Oh, Dolly.

Annie (*trying to calm him*)   I gave you the book about the
Mississippi, Papa. It's a book you loved in your youth, so
you always said.

Thomas (*gripping her arm a bit roughly*)   Where is Maud,
where is she, that she doesn't come in to me?

Annie   She's taken refuge, taken refuge you might say, in
her own difficulties.

Thomas   Is that right? And Dolly, where is Dolly?

Annie   Gone out into the wide world, Papa. Would you
blame her?

Thomas Blame her? (*Formal again.*) How do you do? How is Maud? How are the boys? No, no, I know all that. Don't tell me. I won't waste your time, never you fear. How are you? That's the important thing to establish. That's how people go on among themselves, family people. Is there any word from Dolly in America? Annie, Annie, where is she in America?

Annie Ohio, Papa?

Thomas Ohio, Ohio! That's the place. Ah, I was tormented trying to think of the word. Ohio. Dolly in Ohio. I must write it down. Do you have a dragonfly – a pencil?

Annie No, Papa, I don't. This room is so bare and dark, for all the shillings I give them. I hope they give you your paper. It's all I can manage, Papa, out of your pension. It is a very miserly pension. Matt makes up the rest of it for us. And he has a pittance.

Thomas Don't I have a beautiful pension for my forty-five years of service?

Annie No, Papa, you don't.

Thomas I think I should have.

Annie Look, Papa, what I brought for you. (*She pulls a bunch of heather from the bag.*)

Thomas Oh, Lord, Lord. (*Smelling it in his hands tenderly.*) From the hills above Kiltegan. How the heat of the day makes the heather raise its smell to the grateful native. The peace, the deep peace in the evening as we stared, you and me, into the last lingering flames running across the ashen turf, and the ghostly tiredness in us after slaving about the place all day.

Annie When was that, Papa?

Thomas Those three years in Kiltegan, Annie, when you and me were left to amuse ourselves as we could, Annie. You remember?

Annie   I do, Papa, I remember the three years well enough.
With you sinking lower and lower in your chair beside that
fire, and muttering about this and that, and the way you had
been abandoned, you wouldn't treat a dog like that, you said,
muttering, muttering, till I was driven mad. And all the
work of the dairy and the byre and the hens to do. It was like
living with Hannibal in Abyssinia, when Hannibal was a
leader no more.

Thomas   Who? Where? But didn't the Cullens of Lathaleer
come visiting like royalty in their high trap, and the Dunnes
of Feddin, and the Cullens of Kelsha?

Annie   No, Papa, they did not, not after you drove them
away with insult and passing remarks.

Thomas   I never did. We lived there like, like . . .

Annie   Like, like the dead, Papa.

Thomas (*angry*)   All right. So there were demons in the high
wood, and the screams of the lost from the byres, and the
foul eggs in the rotting hay, and every pitchfork in the barn
was sharp, glinting sharp, for you to thrust into my breast.

Annie   Papa, Papa, calm and ease, calm and ease.

Thomas   Oh, fearsome, fearsome, fearsome. Can I see my
grandsons?

Annie (*holding on to her father*)   Papa, Papa. Your grandsons
are afraid of you.

Thomas   Afraid? Filthy, filthy.

Annie   Papa, Papa. How many miles to Babylon?

Thomas (*smiling*)   Babylon.

Annie   Three score and ten. Remember, Papa, remember?

Thomas   Will I be there by candlelight?

Annie   Sure, and back again.

Thomas Candlelight. Oh, yes, yes. (*Weeping.*) Yes. (*Smiling.*) Yes.

Annie How many times in that last year in Kiltegan did I have to sing you the songs to calm your fears?

Thomas Was it so many?

Annie Many, many, many. Three score and ten, Papa.

Thomas (*after a long breath*) My father was the steward of Humewood, and I was the steward of Christendom. Look at me.

Annie Papa, we've all to grow old.

Thomas (*patting her back with his right hand, like a child*) Oh, yes. Oh, yes.

Annie *goes quietly.* **Thomas** *sits on the stool slowly. The door ajar.*

Candlelight. (*After a little.*) A bit of starch for a new shirt, a bit of spit for my shoes, I could set out for Kiltegan as an ordinary man and see those shining boys. (*After a little.*) No. (*After a little.*) And take them up and smell their hair and kiss their noses and make them do that laughter they have in them. (*After a little.*) No. (*After a little.*) Dear Lord, put the recruits back in their barracks in Fitzgibbon Street, put the stout hearts back into Christendom's Castle, and troop the colours once more for Princess and Prince, for Queen and for King, for Chief Secretary and Lord Lieutenant, for Viceroy and Commander-in-Chief. (*After a little.*) But you cannot. (*After a little.*) Put the song back in the mouth of the beggar, the tune back in the pennywhistle, the rat-tat-tat of the tattoo back in the parade ground, stirring up our hearts. (*After a little.*) But you cannot. (*After a little.*) – Gone. The hearth of Kiltegan. How many miles to Kiltegan, Nineveh and Babylon? The sun amiable in the yard and the moon in the oaks after darkness. The rabbitman stepping out of the woods at dusk with a stick of dangling snags and a dark greeting. – Gone. (*After a little, quietly.*) Candlelight. I walked out through the grounds of Loreto College as far as the sea. The midwife had bade me go. I was a man of fifty.

Rhododendrons. All night she had strained in the bed, she was like a person pinned by a fallen rock, waving her arms and legs and groaning, and shouting. Her shouts escaped from Polly Villa and ran up the road to the station and down the road to the village in darkness. I was becoming distressed myself, so the midwife bade me go. Willie, Maud and Annie had been difficult for her too, because she was small, small and thin and hard-working. Cullen's daughter. And she was like a sort of dancer in the bed, but stuck in the dance. King Edward himself praised her hair, it was mole-black, though there are no moles in Ireland. Out at sea, the lighthouse was hard at work too, warning the mail-packet and the night fishermen. I thought of all the nuns asleep up in the college, asleep in their quiet rooms, the sea asleep herself at the foot of the cliff. And I thought, I would do anything for that woman of mine behind me in the house, where we had done all our talking and laughing and our quarrelling. But my mind was in a peculiar state. I thought of all the Sunday roasts she had made, all piled up somewhere in eternity, a measure of her expertise. And I thought of how much her daughters and her son loved her, and depended on her for every sort of information, and how stupid and silent I was with my son. How she made the world possible and hopeful for him and the two girls. (*Sits on bed.*) I started to tremble, it was a moment in your life when daily things pass away from you, when all your concerns seem to vanish, and you are allowed by God a little space of clarity and grace. When you see that God himself is in your wife and in your children, and they hold in trust for you your own measure of goodness. And in the manner of your treatment of them lies your own salvation. I went back to the house with a lighter heart, a simpler man than the one who had set out. And the house was quiet. It was as if it were itself asleep, the very bricks, living and asleep with a quiet heartbeat. (*Holding the pillow.*) Suddenly I was terribly afeared that my new child was dead, I don't know why. You expect its cries, you long for its cries. I pushed open my front door and hurried down into the back room. The midwife was over by the window, with a little bundle. And Cissy was lying quiet, still, at ease. The midwife came over immediately and placed her bundle in my arms. It was like holding a three-pound bag of loose corn. (*The pillow.*) And there was a little face in the midst of the linen, a little wrinkled face, with red skin, and two big round eyes seeming to look up at me. I pledged all my heart and life to that face, all my blood and strength to that face, all the usefulness of my days to that face. And that was Dolly. And that was just as the need for candlelight fails, and the early riser needs no candle for his task.

Music. Dark after a few moments.

Act Two

Thomas's *room as before,* **Maud** *holding his sword in readiness.*
Annie *near.* **Dolly** *looking at* **Thomas** *with the polished shoes just on. He wears his dress uniform, the helmet as yet on the table.*

Thomas   Oh, Dolly, Dolly, Dolly.

Dolly   Will they do, Papa?

Thomas   They're beautiful shoes now.

Dolly   This whole day reminds me of when I was twelve, and there were snipers on the roofs above the music-hall, and me and Annie and Maud would be crawling along the sandbags outside the gates, trying to get in home from the shops. And laughing. And the soldiers at the gates laughing too.

Annie   That poor lieutenant didn't laugh when they put a bullet in his head.

Maud   And you were only ten then, Miss Dolly, and as wild as a tenement cat.

Dolly   Will it be like that today?

Thomas   No, sweet, that's all done with now. This is an act of peace.

Annie   My foot.

Thomas (*putting an arm about* **Dolly**)   Mr Collins and a small staff will come in, and we'll all meet like gentlemen.

Annie   Ha.

Thomas   And he will take command of the place, in effect. Don't you worry, Dolly, don't you worry.

Dolly   And what time is the meeting, Papa?

Thomas Shortly. The chief secretary wanted to meet at six but Collins sent in a note to say he wasn't a blackbird.

Annie Blackguard more like.

Dolly You are sure no one will try to shoot you?

Thomas Why would they want to shoot me?

Annie They would hardly have offered Papa a position in their new police force if they wanted to shoot him.

Dolly Did they, Papa? Oh, and will you take up that offer, Papa? It would be exciting.

Thomas We'll be Wicklow people again by year's end. Look at your father, Dolly. I am sixty-six years old! I am too old for new things. Indeed, I wish I were a younger man again, and I could kiss your noses, like when you were babies, and make you scream with delight.

Maud Papa! Come along, Papa, and we'll get your sword on you.

Maud *and* **Annie** *attach the sword to its belt.*

Thomas A man with three such daughters, three beautiful daughters, will never be entirely worthless. This January morning is the start of peace, and we may enjoy that peace till September, and then be gone – gone like shadows of an old dispensation.

Dolly A girl of eighteen is never a shadow, Papa.

Thomas Today is – what do you call it – symbolical. (**Maud** *doing the last buttons on the jacket.*) Like those banners in the Chapel Royal for every lord lieutenant that has ruled Ireland. It's a mighty symbolical sort of a day, after all these dark years. I'll be worn out. I'll be practising now. (*Taking* **Dolly**'*s hand.*) Good man, Joe, good man, Harry – that's the constables, because they're young too, Dolly, and will be greatly affected. Oh, big country hands, with rural grips! I'll have crushed fingers, like a visiting king.

Annie   And well, Papa, you are a king, more than some of those other scallywags.

Thomas   That is the whole crux of the matter. I am not a king. I am the servant of a king. I am only one of the stewards of his Irish city.

Annie   Collins is no king either, begging your pardon. With a tally of carnage, intrigue and disloyalty that would shame a tinker. And that King, for all his moustaches and skill on horseback, has betrayed us.

Maud   Annie, Annie, be quiet while Papa goes out. It isn't Papa's fault.

Thomas   I served that King, Annie, and that will suffice me. I hope I guarded his possession well, and helped the people through a terrible time. And now that story is over and I am over with it, and content. I don't grieve.

Maud   Of course you don't. Won't we have the great days soon in Kiltegan?

Thomas   But won't Dolly miss the fashions and the shops and the to-do of the town?

Annie (*before* **Dolly** *can answer*) I'll miss nothing. If they want to destroy everything, let them do so without us. It will be whins and waste everywhere, with bits of stones sticking up that were once Parliament, Castle and Cathedral. And people going round like scarecrows and worse. And Cuckoo Lane and Red Cow Lane and all those places just gaps with rubbish in them.

Maud   Annie, you're giving me a powerful headache.

Annie   The like of Collins and his murdering men won't hold this place together. They haven't the grace or the style for it. So you needn't mourn your shops and hats and haircuts, Dolly Dunne – they won't be there.

Thomas   Will I tell Mr Collins you said so, Annie?

Maud You'll miss the show if you don't go now, Papa. You don't want to be running over the square to them and sweating in your finery.

Thomas Am I shipshape?

Maud Shipshape as a ship.

Dolly Wait, don't let the king go! (*Hurrying out for something.*)

Thomas Where's she off to now?

Annie Who can say where Dolly goes.

Maud Poor Dolly – I do feel sorry for her.

Annie Why for Dolly? Feel sorry for yourself, woman.

Dolly (*coming back with a buttonhole*) I got this for you last night, Papa.

Annie On that dangerous trek back from the dance at the Rotunda . . .

Dolly (*looking at* **Annie**) Fresh up from the country.

Annie I hope you can wear a buttonhole today? It seems frivolous.

Thomas Put it in for me, Dolly. A white rose! Now I'm ready for them.

Dolly (*catching sight of the heather on the table*) Oh, but, Papa, you'd flowers already – maybe you meant to wear a bit of this?

Annie It isn't there at all yet. Just mere hints of flowers. That heather was born in the snow.

Maud (*smelling it*) That heather was born in the snow, right enough, Annie.

Annie (*drawn to the heather, as are* **Thomas** *and* **Dolly**) It came up on the Wicklow train. Sometimes you find you need a hint of home.

Dolly Born in the snow, like a lamb.

Thomas   That's from the hill beside the sloping field. I know that colour. (*Smelling, all of them smelling.*) It smells like God's breath, it does.

Maud   We won't mind going home to such riches.

Thomas   It is the very honeyed lord of a smell, so it is.

Thomas *goes out the door happily. The daughters scatter. Then the noise of a ruckus in the corridor.*

Smith (*off*)   Where are you wandering to? (*After a little.*) Where are you heading, old man?

Thomas (*off*)   What are you saying to me, constable? – Get back from me!

Smith (*off*)   Mrs O'Dea, Mrs O'Dea! Lie in there against the wall, you scarecrow, you. Mrs O'Dea! Come up, come up!

Mrs O'Dea (*off*)   Oh, I'm hurrying, I'm hurrying . . .

Mrs O'Dea *steps into the room.*

Thomas (*off*)   But I have to go and meet Collins!

Smith (*off*)   Collins is stone dead.

Thomas, *in his long johns again, propelled in by* **Smith**.

Thomas   Where are you putting me? This isn't our quarters!

Smith   Who was it left his door open? He might have gone raving up the main street of Baltinglass.

Mrs O'Dea   I don't know. It must have been his daughter.

Thomas   What have you done with my daughters? (*Pushing* **Smith**.) Get back from me, you blackguard. By Christ, assaulting a policeman. That's the Joy for you, you scoundrel.

Smith (*drawing out the pacifier*)   Right, boy, I did warn you. Now you'll get it. (*Raising the implement.*) Mrs O'Dea, fetch the

jacket off the hook in the corridor. (**Mrs O'Dea** *goes out.*)
You'll see the suit she has for you now, Thomas Dunne.

Thomas   You'll see the suit, Tomassy Tom. You'll see the
suit.

Thomas *escapes from him, leaps the bed like a youth.*

Smith   Jesus of Nazareth. (**Smith** *goes after him,* **Thomas**
ducks around to the stool, **Mrs O'Dea** *brings in the strait-jacket.*)

Thomas   Nicks, nicks.

Smith   He's claiming nicks off the three-legged stool.

Smith *strides to* **Thomas** *and strikes him with the pacifier, expertly
enough.*

Why couldn't I go with my brother flensing whales?

Thomas (*wriggling*)   You think I haven't had worse? See
this thumb? See the purple scar there? My own Da Da did
that, with a sheath knife. What do you think of that? (**Smith**
struggles to place the jacket on him.) Do you want to see my
back? I've a mark there was done with a cooper's band, and
on a Sunday too. But he loved me.

Mrs O'Dea   Lie up on your bed, Mr Dunne. (*To* **Smith**.)
He'll be worn out in a minute. I have your suit ready, Mr
Dunne, will I bring it up to you? He'll be good now, Mr
Smith.

Thomas (*lying on the bed awkwardly, bound*)   Give it to Patrick
O'Brien that excelled mightily at the bulleting. He'll eat it
piecemeal like a dog. (**Mrs O'Dea** *and* **Smith** *go out, and lock
the door.*) We're all here, the gang of us, all the heroes of my
youth, in these rooms, crying and imagining, or strung out
like poor paste pearls of people along the rows of the
graveyard. Lizzie Moran and Dorothy Cullen I saw there,
two beauties of Lathaleer, and Hannigan that killed his
mother, under a whinbush. And the five daughters of Joseph
Quinn, the five of them, much to my amazement, side by
side in five short graves. All of them lost their wits and died,
Black Jim. If I could lead those poor souls back across the

meadows and the white lanes to the hearths and niches of
their youth, and fill the farms with them again, with their
hopes and dreams, by God . . . I am a tired old man and I'll
have terrible aches forthwith. Let him hit. What else has he,
but hitting? Does he know why the calf is stupid? No. There
he is in his ignorance, hitting. Let him hit. (*After a little.*) My
two bonny grandsons would cure me. (*After a little.*) It's a
cold wind that blows without forgiveness, as the song says.

There's a sort of darkness in the room now, with a seep of lights.
Willie *stands in the corner, quietly, singing softly.*

My poor son . . . When I was a small child, smaller than
yourself, my Ma Ma brought me home a red fire engine from
Baltinglass. It was wrapped in the newspaper and hid in the
hayshed for the Christmas. But I knew every nook and
cranny of the hayshed, and I soon had it found, and the
paper off it. And quite shortly I had invented a grand game,
where I stood one foot on the engine and propelled myself
across the yard. I kept falling and falling, tearing and
scumming my clothes, but no matter, the game was a
splendid game. And my mother she came out for something,
maybe to fling the grains at the hens in that evening time,
and she saw me skating on the engine and she looked at me.
She looked with a terrible long face, and I looked down and
there was the lovely engine all scratched and bent, and the
wheel half-rubbed off it. So she took the toy quietly from
under my foot, and marched over to the dunghill and shoved
it in deep with her bare hands, tearing at the rubbish there
and the layers of dung. So I sought out her favourite laying
hen and put a yard-bucket over it, and it wasn't found for a
week, by which time the Christmas was over and the poor
hen's wits had gone astray from hunger and darkness and
inertia. Nor did it ever lay eggs again that quickened with
chicks. And that was a black time between my Ma Ma and
me. (*After a little.*) You were six when your Mam died, Willie.
Hardly enough time to be at war with her, the way a son
might. She was very attached to you. Her son. She had a
special way of talking about you, a special music in her
voice. And she was proud of your singing, and knew you

could make a go of it, in the halls, if you wished. I wanted to kill her when she said that. But at six you sang like a linnet, true enough. (*After a little.*) I didn't do as well as she did, with you. I was sorry you never reached six feet. I was a fool. What big loud talking fools are fathers sometimes. Why do we not love our sons simply and be done with it? She did. I would kill, or I would do a great thing, just to see you once more, in the flesh. All I got back was your uniform, with the mud only half-washed out of it. Why do they send the uniforms to the fathers and the mothers? I put it over my head and cried for a night, like an owl in a tree. I cried for a night with your uniform over my head, and no one saw me.

Mrs O'Dea *unlocks the door and comes in with the new suit, a rough black suit that she has joined with her yellow thread. She brings it to his bedside, dispelling* **Willie**.

Mrs O'Dea   Look at the lovely thread I used in it, just like you asked. Do you think you are quiet now?

Thomas   Yes.

Mrs O'Dea *starts to untie him,* **Smith** *comes in with a bowl of food, puts it on the table.*

Mrs O'Dea (*to* **Smith**)   Help me get him into bed. He'll lie quiet. (*To* **Thomas**.) Take off the long johns too, I'll wash them for you. (**Smith** *pulls down the top. The two wounds from the beating are revealed on* **Thomas**'s *chest.*) We should put something on those weals.

Smith   He's only scratched. Let the sleep heal him. He'll spring up in the morning, gabbling as always, crazy as ever. God knows I can't deal with him now, I have a fancy dress to go to in the town.

Mrs O'Dea   Well, I can't wash a man, Mr Smith.

Smith   He doesn't need washing. He's barely marked.

Mrs O'Dea   Won't you at least wash his hands, they're all black from the floor. And I suppose his feet are as bad.

Smith He may be St Thomas, Mrs O'Dea, but I'm not Jesus Christ, to be washing his hands and feet.

Mrs O'Dea What is he talking about, Mr Dunne?

Smith I have to collect my costume at six, Mrs O'Dea, off the Dublin train.

Mrs O'Dea Tuck yourself up, Mr Dunne, and have a rest.

They go out. **Annie** *and* **Dolly** *come on in mid-conversation.*

Dolly Where is my husband to come from, if we're to go back to Wicklow? I'm not marrying a farmer.

Annie Oh, are you not, Dolly? Isn't it pleasant to pick and choose? What farmer would take a woman like me, and I might have had a sailor once for a husband if I'd been let. So you're not the only one with difficulties, though you always think you are. That's the way of the pretty.

Dolly You couldn't go marrying a sailor, Annie. You never see a sailor. They're always away – sailing.

Annie And our father humiliated by renegades. Collins!

Dolly They didn't humiliate him, Annie, indeed, not at all. I'm sure it was all very polite. I think the truth is, Papa is delighted to be going back to Kiltegan, where he can have us all about him, slaving for him, and being his good girls, and never never marrying.

Annie Dolly, that's poor wickedness.

Dolly I know.

Annie He's desolated to be going back.

Dolly I don't believe he is. Or he'd have taken the new post in the whatever you call them. The Civic Guard.

Annie You don't think they were offering him Chief Superintendent?

Dolly   So. Let him be a superintendent again, and stay in Dublin, where a person can buy a decent hat. There's nothing in Baltinglass but soda-bread and eggs.

Annie   There's your father struggling to put a brave face on this day, which is no doubt the death of all good things for this country, and you're worrying about hats.

Dolly   Hats are more dependable than countries.

Annie   You're a nonsensical girl, Dolly. Why don't you go away somewhere with yourself, if you don't want to go back to Wicklow?

Dolly   I might!

Annie   You will not!

Dolly   Aren't you just after telling me to?

Annie   Dolly, don't dream of going and leaving me alone in Wicklow!

Dolly   For you to be giving out to me, like I was a little girl, and telling me I mustn't think of hats?

Annie (*seriously*)   Dolly, Dolly, you wouldn't go?

Dolly   Why not?

Annie (*almost shaking her.*)   Dolly, I'm serious, say you wouldn't. (*After a little.*) Say you wouldn't.

Dolly   All right, all right, I wouldn't! I wouldn't. I wouldn't, Annie, dear.

Annie *nods at her fiercely. They go off.*

Thomas (*from the bed*)   I could scarce get over the sight of him. He was a black-haired handsome man, but with the big face and body of a boxer. He would have made a tremendous policeman in other days. He looked to me like Jack Dempsey, one of those prize-fighting men we admired. I would have been proud to have him as my son. When he walked he was sort of dancing, light on his pins, like a good

bulleter. Like Patrick O'Brien himself. He looked like he
might give Patrick O'Brien a good challenge for his money
on some evening road somewhere, hoisting that ball of
granite. He had glamour about him, like a man that goes
about with the fit-ups, or one of those picture stars that came
on the big ship from New York, to visit us, and there'd be
crowds in the streets like for royalty, and it would be a fierce
job to keep them held back. Big American men and women,
twice the size of any Irish person. And some of them Irish
too, but fed those many years on beef and wild turkeys. He
was like that, Mr Collins. I felt rough near him, that cold
morning, rough, secretly. There never was enough gold in
that uniform, never. I thought too as I looked at him of my
father, as if Collins could have been my son and could have
been my father. I had risen as high as a Catholic could go,
and there wasn't enough braid, in the upshot. I remembered
my father's anger when I failed at my schooling, and how he
said he'd put me into the police, with the other fools of
Ireland. I knew that by then most of the men in my division
were for Collins, that they would have followed him wherever
he wished, if he had called them. And for an instant, as the
Castle was signed over to him, I felt a shadow of that loyalty
pass across my heart. But I closed my heart instantly against
it. We were to have peace. On behalf of the Crown the chief
secretary wished him well. And indeed it was peaceful, that
moment. The savagery and ruin that soon followed broke my
heart again and again and again. My streets and squares
became places for murder and fire. All that spring and
summer, as now and then some brave boy spat at me in the
streets, I could not hold back the tide of ruin. It was a
personal matter. We had restored order in the days of
Larkin. One morning I met a man in St Stephen's Green. He
was looking at a youngster thrown half-in under a bush. No
more than eighteen. The man himself was one of that army
of ordinary, middle-class Irishmen with firm views and
moustaches. He was apoplectic. We looked at each other.
The birds were singing pleasantly, the early sun was up. 'My
grandsons,' he said, 'will be feral in this garden – mark my
words.'

Dolly, **Maud** *and* **Annie** *come on and move* **Thomas**'s *table out a little and start to half-set it. There's a knock, and* **Matt** *appears.*

Annie   Who are you? What do you want?

Dolly   Who is that, Annie?

Annie   What do you want here?

Matt   My name's Matthew Kirwin, ma'am. I was asked to supper by Maud Dunne.

Annie   By Maud Dunne?

Maud (*coming over*)   Oh, hello, Mr Kirwin. How kind of you to come.

Annie   How kind of him to come?

Maud   Come in, Mr Kirwin, and meet my sisters. This is Dolly.

Dolly   How do you do?

Maud   And this is Annie.

Annie   Yes, this is Annie. And who is this, Maud?

Maud   My friend, Annie, Mr Matthew Kirwin.

Annie   Since when do you have friends, Maud, coming to supper?

Maud   I suppose I can have friends just as soon as Dolly? I suppose I can.

Annie   And have you known Mr Kirwin long, Maud?

Maud   We have an acquaintance. Mr Kirwin was painting in Stephen's Green last Saturday, and I happened to look over his shoulder at what he was doing, and as a matter of fact he was quite cross with me, weren't you, Mr Kirwin, for doing so, and we fell to talking then, and I explained my interest in the old masters . . .

Annie   Your interest in the old masters?

Maud   Yes, Annie. And we both agreed that the newer type of painters were all mad, and I invited him to supper.

Annie (*almost pushing him back*)   I'm sorry, Mr Kirwin, but you'll have to go.

Maud   Annie Dunne!

Annie   I don't know how you got past the gates, but there are to be no strangers coming in here. (*Pushing him elegantly.*)

Matt   If it isn't convenient . . .

Annie   It isn't even desirable, Mr Kirwin.

Maud   Annie, lay your hands off that man, he is my artist that I found in Stephen's Green.

Annie   And do you go out into the street, these times, Maud, and shake hands with everyone you see, and ask them to supper, if they are not doing anything better that night?

Maud   I do not, Annie Dunne.

Annie   What do you know about a man like this, with the leisure to be painting in daylight . . .

Matt   It was my day off, Miss Dunne . . .

Annie   And with a foreign accent . . .

Matt   I'm from Cork city . . .

Annie   And who may be the greatest rogue or the greatest saint that ever came out of – Cork city . . .

Maud   You are not my mother, Annie, in fact I am older and wiser than you . . .

Dolly   Let him stay till Papa comes, Annie, and if Papa says he is all right, we can have him to supper. It would be lovely to have friends to supper again. Let's, Annie.

Annie   And if he is an assassin?

Dolly   He's just a young man like any other young man.

Annie   So are assassins. No, it cannot be. (*Pushing him more vigorously.*) Out with you, Mr Kirwin.

Maud   Leave him be, oh, Annie, leave him be! (*She seems faint now, her legs buckling under her.*) Leave my artist be . . .

Dolly *tries to hold her up.*

Dolly   Help me, please.

Matt *holds her too.*

Annie   Let go of her, let go of her!

Maud *falls to the ground.*

Dolly   Oh, Annie, look what you've done now. Now we're the assassins, and Maud is killed.

The banging of a door below.

Annie   That's Papa. Papa always bangs the lower door for us, Mr Kirwin, because he has a house of girls. Now you'll get your supper!

Matt   I assure you, Miss Dunne . . .

Thomas *comes from the bed and stops by them. He doesn't speak.* **Maud** *opens her eyes, looks at him, gets up.* **Dolly** *goes and kisses her father.*

Dolly   What is it, Papa? You look so pale.

Maud   Do you have a chill, Papa?

Matt (*to* **Annie**)   I'll go, I'll go . . .

Annie (*not hearing him*)   Are you all right, Papa?

Thomas (*after a little*)   The city is full of death. (*After a little, crying.*) The city is full of death.

Annie (*hissing, to* **Maud**)   Look at the state Papa is in – it's no night for a visitor.

Thomas   How do you do, how do you do.

Maud (*to* **Matt**)   By the pillar, Saturday noon.

Matt *nods and goes.*

Thomas   Do I smell a stew, a real stew? Is that the aroma of lamb, bless me?

Annie   It is, Papa.

Thomas   Where did you get lamb, Annie?

Annie   The Dunnes of Feddin sent it up. It's Wicklow lamb.

Thomas   Wicklow. It is – Elysium. It is paradise . . . We'll be happy there, girls . . .

Annie   We will, Papa. We'll fetch the supper, Papa.

But they go out taking the things from the table with them. The door unlocks behind **Thomas**, *and* **Smith** *enters with a basin and a bottle of ointment. He is dressed like a cowboy complete with six-shooters.* **Thomas** *stares at him.*

Thomas   Black Jim!

Smith   Ah, never let it be said I left you alone with those cuts. Come here and sit, if you will. (**Thomas** *obediently goes to the stool.* **Smith** *puts down the bowl and begins to tend to* **Thomas**.) What's got into me? There's a lovely party going on in the town.

Thomas   I could be a man war-wounded.

Smith   You could. Or the outcome of a punch-up in a western saloon.

Thomas (*laughing*)   You think so?

Smith (*posing with the ointment*)   Do I not remind you of anyone in this get-up?

Thomas (*trying*)   No.

Smith   Maybe you never fancied the pictures, did you?

Thomas   I went the odd time to the magic lanthorn show.

Smith You couldn't guess then who I am, besides being Mr Smith, I mean?

Thomas Black Jim?

Smith Gary Cooper, Gary Cooper. Ah, you're no use.

Thomas Gary Cooper? Is that the Coopers of Rathdangan?

Smith (*putting on the ointment*) *Lilac Time*. Did you never catch that? You haven't lived. Of course, it wasn't a cowboy as such. *Redemption* was a hell of a good cowboy.

Thomas No man is beyond redemption, my Ma Ma said, when he let the dog live.

Smith Who, Thomas? If men were beyond redemption, Thomas, what would we do in Ireland for Presidents?

Thomas That's a fair question. (*Laughing.*)

Smith (*doing a cowboy*) You dirty dog, you dirty dog. (*After a little.*) Did you go to the war, Thomas?

Thomas Me? No – I was too old. My son was with the Dublin Rifles.

Smith Oh, I think I knew that. He was the boy that was killed.

Thomas He was that boy.

Smith I had a first cousin in it. A lot of men went out.

Thomas Did he come home?

Smith Not at all. They sent the uniform.

Thomas That's right, they do. I've only a letter from him, that's all I have in the world of him.

Smith Written from the battlefield?

Thomas Oh, aye, from the trenches themselves.

Smith I'd be very interested to see that letter.

Thomas Would you, Mr Smith? Of course. I have it somewhere, stuck in Annie's book. Will I get it?

Smith   Do, get it, man, and we'll have a read of it. Why not?

Thomas (*fetching the letter*)   Do you not want to get to your fancy dress?

Smith   The party can wait. (*Taking the old letter.*) It looks old enough.

Thomas   Well, it's coming up to twenty year ago now.

Smith (*opening it carefully*)   It's an historical document.

Thomas (*laughing*)   Oh, aye. Historical.

Smith (*reading*)   He has a good hand at the writing, anyhow. (*Reading.*)

Thomas (*nudging his knee*)   Would you not . . .

Smith   Read it aloud? You want me to?

Thomas   I do. I would greatly like that.

Smith   Fair enough. Okay. (*Settling himself to read it, clearing his voice, a little self-conscious.*) Of course, I don't read aloud much, so . . . (**Thomas** *smiles.*) Right. – My dearest Papa, Here I am writing to you in the midst of all these troubles. We are three weeks now in the one spot and we all feel we are dug in here for an eternity. The shells going over have become familiar to us, and my friend the first lieutenant from Leitrim, Barney Miles, has given our regular rats names. Our first idea was to thump them with spades because they eat the corpses up on the field but surely there has been enough death. We have not got it as bad as some companies, because our position is raised, and we get drainage, but all the same we know what real mud is by now. We have had some miracles, in that last week deep in the night one of our men was thrown back over the rampart wounded, by what hands we do not know. Another man was sent out with a dispatch and on his way back found a big sow thrashing in the mud. He would have taken her on with him for chops except she was twice his weight and not keen. It made us remember that all hereabout was once farms, houses and farms and grass and stock, and surely the farmer in you would weep, Papa, to see the changes. I hope you don't mind my letter going on. It gives me great comfort to write to my father. You will probably think I am raving a bit, and ranting, but nevertheless, since I am so far distant, I tell myself you will be interested to get news of me here. I wish I could tell you that I am a hero, but truth to tell, there are few opportunities for valour, in the way we all imagined when we set out. I have not seen the enemy. Sometimes in the dark and still of the night-times I see lights over where their position is, and on the stillest evenings you can just hear their voices. Sometimes they sing! Sometimes we sing, low and quiet, we have quite a repertoire now of risky songs, that you wouldn't approve at all. But it is a grand thing that we can still use our voices, and when I sing I think of home, and my sisters, and my father, and hope and know that my mother is watching over me here. God keep you all safe, because we have been told of the ruckus at home, and some of the country men are as much upset by that as they would be by their present emergency. I know you are in the front line there, Papa, so keep yourself safe for my return, when Maud will cook the fatted calf! The plain truth is, Papa, this is a strange war and a strange time, and my whole wish is to be home with you all in Dublin, and to abide by your wishes, whatever they be. I wish to be a more dutiful son because, Papa, in the mire of this wasteland, you stand before my eyes as the finest man I know, and in my dreams you comfort me, and keep my spirits lifted. Your son, Willie.

Thomas (*after a little, while* **Smith** *folds the letter and gives it back to him*)   In my dreams you comfort me . . .

Smith   That's a beautiful letter, Mr Dunne. A memento. A keepsake.

Thomas *nods his head, thinking.*

(*Getting up to go.*) Good man, good man. (*Goes, locks the door.*)

Thomas *puts away his letter and climbs into bed. After a little* **Dolly** *enters and goes to his bedside, with a big ticket in her hand.* **Thomas** *looks at her, takes the ticket, reads it, looks at her.*

Dolly   You aren't angry, Papa? It took all my courage to buy it, every ounce I had, you can't imagine. (*After a little.*) You are wondering how I could afford it? It was quite expensive, but it's only steerage. I had to sell Mam's bracelet that I was given, the ruby one you gave me, and I've to work for an agency the first two years, as a domestic, in Cleveland, Ohio.

Thomas (*after a little*)   Is it because she died on us? She was mortally sorry to die. She died as the need for candlelight failed. She would have adored you, even as she gave her life for you.

Dolly   Papa, don't be angry with me, please, I could not bear it, it took all my courage.

Thomas   Why would you go, Dolly, that is loved by us all, and young men going crazy over you here, and queuing up to marry you?

Dolly   They're not, Papa. I want to be liked and loved, but people are cold towards me, Papa.

Thomas   Why would they be, Dolly?

Dolly   Because – because of you, Papa, I suppose.

Thomas   It will pass, Dolly. In Wicklow we will be among our own people.

Dolly   I don't want to be like the Dunnes of Feddin, three wild women with unkept hair and slits on the backs of their hands from ploughing. You're old, Papa, it's not the same for you.

Thomas (*smiling, giving back the ticket*)   Yes, I am old.

Dolly   I didn't mean to say that, Papa. I knew you would be angry with me, I prayed you wouldn't be.

Thomas   Come here to me. (*He embraces her.*) How could I be angry with you? It's a poor look-out if I am angry with my own baby because she is afraid.

Dolly   I didn't want to hurt you, Papa.

Thomas   Papa is strong enough for all these things.

Dolly   You'll take care, Papa, and write to me, about all the goings-on in Kiltegan?

Thomas   I will of course. (*The lock turns in the door,* **Dolly** *breaks from him, goes.*) I will of course!

Mrs O'Dea *pops in and places a pair of black shoes by his bed.*

Mrs O'Dea   I'm just putting these here for you. I found you shoes at last, to go with the beautiful suit. I didn't mean to disturb you. You're the neatest sleeper I ever did meet, Mr Dunne. Never a ruffle in the sheets, just a long warm nest where your body lies.

Thomas   That's about the height of it.

Mrs O'Dea   Oh, you're a man for a bit of philosophy, I know.

Thomas   Whose shoes were they, Mrs O'Dea?

Mrs O'Dea   Let's see now. They were Patrick O'Brien's, Mr Dunne.

Thomas (*after a moment*)   You must take them for another man. I'd never fill them.

Mrs O'Dea   But what if your grandsons come to see you and you've nothing to put on your feet?

Thomas   There's no chance of that now.

Mrs O'Dea (*taking up the bowl of food*)   It's stone cold and you ate nothing. (*Going.*) Didn't I make you a beautiful suit?

She goes, locks the door. **Annie** *comes on with one of his big socks to darn and sits on the stool and works on the darning.* **Thomas** *dons* **Mrs O'Dea**'s *suit.*

Annie   Three days now, Papa.

Thomas   Three days, Annie. And we'll be set up in the old house again. We'll get that dairy going again first thing, a good scrub-down with the carbolic.

Annie   Yes.

Thomas   And I'll have our milking cow fetched over from Feddin, and the Dunnes of Feddin can hire someone else's fields, because we'll need them presently.

Annie   We will.

Thomas   And we'll be dog tired every night from the wealth of work, and be proud. And we have eight Rhode Island Reds and a crowing cock, that they are keeping for me in Lathaleer. And they're looking out for a pony, they say they know a fair-minded tinker will sell us something apt, and two hours at the most with a pot of polish will have those high lamps on the old trap gleaming. And we will cut a fine figure, you and I, Annie, Thomas Dunne and his daughter, throughout Kiltegan, Feddin and Kelsha.

Annie   We'll enjoy ourselves.

Thomas   And I'll lime the whole place. The house will be blinding white. We'll have red geraniums on the sills like the very dark conscience of summer or we're not Christians at all.

Annie   And Maud to visit, and we'll be peering at her, you know? (*Winking.*)

Thomas   And letters from Dolly, in the meantime, till she wishes to come home.

A knocking. The **Recruit**, *now a constable, comes on.* **Annie** *goes to him. The* **Constable** *whispers in her ear.* **Annie** *comes back to* **Thomas**.

Annie   It's one of the constables, Papa. He wants a word with you privately.

Thomas *goes over to him. The* **Constable** *whispers to him.* **Thomas** *at length pats the man briefly on the arm. The* **Constable** *goes.* **Thomas** *returns slowly to* **Annie**.

What, Papa?

Thomas   They have killed Collins in Cork.

Annie (*after a little*)   We'll be doubly glad to be going home now, and free of it all, Papa.

Thomas *can say nothing.*

Doubly glad.

A country music, and the wide ash-glow of a fire in the grate.

Thomas (*to himself*)   She died as many persons do, at the death of candlelight, as the birds begin to sing. She was a child again at the end, as if she was back again years ago in Lathaleer, and talking to her father, Cullen the coppicer. I stood by her bed, holding Dolly in my arms like a three-pound bag of loose corn, and Cissy spoke to me as if I were her own father. But our account was clear. (*Calling.*) Annie! When I went out that day to stop Larkin in Sackville Street, all the world of my youth, the world of Ireland that I knew, was still in place, loyal, united and true. I had three lovely daughters, and a little son as glad as a rose. And I had risen as high as Catholic could in the Dublin Metropolitan Police. And we were drawn up, ready to dispell them. (*Sits in near fire.*) Annie!

Annie   Yes, Papa?

Thomas   Bring my sword, would you?

Annie   No, Papa, I'm not bringing your sword.

Thomas   There's fellas roaming the countryside seeking out the maiming of this man and the death of that man, old scores must be settled, they're whispering and conspiring in the dark.

Annie   There's nothing and no one out there, Papa.

Thomas   But there is. I can smell them. Dark boys in black suits bought off the back of carts in county fairs, with old guns that might as soon blow off their own fingers when they fire. They won't get us. You must bring the sword.

Annie   There's nothing but your own fears. Go in to your bed and pull the blankets over your face and get a sleep, Papa.

Thomas   And lose my last daughter to ruffians and murderers?

Annie   You have the respect of the district, Papa.

Thomas   And what about that filthy mass of men that came up the yard last week and rattled our latch, and shouted in at me, while you were away at the well?

Annie   It was only a crowd of tinkers, Papa, that thought you were a woman alone, and wanted to frighten you. They took two churns from the shed and a length of rope because you wouldn't go out to them.

Thomas   I didn't dare breathe, I didn't dare breathe. I held fast to the fire.

Annie   Papa, you know country life better than me, but you are not suited to it, I think.

A soughing in the maples outside.

Thomas   There's them breathing now. Fetch the sword!

The soughing. **Thomas** *bolts from the stool and gets the sword, comes back and stands in the middle of the room holding it high.*

Come in now to us, and see what you'll get!

Annie   Papa, Papa, please. (*She tries to hold him and take the sword.*) If you'll be quiet, I'll make us another pot of tea and then we can go to our rest.

Thomas (*breaking from her*)   I must strike, I must strike. (*He goes about hitting at whatever he can, table and stool and such.*) Look at them running about like rats! Annie, there's rats come in, down the chimney! (*Striking the floor.*) Look at them, they're too quick for me!

Annie   There's no rats in my house! (*She covers her face with her hands.*) It's a clean house.

Thomas (*raving*)   What a to-do and a turmoil it is, with all their heroes lying in state about the city! They're bringing him up tonight to lie in state in the Pro-cathedral! Collins!

We'll be doubly glad to be going home, now, she said!
Because of you, Papa, I suppose, says Dolly. Says Dolly, says
Dolly, says Dolly, says Dolly . . .

Annie   Papa! Stop it!

*He does. He stands still where he is, the sword loose in his grip. He
breathes heavily. He sinks to his knees, offers **Annie** the sword.*

Thomas   Please, child . . .

Annie   What now?

Thomas   I am quiet now, Annie. I ask you a simple favour.

Annie   What favour, Papa?

Thomas   Take the sword, Annie, and raise it up like a
slash-hook, and bring it down on top of me like I was
brambles, with all your might.

Annie *looks at him. She goes to him and pulls the sword roughly
from him. Maybe she considers using it for a moment. She goes, taking
the sword with her.* **Thomas** *stares after her. He closes his eyes and
cries like a child. The fire fades away, and the colder light of his room
in the Baltinglass home returns.* **Willie** *comes, his uniform flecked
with gold.*

Thomas (*head down*)   Da Da, Ma Ma, Ba Ba . . . (*After a
little, seeing his son.*)   Oh, Willie . . . (*Humorously.*) The great
appear great because we are on our knees. Let us rise.

Willie *holds out a hand to help him get up.* **Thomas** *is surprised to
find it solid enough when he takes it.*

Oh, Willie . . .

Willie *brings him over to the bed and helps him get in.*

It's all topsy-turvy, Willie. (*After a little.*) Sure, Willie, I
think the last order I gave to the men was to be sure and
salute Mr Collins's coffin as it went by . . . (*After a little.*)
One time, Willie, and it was Christmastime too, and I was a
young fellow in Kiltegan, our dog Shep went missing for
some days, as dogs in winter will. I was maybe ten or eleven,

and I loved that Shep, and feared he was gone forever. We had got him as a young dog that had been beaten somewhere, and broken, till he reached our haven, and uncoiled, and learned to bark like a baby learns to laugh, and he shone at his work.

Willie *gets up on the bed beside his father.*

One morning early after a fall of snow I went out to break the ice on the rain-barrel to plash my face, and I saw his tracks in the snow going up the sloping field, high to the fringes of the wood, and I was greatly afeared, because there were drops of blood now and then as he went, little smears of it on the cleanly snow. So I followed him up, sinking here and there in the drifts, well used to it, well used to it, and on a piece of field we called the upper garden, because it was flat there and you could see across to Baltinglass and some said even to Shillelagh and the dark woods of Coollattin, I found our dog there with the carcass of a ewe well-eaten, only the hindquarters remaining. I saw my father's blue sign on the wool and knew the worst. For a dog that would kill a sheep would die himself. So in my innocence I went down to my father and told him and he instructed me, as was right and proper, to go back up with a rope and lead Shep down so the killing could take place. The loss of a ewe was a disaster, a disaster, there'd be pounds of money gone into her. But I loved the dog so sorely, I hesitated when I had the rope tied about him, and at length led him off further up the hill, across the little stand of scrubby pines, and on into the low woods dark with snow and moss. And we went through by a snaking path I knew, till we got to the other side, where there was a simple man living, that made his living from the rabbits, and maybe had need of a watchful dog. But he wouldn't take a dog that had killed, though he was a tender man enough, and it behoved me to retrace my steps back into the woods, now moving along but slowly, and the dog sort of dragging behind, as if he knew well his misdeed and his fate. And I stopped in the centre of the trees, and do you know my young legs would not go forward, they would not proceed, try as I might, and there I was all that afternoon and night with the dog and the hazels. How is it that the drear of winter didn't eat my bones and murder me for my foolishness? Love of the dog kept me standing there, as only a child can stand, without moving, thinking, the poor dog whimpering with the cold. About five o'clock I went on, because I heard calling over the hill, here and there, and I could see black figures with lights moving and calling, calling out to me and the dog to come home. We came down the sloping field with the neighbours about us, them not saying a word, maybe marvelling at me, thinking I had been dead, and the torches and lamps making everything crazy with light, the old crab apple enlarging to the size of the field, its branches wild like arms. Down at last into the yard we came, the dog skulking on the rope just the same as the day he had arrived to us, and my father came out from the house in his big clothes. All brown with clothes and hair. It was as if I had never seen him before, never looked at him in his entirety, from head to toe. And I knew then that the dog and me were for slaughter. My feet carried me on to where he stood, immortal you would say in the door. And he put his right hand on the back of my head, and pulled me to him so that my cheek rested against the buckle of his belt. And he raised his own face to the brightening sky and praised someone, in a crushed voice, God maybe, for my safety, and stroked my hair. And the dog's crime was never spoken of, but that he lived till he died. And I would call that the mercy of fathers, when the love that lies in them deeply like the glittering face of a well is betrayed by an emergency, and the child sees at last that he is loved, loved and needed and not to be lived without, and greatly.

He sleeps. **Willie** *lies in close to him. Sleeps. Music. Dark.*